New Perspectives on
James Weldon Johnson's
*The Autobiography of
an Ex-Colored Man*

New Perspectives on James Weldon Johnson's *The Autobiography of an Ex-Colored Man*

EDITED BY Noelle Morrissette

The University of Georgia Press
ATHENS

A Sarah Mills Hodge Fund Publication
This publication is made possible in part through a grant from the Hodge Foundation in memory of its founder, Sarah Mills Hodge, who devoted her life to the relief and education of African Americans in Savannah, Georgia.

Paperback edition, 2019
© 2017 by the University of Georgia Press
Athens, Georgia 30602
www.ugapress.org
All rights reserved
Set in 10/13 Kepler by Graphic Composition, Inc., Bogart, Georgia.

Most University of Georgia Press titles are available from popular e-book vendors.

Printed digitally

The Library of Congress has cataloged the hardcover edition of this book as follows:

Names: Morrissette, Noelle editor.
Title: New perspectives on James Weldon Johnson's The autobiography of an ex-colored man / edited by Noelle Morrissette.
Description: Athens : The University of Georgia Press, 2017. | Includes bibliographical references and index.
Identifiers: LCCN 2016049000| ISBN 9780820350974 (hard bound : alk. paper) | ISBN 9780820350967 (e-book)
Subjects: LCSH: Johnson, James Weldon, 1871–1938. Autobiography of an ex-colored man. | African American men in literature. | Race in literature.
Classification: LCC PS3519.O2625 A9535 2017 | DDC 818/.5209—dc23 LC record available at https://lccn.loc.gov/2016049000
Paperback ISBN 978-0-8203-5683-9

To Robert and Michele, Frank and Nancy,
ancestors and family

CONTENTS

ACKNOWLEDGMENTS ix

INTRODUCTION Biography of an Author, Biography of a Text: James Weldon Johnson's Ultimate American Work
NOELLE MORRISSETTE 1

PART ONE CULTURES OF READING, CULTURES OF WRITING: CANONS AND AUTHENTICITY

"Stepping across the Confines of Language and Race": Brander Matthews, James Weldon Johnson, and Racial Cosmopolitanism
LAWRENCE J. OLIVER 23

How *The Autobiography of an Ex-Colored Man* Became an Unlikely Literary Classic
MICHAEL NOWLIN 41

Authenticity and Transparency in *The Autobiography of an Ex-Colored Man*
JEFF KAREM 64

PART TWO RELATIONAL TROPES: TRANSNATIONALISM, FUTURITY, AND THE EX-COLORED MAN

The Futurity of Miscegenation: James Weldon Johnson's *The Autobiography of an Ex-Colored Man* and Pauline Hopkins's *Of One Blood*
DIANA PAULIN 87

Blackness Written, Erased, Rewritten: James Weldon Johnson, Teju Cole, and the Palimpsest of Modernity
DAPHNE LAMOTHE 112

Dead Ambitions and Repeated Interruptions: Economies of Race and Temporality in *The Autobiography of an Ex-Coloured Man*
BRUCE BARNHART 128

PART THREE POETICS: SOUND, AFFECT, AND THE ARCHIVE

The Autobiography as *Ars Poetica*: Satire and Rhythmic Exegesis in "Saint Peter Relates an Incident"
BEN GLASER   147

The Composer versus the "Perfessor": Writing Race and (Rag)Time
LORI BROOKS   169

James Weldon Johnson's
The Autobiography of an Ex-Colored Man, Archived and Live
NOELLE MORRISSETTE   189

PART FOUR LEGACIES

W. E. B. Du Bois, Barack Obama, and the Search for Race: School House Blues
ROBERT B. STEPTO   213

AFTERWORD The Ex-Colored Man for a New Century
NOELLE MORRISSETTE AND AMRITJIT SINGH   230

SUGGESTED FURTHER READING   239

CONTRIBUTORS   243

INDEX   245

ACKNOWLEDGMENTS

              I am thankful to the contributors to this collection who, through their distinct lines of critical inquiry, have taught me new things about James Weldon Johnson, his writing, and our shared endeavors as scholars, authors, and educators. Our work in this volume rests on the rigorous and lasting scholarship of too many authors to name. All of our efforts are indicative of a collaboration that honors Johnson's scholarly and creative legacy and his deep regard for African American culture. Together we acknowledge the "black and unknown bards" and the placement of African American literature in America and the world.

Several colleagues, particularly Robert Stepto and Louise Bernard, encouraged me to bring together this collection. Robert's critical legacy has inspired and guided my work; his friendship has sustained me. Louise helped shape the critical vision of this collection and has offered her support at every stage. Keen critical feedback from my colleagues at the University of North Carolina at Greensboro helped me see the way through this endeavor. Karen Kilcup, friend and mentor, guided me as I assumed the challenging role of editor, patiently providing advice about the numerous and nuanced editorial decisions involved in a collaborative critical anthology. María Carla Sánchez, Karen Weyler, Ana Hontanilla, Hepzibah Roskelly, and Mary Ellis Gibson provided perceptive criticism and a supportive audience. I have presented portions of this work at the American Literature Association, on a panel addressing practices of African American biography with Emily Bernard, Carla Kaplan, and Louise Bernard; and at a symposium at Yale University honoring Stepto's teaching and scholarship.

Support from the Marc C. Friedlaender Faculty Excellence Award from the Department of English at the University of North Carolina at Greensboro helped me complete this book. Special thanks go to Sue Williams for her support of this project.

A work such as this is the product of the labors of many. I would like to thank the University of Georgia Press, particularly Walter Biggins, who embraced this project from the start. Jon Davies, assistant director for EDP at the press, and Merryl A. Sloane, our copyeditor, provided keen editorial insight to bring this book into its best, most readable form. Any errors that remain are entirely my own.

I gratefully acknowledge the University of Minnesota Press for permission to publish a modified version of Diana Paulin's "The Futurity of Miscegenation," from her monograph *Imperfect Unions*, and Harvard University Press for permission to publish Robert Stepto's "W. E. B. Du Bois, Barack Obama, and the Search for Race: School House Blues," the second of his W. E. B. Du Bois lectures from *A Home Elsewhere: Reading African American Classics in the Age of Obama* (Cambridge, Mass.: Harvard University Press), Copyright © 2010 by the President and Fellows of Harvard College. I also acknowledge the University of Iowa Press, which published my *James Weldon Johnson's Modern Soundscapes* (2013). The James Weldon Johnson and Grace Nail Johnson Papers in Yale University's Collection of American Literature at the Beinecke Rare Book and Manuscript Library are cited frequently in this book. I thank the Beinecke staff and Nancy Kuhl, the curator of the collection.

In memoriam: Joseph T. Skerrett Jr. (1943–2015)

New Perspectives on
James Weldon Johnson's
*The Autobiography of
an Ex-Colored Man*

INTRODUCTION

Biography of an Author, Biography of a Text
James Weldon Johnson's Ultimate American Work

NOELLE MORRISSETTE

> It seems probable that, instead of developing them independently to the utmost, the Negro will fuse his qualities with those of the other groups in the making of the ultimate American people; and that he will add a tint to America's complexion and put a perceptible permanent wave in America's hair.
>
> —James Weldon Johnson, *Along This Way*

When James Weldon Johnson wrote these words, he possessed not only the hindsight of sixty-two years in America but a carefully considered knowledge of centuries of New World blacks. His knowledge was familial and represented an expansive geography, based on his mother's Bahamian and Haitian heritage and his father's experiences as a free black man in Virginia who worked at hotels for wintering vacationers in Florida and had family in New York City. Johnson's knowledge was personal, based on his experiences with Jim Crow and with the geographic, linguistic, and visual diversity of New World black cultures: Cuban itinerant workers in Jacksonville and boyhood friendships with other young black men, including a Cuban exchange student (Ricardo Rodriguez) and the impetuous Judson Douglas Wetmore, who was light enough to pass. Johnson's knowledge also was scholarly and multilingual: he had finished his detailed historical and sociological account of black New York, which broadly extended to world citizenship rights for African Americans, in *Black Manhattan* (1930) just three years prior to this reflection, and he had translated into English poems by the Cuban Plácido as well as petitions for just treatment made by Haitians under U.S. occupation.

In his "real" autobiography, *Along This Way*, Johnson wrote from a hard-earned status, having devoted his life to making sure America dealt with "the Negro" "right and righteously," making this case through his high-profile engagement in many of the National Association for the Advancement of

Colored People's most celebrated causes for racial justice: the Silent Protest Parade marking the racial atrocity of the East St. Louis riots (1917), the Dyer Anti-Lynching Bill (1918–22), and the Ossian Sweet case challenging restrictive real estate covenants (1925–26). "If the Negro is made to fail, America fails with him," Johnson wrote.[1] Serving as field secretary, secretary, and executive secretary in ascending order within the ranks of the NAACP, Johnson deeply shaped that institution's endeavors, correctly viewing racial diplomacy as crucial in a segregated nation largely ignorant of its African American citizens.

Johnson paired his role as a domestic diplomat—who constantly invoked a national conscience in matters of Jim Crow segregation and race-targeted brutality—with his prose writings, both fiction and nonfiction, on the Negro in America. *The Autobiography of an Ex-Colored Man* initiated this call to conscience, placing black culture in multiple geographic, linguistic, and expressive modes that were indicative of the forced diaspora of black people in a global context. Between 1912 and 1935 Johnson authored this anonymously published novel, extensive editorials and articles for major black and white publications such as the *New York Age* and the *Nation*, two substantial prefaces to collections of African American poetry and spirituals, a cultural history of black New York, and an autobiography that originally contained enough material for two volumes.[2] Johnson also helped compose materials that did not include his name, including the publisher's preface to his 1912 *The Autobiography of an Ex-Colored Man*, reviews, film scripts, entries on "Negro, American" and "Negro, Literature" for the *Encyclopaedia Britannica*, and advertisements and flyers in support of the Dyer Anti-Lynching Bill.[3] These prose works augmented Johnson's endeavors in racial diplomacy within and outside the nation, including Latin America and Haiti, where he held official roles as the U.S. consul to Venezuela and later Nicaragua and an unofficial one (following his resignation from the consulate) as an NAACP investigator of America's occupation of Haiti. He published three volumes of poetry during 1914–34, and considered these works artistic contributions to African American equality.

Johnson never again published a work of fiction like *The Autobiography of an Ex-Colored Man*, although his unpublished papers contain notes for short stories, operettas, and another novel in which he planned to force racial inheritance and racial identity into confrontation, showing their misappropriation and reconfiguration based on a changing affiliation with and valuation of black culture. The author did, however, borrow verbatim from his 1912 work, transferring passages to his preface to *The Book of American Negro Poetry* (1922), *Black Manhattan*, and even *Along This Way*. While one might argue that Johnson simply found aspects of the 1912 book worthy of repetition, the multiplicity of genres into which he inserted this work—a preface to an anthology, a history, and an autobiography—suggests a deeper, more coherent intent. Johnson confirmed the dynamic processes of African American cultural practices, inclusive of multiple languages, geographies, and experiences, through these repetitions. Reusing passages from *The Autobiography of an Ex-Colored Man* underscored how he understood this dynamism: moving through but not contained by a single song or text or, for that matter, by a single voice.

Johnson's efforts to recover, revalue, and make relevant African American culture to the United States was part of the wave of modern black cultural identity sweeping the nation. The "New Negro" had been invoked by authors and speechmakers as varied as Booker T. Washington, A. Philip Randolph, and Johnson's brother, Rosamond, since the late 1890s as the symbol of radical social change. Johnson understood the crucial nature of knowing and valuing a racial past that located one's African or New World black ancestors in the contemporary world by acknowledging their creative contributions. "A people may become great through many means, but there is only one measure by which its greatness is recognized and acknowledged. The final measure of the greatness of all peoples is the amount and standard of the literature and art they have produced. The world does not know that a people is great until that people produces great literature and art," Johnson wrote in his preface to *The Book of American Negro Poetry*.[4] He realized it was essential to link that racial past to a national history, because without a nation African Americans would lack citizenship and remain without a homeland. Public discourse, Johnson realized, had to propel forward this useable, even definitive, past of black culture and its literature, art, and history as a distinct voice *within* a nation. This racial voice could "become lost" and be "shut out from historical greatness" as determined by nations, Johnson observed from his diplomatic post in Venezuela. Of the black man in Venezuela, Johnson wrote to Booker T. Washington, "he will make no name here because he has no obstacle. And I believe that should the same conditions obtain in the United States he would make no name there."[5] The "fusion" of the Negro that Johnson referenced in the creation of "the ultimate American" must retain an identifiable, defining, and crucial component that is African American. The Negro past became, in Johnson's writing, an anticipation of the future—a future that would do more than simply accommodate or conjoin African American culture to a white American majority. Rather, Johnson's anticipated future makes African Americanness a perceptible, distinctive quality central to American culture, society, and political life.

Has the "permanent wave" Johnson anticipated found contemporary expression? The Reverend Joseph E. Lowery explicitly linked Johnson and President Barack Obama in his inaugural benediction of 2009, where he invoked Johnson's "Lift Every Voice and Sing."[6] Familiarly known as the "black national anthem" to African Americans, this song presents the imperative that *every* voice sing of black trials in accessing citizenship and of spiritual fellowship in America. The web of references, influences, and legacies among Johnson, Obama, and Lowery himself as a civil rights leader is indicative of the diversity and motion of a continuing, distinctly national conversation about understanding, equality, and black value.[7] The twenty-first-century media's preoccupation with the candidacy and election of Barack Obama as the first black president demonstrates America's continued obsession with racial categories and their ownership, as well as the nation's reluctance to share voice and power with its minority citizens. The focus on Obama's ability to inhabit the statuses of "black" and "president" illustrates how the very categories by which the nation measures progress toward liberation often become entangled with the constraining, limited categories it seeks to transcend. There is no futurity for African Americans in these measurements. Time stops in conversations about blackness, legitimacy, and ownership: there never can be successive black presidents to propel this conversation to the future through the expansion of thought represented by diverse individuals and more complex modes of social connection, such as affiliation.[8]

Both Johnson and Obama address this denial of futurity by writing themselves into the distinct literary category of American autobiography.[9] These leaders use the unique mode and conventions of American autobiography to engage the racial past, insist upon their individuality, and assert their ability to speak for the collective nation. To write oneself into the canon of American literature through this distinct type of autobiography, Johnson and Obama suggest, is to write oneself into history—as American authors, citizens, and spokespeople. And Johnson tested the limits of autobiographical texts by referencing several prior works written by black authors in his self-consciously modern tale, *The Autobiography of an Ex-Colored Man*. Drawing from earlier writers such as Harriet Jacobs, Josiah Henson, and Booker T. Washington, Johnson's improvised autobiography emphasizes the performative nature of the slave narrative, calling attention to tropes of African American autobiography, such as the "cabin in the woods," which is the site of sexual transgression between black and white and the narrator's dimly recalled first home. At the same time Johnson's work appropriates the larger national discourse of autobiography seemingly reserved for white authors, such as Benjamin Franklin and Henry Adams.

Historical-Cultural Background of the Novel

Through *The Autobiography of an Ex-Colored Man*, Johnson established a legacy of African American culture that looked backward and forward, making an argument for black futurity and citizenship in America. Subsequent to its anonymous publication in 1912, Johnson began to reveal his authorship, using the work to propel himself and African American culture forward. Johnson was well aware that the white press and politicians framed conversations about African American citizenship and social equality as the question of whether black people could maintain their racial and national identities simultaneously and be ideal citizens. He does not depict the crucial issue of racial versus national loyalty in *The Autobiography* as black rebellion against American civic life, but instead objectively emphasizes the "race-drama" invoked by the work's preface,[10] showing that America's enforced segregation of black people imposes a protective insularity on them. Black citizenship is contingent upon white America's realization of the error of Jim Crow, a realization that *its* soul is at stake in the denial of the souls of black Americans.

Despite its retrospective narration, *The Autobiography of an Ex-Colored Man* provides the way forward for an African American, and ultimately American, futurity. Much like W. E. B. Du Bois's *The Souls of Black Folk* (1903), a work that deeply influenced Johnson, *The Autobiography* predicts more than African American culture's future evolution; it anticipates twentieth- and twenty-first-century America's defining struggles over the extension of democratic principles to all its citizens. Du Bois, whose work's "forethought"—initially called an "outlook"—declared, "the problem of the Twentieth Century is the problem of the color-line,"[11] outlined the critical role of African American futurity in the new century. If left to the past African Americans would languish in the continued aftermath of Reconstruction's death. If given agency, African Americans would prove to the world America's worthiness as a democratic nation. Developing Du Bois's claims for futurity, Johnson's projection of the United States offered consciously crafted argumentation, but his aim was not speculation. Rather, this future nation created a space for the future Johnson and for his legacy as well as the legacy of all the African American creators of the New World.

Building on the historiography and autobiography of Du Bois's essay collection *The Souls of Black Folk*, which has been referred to aptly as "the Old Testament of twentieth-century African American letters,"[12] Johnson's *The Autobiography of an Ex-Colored Man* engages the practices of multiple genres in American letters. Not only the slave narrative, but also abolitionist speeches, African American sermons, Cuban communal talk, discourse on the "Negro problem," popular song lyrics, and even the preface itself are presented as diverse, sometimes divergent acts of writing and representation.[13] In his narrative, the nameless narrator (the Ex-Colored Man) emphasizes the accretive processes of identification through these various genre practices. Reading in the twenty-first century, it is difficult not to associate Johnson's work with Ralph Ellison's *Invisible Man* (1952) and the invisible protagonist who must confront a series of racial symbols and rituals in order to discard their claims to truth and begin anew.[14] These secret cultural signs, called "freemasonry" in Johnson's novel, must be learned, yes, but Johnson's and Ellison's texts suggest that it is imperative that translation occur from within to without, individually and communally, for blacks to survive in modern America.

Du Bois presents this survival through the dilemma of citizenship and equality. Like Du Bois, Johnson explores the double life of being "an American, a Negro,"[15] pursuing the duality using many of his precursor's tropes of African American identity, such as the veil and double-consciousness (in Johnson, "dual personality"). Johnson distinguishes *The Autobiography of an Ex-Colored Man* from Du Bois's work by addressing the interracialism taboo head-on, an issue that forcefully dramatizes the dilemma of sharing the United States. Using nineteenth- and twentieth-century American discourses centered on racial and national categories of identity and citizenship, Johnson demonstrates the intimate bonds of sexual union between black and white. The experiences of the narrator's black mother chart the exploitation of African Americans as labor and goods with limited access to social advancement: his white, aristocratic father "was all to us that custom and the law would allow" (*The Autobiography*, 27).[16] In *The Autobiography of an Ex-Colored Man*, the rape and sexual exploitation of black women in slavery and in Reconstruction produces miscegenated blacks, such as the narrator's mother and the narrator himself. In turn, these individuals force amalgamation by passing in white society and marrying whites. The preface asserts, "It is curiously interesting and even vitally important to know what are the thoughts of ten millions of them concerning the people among whom they live" (1). Johnson forewarns that America's path will lead the nation to the opposite of what it believes Jim Crow segregation will achieve.

Johnson's focus on sex and labor fosters scrutiny of the very concept of U.S. citizenship. Such citizenship is, as Werner Sollors has shown, "based on consent, not descent, which further blend[s] the rhetoric of America with the language of love and the concept of romantic love with American identity."[17] *The Autobiography of an Ex-Colored Man*, reviewed with Russian Jewish immigrant Mary Antin's autobiography, *The Promised Land*, also published in 1912, displays this love of nation. Johnson uses his narrator's interracial union with his white lover to claim a full American identity through a "declaration of will," effectively creating a position from which to criticize the nation's nativist exclusions and to praise a yet-to-be-fulfilled future inclusiveness.[18]

Simultaneously with the preface's forewarning of defiant acts of interracialism, *The Autobiography of an Ex-Colored Man* presents the bonds of love and music that entitle African Americans to U.S. citizenship. In *The Souls of Black Folk*, Du Bois had initiated acknowledgment of the story that the spirituals tell, prefacing each chapter with an unidentified bar of a spiritual, musically notated but eliding author and title. He paired these unnamed musical epigraphs with verses from Arthur Symons, Robert Browning, and other canonical British and European authors. As Du Bois's biographer David Levering Lewis notes, "Du Bois meant the cultural symbolism of these double epigraphs to be profoundly subversive of the cultural hierarchy of his time."[19] Johnson extends this subversive symbolism, incorporating ragtime-inflected classics and classically inflected ragtime into *The Autobiography*. He references popular gems by Beethoven, Chopin, and Mendelssohn alongside ragtime, which he suggests could, on the one hand, potentially hybridize the United States and, on the other, carry the nation's distinct music forth as a form of international diplomacy. Tracing the American character through the extremes of racial terror and racial interdependency, Johnson's novel emphasizes the poles of Americanness: its destructive forces and its creative potential.

The novel has proved to be profoundly subversive, defiantly resisting the limitations of categories circumscribed by racial identity within character, nation, and genre. The idea of the Ex-Colored Man himself did much to undo racial categories. One contemporary reviewer wondered, "What is an ex-colored man?" questioning whether such an individual could exist. That the narrator is often as ignorant as his white reader challenges the very premise of the faithful transcription of experience expected of the genre of black autobiography. The defiant and contradictory acts of this work undo static categories, proposing instead moving, intertwined, and contingent American identities and genres composing an American discourse of people, cultures, and letters.

Johnson describes African American music's intervening role in American culture as he traces distinct racial experiences, noting the music's fleeting, ephemeral nature, traveling through and yet not contained by bodies. Johnson and Du Bois both recognized the importance of inserting African-descended people into U.S. history while connecting black peoples the world over. In incorporating both spirituals and ragtime music, however, Johnson develops Du Bois's thesis that the fullness of African American citizenship can be measured by the degree to which African American music has been both recognized for its distinct racial nature and assimilated into the nation's culture.[20] The spirituals appear in Du Bois's and Johnson's texts as a "mystified," originary music of America,[21] but in Johnson's work, black music's past in the spirituals is part of an as-yet-unwritten future vision. *The Autobiography of an Ex-Colored Man*'s intervention in twentieth-century African American letters was to present a theory of black cultural transcription through continuously shifting discursive forms—texts and expressive culture—that highlight the dual status of African American music as simultaneously racially distinct and interracial.[22]

Textual Questions: Challenges to Readers

Readers have responded to *The Autobiography of an Ex-Colored Man*'s provocative ambiguities and discursive engagements from its initial anonymous publication in 1912 through the present day, adding ancillary discursive forms—prefaces, introductions, and annotations—to Johnson's intervening, ambiguous text. One scholar called it the first "pseudo-autobiography" in African American literature,[23] and another described it as a "landmark" in "American literary history more generally," describing the novel as an allegory of life across the black-white color line—a "mulatto pilgrim's progress."[24] Therefore, the text itself—not just its narrator—draws attention to the accretive and ambiguous practices of an interracial culture and literature in America. The text demands that interpretative practices acknowledge its critical complexities as it continues to be framed and reframed.

Different editions of *The Autobiography of an Ex-Colored Man* typically reflect one of its two most significant and significantly different publication moments, 1912 and 1927. When Johnson first released the novel in 1912 through Sherman, French and Company, he chose to issue the work anonymously, reasoning that if the identity of the author were known, the sensation elicited by the novel's conclusion—a man and his children passing into white society—would no longer be provocative, and the work would "fall flat."[25] The original work's cover had a partially unfurled scroll bearing the title but with the author's name obscured, which reinforced the author's anonymity, as did the publisher's preface (written by Johnson at the publisher's request), which discusses the narrative sociologically, obscuring the individual author as one of many who have "passed over into the white race" (*The Autobiography*, 1).

Johnson promoted the book as best he could without revealing his authorship, passing it along to white men in the consulate and the U.S. Navy and arranging for its review by his professor of literature at Columbia, the influential literary authority Brander Matthews. But the Great War devastated the Boston publishing world and Johnson's press. By the time he offered the book's serial publication to the *Chicago Defender* in 1919, he had become rather careless about protecting his identity as its author. His meeting with Heywood Broun in 1924 and with Carl Van Vechten shortly after helped propel a very different edition of *The Autobiography of an Ex-Colored Man*, not so much because he substantially revised its content but because he layered new meanings on the original text. The 1927 edition bears Johnson's name as the author; an introduction by Van Vechten, then the *Vanity Fair* music columnist and a profiler of the black artists of the Harlem Renaissance; and an edgy graphic by the New Negro artist Aaron Douglas: a man sits in a diminutive natural landscape on the outskirts of a city, overshadowed by the skyscrapers.

British spellings, a vogue of the decade, were adopted, changing the title to "Ex-Coloured"; the edition was part of Alfred A. Knopf's Blue Jade series of fine books, printed in an innovative font on acid-free paper, with the striking orange-and-black (uncredited) design of Douglas's dust jacket wrapping the book.

Since the 1912 edition, *The Autobiography of an Ex-Colored Man*'s inside matter—from the publisher's preface to Van Vechten's introduction, from American to British spellings and back again—has changed, as has its ancillary material, such as introductions, notes, and biographical and chronological information. Authorities such as Charles S. Johnson (Johnson's contemporary, a sociologist and National Urban League activist), Arna Bontemps (a literary scholar and author, also Johnson's contemporary), John Hope Franklin (a historian who studied with Johnson at Fisk University), and Henry Louis Gates Jr. (a literary scholar and influential spokesperson on African American and African diaspora issues) have written introductions that increase the novel's multiple meanings. The introductions and annotations of editions that now span more than a century reflect scholars' continued and incomplete endeavors to capture the narrative's meaning. Some of these additions have become part of the work itself. Its framing in 1965 as one of "three Negro classics" in John Hope Franklin's edited collection of that name has presented the text, and Johnson himself, as timeless and definitive, creating a tradition of African American letters. A much-anticipated critical edition of the work was issued in 2015.[26]

Such extensions enrich Johnson's endeavor, continuing the author's evolving relationship to his narrator and his story a hundred years after its initial publication. We continue to read *The Autobiography of an Ex-Colored Man* because of its engagement with modernity, internationalism, and citizenship, not only of the narrator's new (twentieth) century, but also our own: it anticipated the troubling relations among art, capitalism, and labor as well as the history and historiography of raced peoples in the New World. The series of paradoxes Johnson's novel examines crucially inform twenty-first-century readers' dynamic understanding of America as a nation. Johnson's work imagines a nationless cosmopolitanism that nevertheless espouses American culture's distinctiveness through its black folk art forms, presents the American South as the ground of the new colonial enterprise of industrialized labor, and ambivalently describes how black art forms become commodified. The term "ex-colored" only begins the inquiry into the contradictions of being "an American, a Negro," as Du Bois described it in 1903. The 2008 election of Barack Obama, heralded as bringing forth a "postracial" society, has proven something quite the opposite, true to the phrase's internal paradox: a culture continually obsessed with racial difference.

History of Criticism

The essays in this collection respond to Johnson's invocation in *The Autobiography of an Ex-Colored Man* of the futurity of African America. The centenary of his first book provides an opportunity for critical reassessments of its importance to African American literary canons, particularly through the critical discourses of African American studies and African American literary criticism that emerged in the twentieth century. Read now, *The Autobiography of an Ex-Colored Man* demands broader interpretation within the trajectory and meaning of African American literary criticism.

Prior interpretations of *The Autobiography of an Ex-Colored Man* followed historical trends in African American literary criticism. Studies in the 1960s and 1970s, seeking to establish a pantheon of African American authors whose works affirmed the value of African American subject matter, focused on biographical and celebratory readings of fictional works. Within this critical paradigm Johnson's accomplishments often were emphasized above his narrator's, giving the impression that the text was merely incidental to this extraordinary man's arc of success. Yet the 1960s and 1970s criticism also introduced a documentary, at times polemical, negative phase, presenting African American city life in a social realist or protest mode, exemplified by contemporary, loosely autobiographical works, such as Claude Brown's *Manchild in the Promised Land* (1965), Iceberg Slim's *Pimp* (1967), and *The Autobiography of Malcolm X* (1965). Critics using this conceptual framework contended that Johnson's novel revealed, also in social realist mode, the city's vice and corruption, which so challenged black manhood. They paralleled the narrator's tragic loss of his black cultural roots with the endangerment facing blacks generally as they sought civil rights through nonviolent or more militant means. Black arts critics of this same period dismissed Johnson's work, however, perceiving an affiliation of the text, and Johnson himself, with a white standard for judging black matters—it was "slavemaster, bourgeois art"—and with a lack of a "politically revolutionary" ideology, as Amiri Baraka made clear in an essay called "The Revolutionary Tradition in Afro-American Literature."[27]

So which is it? A celebration of the author, a work of social realism, or a bourgeois commodity? Might it be that Johnson wished to trouble these shorthand categories for black voices and experiences?

In an effort to address these contradictions, studies of Afro-American narrative during the late 1970s and early 1980s charted a literary tradition of black writers as an intraracial practice formed not only by ideology but also by narrative practices. Robert Stepto's groundbreaking and critically rigorous *From behind the Veil* (1979) placed a cluster of slave narratives in a line of influence extending to Ralph Ellison, showing how each work initiated a call for a fulfillment of authorial authority, and the writers responded by revising prior texts.[28] This work deepened the examination of black narrative by focusing on the in-group field of reference among black writers over time while succinctly compiling information about their publication venues, sales, and reception. Stepto's study is still in print today, suggesting its lasting explanatory power. Several important works on Johnson's first book, including Joseph Skerrett's "Irony and Symbolic Action in James Weldon Johnson's *The Autobiography of an Ex-Coloured Man*" and Valerie Smith's "Privilege and Evasion in *The Autobiography of an Ex-Colored Man*," advanced this approach, focusing particularly on how Johnson used irony and ironic distancing between author and narrator.[29]

Such intraracial studies of narrative were themselves a narrative history. For many, the early decades of the twentieth century, the era that became known as the Harlem Renaissance, provided many parallels to the flowering of the black arts in the 1960s and 1970s. Nathan Irvin Huggins and others appropriately situated Johnson in these studies as a major participant.[30] The language of "literary tradition" and "literary classic" affirmed this alternative canon of American literature. But this new tradition possessed many of the same flaws of exclusion. Black feminist scholars critiqued Stepto's work for its lack of women writers, and they proposed a black female lineage of creativity.[31]

Comparative ethnic and modernist studies, including works by Werner Sollors and Samira Kawash, developed these intraracial studies by considering the experiential intersections of hyphenated Americans—immigrants and minorities—and their experimental art forms.[32] The trope of racial passing gained critical currency and had broad application to other forms of transgression, be they the identity formations of gender and sexuality or the presence of immigrants in a changing America.[33] These critical frameworks fruitfully complicated narrative studies of *The Autobiography of an Ex-Colored Man*, breaking out of the fact-versus-fiction divide over its "truth" and crossing the divide between African American studies and ethnic studies to discuss hybrid or indeterminate genres and peoples. African American literature was deepened by conversation with the emerging field of whiteness studies, which drew attention to the racialization of ethnic groups considered white but "of a different color."[34] Comparative American modernist studies placed the language projects of writers like Johnson and Zora Neale Hurston in conversation with those of T. S. Eliot and William Carlos Williams and opened a window into the interracial collaborations of writers and publishers of the 1920s, like Johnson and H. L. Mencken. George Hutchinson's *The Harlem Renaissance in Black and White* influenced a generation of scholars, opening up consideration of the Harlem Renaissance as an interracial event not divided by the boundaries erected by academic studies of this period.[35]

Disciplinary study has indeed both limited and expanded readings of *The Autobiography of an Ex-Colored Man*. Brent Edwards has led an entire subdiscipline of twenty-first-century literary criticism and theory—translation studies—that is focused on the comparative work of racial formation in a global context, so that New Negro representations converse with the cultural contexts and insights of other arts-based movements occurring in Latin America, France, and Germany. *Décalage*—Edwards's key term for the gaps between the translations of linguistic terms—also indicates his view of the fluid notion of identity and of knowledge itself. As the categories of knowledge and of cultural value have been called into question, several important new fields—translation studies, performance studies, and sound studies, among them—interrogate the status of the archive and of static categories of knowledge themselves through the more ephemeral, transient acts of sound, gesture, and performance.[36] These theoretical interpretations focus on the Ex-Colored Man's racial performativity and on theatrical performances contemporary with the novel's composition as the sites of culturally, historically, and temporally complex racial negotiations. Developing the poststructuralist models of thought offered by Jacques Derrida and Michel Foucault, scholars have questioned whether the institutionalized stores of knowledge represented by the archive can voice the powerful negotiations that occur between body and text. Here the Ex-Colored Man emerges as one who collects and archives knowledge or who, in his position of retreat from the world, himself represents an archive.

In the twenty-first century, the shifting criticism has looked not only to the origins of African American literature, but also to its end. While some authors have placed particular emphasis on African American literature as a historical and now defunct category,[37] others have emphasized the simultaneous growth of twentieth-century African American literature and a corpus of African American literary criticism.[38] In *What Was African American Literature?* Kenneth Warren argues that the oppressive, segregated racial hierarchy of Jim Crow defined African American literature. Writers produced works from within that system, responding to Jim Crow while also trying to imagine an existence outside of the black-white categorization of authors and citizens. Warren argues for the disappearance of race as an organizing literary category for African American writing with the advent of the 1970s.

Similarly, Gene Jarrett's alternative reader, *African American Literature beyond Race*, the companion to his monograph *Deans and Truants: Race and Realism in African American Literature*, proposes an African American literature that, from the latter half of the nineteenth century to today, exists outside the confines of race, separate from the dominating narrative of social realism and the racially grounded mythos that have almost exclusively become *the* literary history of an African American tradition.[39] Jarrett, like Warren, is concerned that what is a vital, diverse, multigenre intellectual tradition has become reduced to a single framework of thought that perpetuates racial myths. Adding to this innovative work that charts the intellectual diversity of African American writing, Lawrence Jackson's *Indignant Generation* (2011) investigates the crucial nature of midcentury African American authors intent on citizenship amid a global politics shaped by World War II and communism while acutely aware of the continued domestic oppression of Jim Crow. These groundbreaking monographs have developed the current, still-evolving meaning of African American studies as a discipline and have therefore expanded the available readings of Johnson's *The Autobiography of an Ex-Colored Man*. While interrogating the value systems that construct what we call "literary history," these works acknowledge the interdisciplinarity that makes African American studies a dynamic and changing practice, providing a comparative framework for understanding the forced movement of African-descended peoples through a global system of power and capital.

The Essays in This Book

New Perspectives on James Weldon Johnson's "The Autobiography of an Ex-Colored Man" redirects critical conversation about the book through these recent developments in African American literary studies, setting the stage for future work on Johnson's novel, his other writings, and broader topics in African American literature and literary-critical practice. The essays in this book range from literary-cultural history to comparative/influence studies, from close readings to literary theory, but they cross over a conceptual framework that importantly organizes Johnson criticism: the critical trajectory of American and African American cultural traditions and scholarly practices, which were initiated by Johnson and others, like Du Bois and Alain Locke in the early twentieth century, and which continue to develop interpretative models for reading Johnson's signal work and historic and contemporary productions of African American culture in national, hemispheric, and global contexts.

The four parts of this collection reflect the complexity of Johnson's 1912 work and are representative of the range of critical and theoretical conversations about *The Autobiography of an Ex-Colored Man*, African American literature, and American literary cultures. Part I, "Cultures of Reading, Cultures of Writing: Canons and Authenticity," addresses Johnson's authorship by discussing his literary and cultural milieu (models of influence and writing profoundly shaped by Brander Matthews, Johnson's professor of literature at Columbia University, as Lawrence J. Oliver shows), his development as an author through and in relation to this text (an "unlikely" classic that should have, but did not, lead to a more substantial oeuvre, as Michael Nowlin convincingly demonstrates), and the signals he generated for its interpretation (Jeff Karem discusses the signposts of authenticity in the work as the "promise of the secret").

Part II, "Relational Tropes: Transnationalism, Futurity, and the Ex-Colored Man," discusses the ways that Johnson's work intervenes in transnational discourses of race that are enforced, staged, and imagined. Diana Paulin and Daphne Lamothe place *The Autobiography of an Ex-Colored Man* in conversation with prior and contemporary authors (Pauline Hopkins and Teju Cole) engaged in tracing the regional, hemispheric, and global movement of black cultures in and around national identity. The "temporal orientations" of Johnson's 1912 work are shown by Bruce Barnhart to create "psychic rhythms" in the text, which are the outcome of its orientation to the present. This attentiveness to time results in a heightened awareness of the narrator's orientation in the racialized logic of the present and his inability to engage futurity. Paulin's, Lamothe's, and Barnhart's investigations reveal ongoing practices of racial formation and subjectivity in time and space, underscoring the potential of categories of blackness and whiteness to perpetuate opposition and oppression or to open up an understanding of heterogeneity and possibility.

Part III, "Poetics: Sound, Affect, and the Archive," presents multiple dimensions of Johnson's endeavor to represent in his writing an aesthetic inclusive of black expressive culture. Ben Glaser provides a much-needed exegesis of Johnson's poetry, placing it in relation to *The Autobiography of an Ex-Colored Man* to show the author's limited—or tentative—use of a poetics inclusive of black expression. Lori Brooks furthers this discussion of poetics by providing a cultural history of the significance of Johnson and his brother's production of a learned professor of ragtime, who supplanted the innately musical but uneducated black musician to engage and inform a musical nationalism emerging in the first decades of the twentieth century. The performative elements of Johnson's work are taken up in my essay in this portion of the book, which engages the idea of an African American archive operating in Johnson's text and examines the author's understanding and use of such a repository in developing his aesthetic of sound. Discussing the complicated combinations of popular and classical music that formed the compositional aesthetic of Cole and Johnson Brothers and Johnson's 1912 text itself, I show how Johnson conceived of a living, breathing archive inclusive of sound and biography—an archive that was mutually constitutive of Johnson's self and the sounds of American culture he wished to represent.

Part IV, "Legacies," features Robert Stepto's critical return to Johnson as he rereads *The Autobiography of an Ex-Colored Man* as an African American classic in the "age of Obama." His work initiates a call for new critical conversations about such texts as we look backward and forward, anticipating our claim to a shared inheritance of interracial cultural gifts that yield a greater understanding of ourselves.

The collection's coauthored afterword, written by Amritjit Singh and me, responds to the other essays in this volume. For more than three decades Singh has facilitated literary-critical conversations about the domestic and international relevance of African American novelists' works. As one of the editors, with William S. Shiver and Stanley Brodwin, of *The Harlem Renaissance: Revaluations* (1989) and the author of a study of twelve novelists from the period (1976), he has presented works by Harlem Renaissance authors as both an aesthetic and a form of social action.[40] In the present collection, influential scholars who have offered definitive interpretations in the field of Johnson studies—Oliver and Stepto[41]—offer new analyses reflective of the literary-critical and social changes that have provided fresh context to *The Autobiography of an Ex-Colored Man*. Several other contributors to this collection have previously published essays on Johnson's work and offer interpretations here that add to their prior scholarship.[42]

Together, these new essays on *The Autobiography of an Ex-Colored Man* represent exciting, critically innovative work in the field of Johnson studies, directing attention to a reassessment of the author's writing and legacy and the racial futurity he called for, to which we continue to respond.

A Note on the Editions

The two different spellings of Johnson's work—Ex-Colored versus Ex-Coloured—reference two different editions of his text. *The Autobiography of an Ex-Colored Man* refers to the anonymous edition of Johnson's work, published in 1912, while *The Autobiography of an Ex-Coloured Man* indicates the 1927 edition, which was published under Johnson's name and with an introduction by Carl Van Vechten. The different reissues tend to reference one or the other of these editions, sometimes leaving out, changing, or adding to the publisher's preface of 1912 (penned by Johnson) and Van Vechten's 1927 introduction. The essays in this collection draw from numerous editions, which represent this text's multiple, extended lives.

NOTES

1. James Weldon Johnson, *Along This Way: The Autobiography of James Weldon Johnson* (1933; rpt., New York: Viking, 1961), 412.

2. Anonymous, *The Autobiography of an Ex-Colored Man* (Boston: Sherman, French, 1912); James Weldon Johnson, *Fifty Years and Other Poems* (Boston: Cornhill, 1917); Johnson, preface, *The Book of American Negro Poetry* (New York: Harcourt, Brace, 1922);

Johnson, preface, *The Book of American Negro Spirituals* (New York: Viking, 1925); Johnson, preface, *The Second Book of American Negro Spirituals* (New York: Viking, 1926); Johnson, *God's Trombones: Seven Negro Sermons in Verse* (New York: Viking, 1927); Johnson, *The Autobiography of an Ex-Colored Man* (New York: Knopf, 1927); Johnson, *Saint Peter Relates an Incident* (New York: Viking, 1935); Johnson, *Black Manhattan* (New York: Knopf, 1930); Johnson, *Along This Way;* Johnson, *Negro Americans, What Now?* (New York: Viking, 1935). Johnson's editorials and essays for the *New York Age*, the *Nation*, *Harper's*, *American Mercury*, the *Crisis*, and *Opportunity*, among others, have been collected in Sondra Kathryn Wilson, ed., *The Selected Writings of James Weldon Johnson* (New York: Oxford University Press, 1995).

3. Johnson's authorship of the publisher's preface to *The Autobiography* was not established until 1990. A facsimile letter in his papers, addressed to his publisher Sherman, French and Company, responds to its request that he write a preface to the work. Some phrases Johnson proposes, including "biography of the race" and "truth stranger than fiction" were excised. The rest remains as the preface. See Johnson's correspondence in the James Weldon Johnson and Grace Nail Johnson Papers, Beinecke Rare Book and Manuscript Library, Collection of American Literature, Yale University, hereafter JWJ BRBL. Johnson to Sherman, French and Company, February 7, 1912, ser. 1, JWJ Correspondence, box 41, folder 22, JWJ BRBL. The distinct prose style of *The Autobiography of an Ex-Colored Man* (and its preface) is reflected in several reviews of the work, which borrow heavily from its phrasing. Johnson collected these reviews for years; in the 1920s his secretary and close confidante Richetta Randolph placed the clippings into two scrapbooks, which are now housed in the Johnson Memorial Collection at BRBL. For Johnson's authorship of film scripts, see Noelle Morrissette, *James Weldon Johnson's Modern Soundscapes* (Iowa City: University of Iowa Press, 2013), 103–4. For his engineering and authorship of the Dyer Anti-Lynching bill, see Johnson's autobiography, *Along This Way*, 361–73.

4. Johnson, preface, *Book of American Negro Poetry*, 9.

5. Johnson to Washington, August 30, 1906, Booker T. Washington Papers, Manuscripts Division, Library of Congress, Washington, D.C.

6. Lynn Sweet, "Rev. Lowery Inauguration Benediction: Transcript," *Washington Post*, January 20, 2009, http://voices.washingtonpost.com/inauguration-watch/2009/01/transcript_of_rev_lowerys_inau.html/

7. See, for example, Patricia Williams, *Alchemy of Race and Rights: The Diary of a Law Professor* (Cambridge, Mass.: Harvard University Press, 1992); Randall Robinson, *The Debt: What America Owes to Blacks* (New York: Random House, 2001); and Michelle Alexander, *The New Jim Crow: Mass Incarceration in the Age of Color-Blindness* (New York: New Press, 2011).

8. The satirist and blogger Baratunde Thurston discusses "how to be the second black president" in his bestseller, *How to Be Black* (New York: Harper, 2012). It may well be that satiric humor will initiate more serious conversations about racial legacies in U.S. politics.

9. For example, Barack Obama, *Dreams from My Father: A Story of Race and Inheritance* (New York: Three Rivers, 1995).

10. Publisher's preface in Johnson, *The Autobiography of an Ex-Colored Man and Other Writings*, ed. Noelle Morrissette (New York: Fine Creative Media, Barnes and Noble Classics, 2007), 2. Future references are to this edition and are given parenthetically in the text.

11. John Cullen Gruesser, *The Empire Abroad and the Empire at Home: African American Literature and the Era of Overseas Expansion* (Athens: University of Georgia Press, 2012), 1; W. E. B. Du Bois, *The Souls of Black Folk* (1903), ed. Farah Jasmine Griffin (rpt., New York: Fine Creative Media, Barnes and Noble Classics, 2003), 3.

12. Dolan Hubbard, ed., *"The Souls of Black Folk" One Hundred Years Later* (Columbia: University of Missouri Press, 2003), 1.

13. See Morrissette, "Biography of the Race: Musical Comedy and the Modern Soundscape of *The Autobiography of an Ex-Colored Man*," in Morrissette, *Modern Soundscapes*, 33–64.

14. Robert B. Stepto, "Literacy and Hibernation: Ralph Ellison's *Invisible Man*," in his *From behind the Veil: A Study of Afro-American Narrative*, 2nd ed. (Urbana: University of Illinois Press, 1991), 163–94; Houston Baker, "A Forgotten Prototype: *The Autobiography of an Ex-Colored Man* and *Invisible Man*," in *Critical Essays on James Weldon Johnson*, ed. Kenneth M. Price and Lawrence J. Oliver (New York: G. K. Hall, 1997), 31–42.

15. Du Bois, *Souls of Black Folk*, 9.

16. See bell hooks, "Reflections on Race and Sex," in her *Yearning: Race, Gender, and Cultural Politics* (Boston: South End, 1990), 58–59.

17. Werner Sollors, *Beyond Ethnicity: Consent and Descent in American Culture* (New York: Oxford University Press, 1987), 112.

18. Sollors writes, "It was assimilation, full American identity, even if claimed unilaterally by declaration of will rather than by American birth or by easy acceptance by old-stock Americans that enabled Antin to criticize her adopted 'promised land'—or to praise it for qualities the United States would still have to acquire by fully including people like her" (*Ethnic Modernism* [Cambridge, Mass.: Harvard University Press, 2008], 80).

19. David Levering Lewis, *W. E. B Du Bois: Biography of a Race, 1868–1919* (New York: Henry Holt, 1993), 1:278.

20. Ronald Radano's *Lying Up a Nation: Race and Black Music* (Chicago: University of Chicago Press, 2003) specifically explores "how black music influences and reflects the social forces of American life" (xiii).

21. Ibid., 280.

22. Writes Radano, "In its seemingly endless capacity, black music both affirms evolving myths of blackness that cast African Americans apart from a dominant whiteness and serves to overcome the color line, proposing in sound a broader, interracial involvement. Its power derives above all from its ambiguity, from its contradictory articulation of two key realms of symbolism" (ibid., xiv).

23. Eugene Levy, *James Weldon Johnson: Black Leader, Black Voice* (Chicago: University of Chicago Press, 1973), 130.

24. Henry Louis Gates Jr., introduction to *The Autobiography of an Ex-Coloured Man* by James Weldon Johnson (1927; rpt., New York: Vintage, 1989), xvi.

25. Johnson wrote letters warning them to "keep the secret" to his brother, Rosamond; his wife, Grace; and an Atlanta University friend, George Towns. See Miles Jackson, ed., "Letters to a Friend: Correspondence from James Weldon Johnson to George A. Towns," *Phylon* 29, no. 2 (1968): 189.

26. Charles S. Johnson, introduction to *The Autobiography of an Ex-Colored Man* (New York: Pelican, 1948); Arna Bontemps, introduction to *The Autobiography of an Ex-Coloured Man* (New York: Hill and Wang, 1960); William L. Andrews, introduction to *The Autobiography of an Ex-Colored Man* (New York: Penguin, 1990); Gates, introduction; Jacqueline Goldsby, introduction to *The Autobiography of an Ex-Colored Man* (New York: Norton, 2015).

27. Amiri Baraka, "The Revolutionary Tradition in Afro-American Literature" (1979), in *The LeRoi Jones/Amiri Baraka Reader*, ed. William J. Harris (New York: Basic, 2000), 316.

28. Robert B. Stepto, *From behind the Veil: A Study of Afro-American Narrative*, 2nd ed. (Urbana: University of Illinois Press, 1991).

29. Skerrett, "Irony and Symbolic Action in James Weldon Johnson's *The Autobiography of an Ex-Coloured Man*," *American Quarterly* 32 (Winter 1980): 540–58; Smith, "Privilege and Evasion in *The Autobiography of an Ex-Colored Man*," in her *Self-Discovery and Authority in Afro-American Narrative* (Cambridge, Mass.: Harvard University Press, 1987), 44–64. Both are reprinted in Price and Oliver, *Critical Essays*.

30. Nathan Irvin Huggins, *Harlem Renaissance* (New York: Oxford University Press, 1971).

31. For example, Cheryl Wall, "Histories and Heresies: En-Gendering the Harlem Renaissance," *Meridians* 2, no. 1 (2001): 59–76.

32. Sollors, *Beyond Ethnicity*; Samira Kawash, *Dislocating the Color Line: Identity, Hybridity, and Singularity in African-American Literature* (Stanford, Calif.: Stanford University Press, 1997).

33. See M. Giulia Fabi, *Passing and the Rise of the African American Novel* (Urbana: University of Illinois Press, 2001); Elaine K. Ginsberg, ed., *Passing and the Fictions of Identity* (Durham, N.C.: Duke University Press, 1996); Phillip Brian Harper, *Are We Not Men? Masculine Anxiety and the Problem of African American Identity* (New York: Oxford University Press, 1998); Judith Butler, *Bodies That Matter: On the Discursive Limits of Sex* (New York: Routledge, 1993); Kevin Mumford, *Interzones: Black/White Sex Districts in Chicago and New York in the Early Twentieth Century* (New York: Columbia University Press, 1997); George Chauncey, *Gay New York: Gender, Urban Culture, and the Making of the Gay Male World, 1890–1940* (New York: Basic, 1994).

34. Matthew Frye Jacobson, *Whiteness of a Different Color* (Cambridge, Mass.: Harvard University Press, 1998).

35. Hutchinson, *The Harlem Renaissance in Black and White* (Cambridge, Mass.: Belknap, 1997); Michael North, *The Dialect of Modernism: Race, Language, and Twentieth-Century Literature* (New York: Oxford University Press, 1998). The boundaries between disciplines are racially inflected and have been symptoms of segregated social practices. Despite this legacy, authors and scholars do collaborate beyond the imposed limitations.

36. Brent Edwards, *The Practice of Diaspora: Literature, Translation, and the Rise of Black Internationalism* (Cambridge, Mass.: Harvard University Press, 2003); Daphne

Brooks, *Bodies in Dissent: Spectacular Performances of Race and Freedom, 1850–1910* (Durham, N.C.: Duke University Press, 2006); Alexander Weheliye, *Phonographies: Grooves in Sonic Afro-Modernity* (Durham, N.C.: Duke University Press, 2005); Fred Moten, *In the Break: The Aesthetics of the Black Radical Tradition* (Minneapolis: University of Minnesota Press, 2003); Diana Taylor, *The Archive and the Repertoire: Performing Cultural Memory in the Americas* (Durham, N.C.: Duke University Press, 2003); Mark Goble, *Beautiful Circuits: Modernism and the Mediated Life* (New York: Columbia University Press, 2010); Katherine Biers, *Virtual Modernism: Writing and Technology in the Progressive Era* (Minneapolis: University of Minnesota Press, 2013).

37. Kenneth Warren, *What Was African American Literature?* (Cambridge, Mass.: Harvard University Press, 2011).

38. Lawrence Jackson, *The Indignant Generation: A Narrative History of African American Writers and Critics, 1934–60* (Princeton, N.J.: Princeton University Press, 2011).

39. Gene Jarrett, *Deans and Truants: Race and Realism in African American Literature* (Philadelphia: University of Pennsylvania Press, 2006); Jarrett, ed., *African American Literature beyond Race* (New York: New York University Press, 2006).

40. Amritjit Singh et al., eds., *The Harlem Renaissance: Revaluations* (New York: Garland, 1989); Singh, *The Novels of the Harlem Renaissance* (University Park: Pennsylvania State University Press, 1976).

41. Robert B. Stepto, "Lost in a Quest: James Weldon Johnson's *The Autobiography of an Ex-Coloured Man*," in *Critical Essays on James Weldon Johnson*, edited by Kenneth M. Price and Lawrence J. Oliver, 43–69 (New York: G. K. Hall, 1997); Lawrence Oliver, *Brander Matthews, Theodore Roosevelt, and the Politics of American Literature, 1880–1920* (Knoxville: University of Tennessee Press, 1992); Oliver, "'Jim Crowed' in Their Own Countries: James Weldon Johnson's *New York Age* Essays on Colonialism during the Wilson Years," in Price and Oliver, *Critical Essays*, 209–22.

42. Michael Nowlin, "Race Literature, Modernism, and Normal Literature: James Weldon Johnson's Groundwork for an African American Literary Renaissance, 1912–20," *Modernism/Modernity* 20, no. 3 (2013): 503–18; Nowlin, "James Weldon Johnson's *Black Manhattan* and the Kingdom of American Culture," *African American Review* 39 (Fall 2005): 315–25; Daphne Lamothe, "Striking Out into the Interior: Travel, Imperialism, and Ethnographic Perspectives in *The Autobiography of an Ex-Colored Man*," in her *Inventing the New Negro: Narrative, Culture, and Ethnography* (Philadelphia: University of Pennsylvania Press, 2008), 69–90; Bruce Barnhart, "Music, Race, and Sublimation: Ragtime and Symphonic Time in *The Autobiography of an Ex-Colored Man*," in his *Jazz in the Time of the Novel: The Temporal Politics of American Race and Culture* (Tuscaloosa: University of Alabama Press, 2013), 41–81.

PART ONE

Cultures of Reading, Cultures of Writing

Canons and Authenticity

"Stepping across the Confines of Language and Race"
Brander Matthews, James Weldon Johnson, and Racial Cosmopolitanism

LAWRENCE J. OLIVER

> It would not have taken a psychologist to understand that I was born to be a New Yorker.... But being born a New Yorker means being born, no matter where, with a love for cosmopolitanism; and one either is or isn't.
>
> —James Weldon Johnson, *Along This Way*

> We New Yorkers have to make traditions for ourselves, as best we may, in the welter and vortex of conflicting influences. We come of stocks so varied, and yet so ill fused, that although the new American begins to emerge, he is surrounded and encompassed about by men of every heredity; and he is receptive perforce; and he is not hostile to the foreigner; and he cannot but be cosmopolitan.
>
> —Brander Matthews, "More American Stories"

In his autobiography, *Along This Way*, James Weldon Johnson relates that after he moved from Jacksonville to New York City in 1902, intent on making his career as a songwriter with his brother, Rosamond, and Bob Cole, he began taking literature classes at Columbia University (then Columbia College) from Brander Matthews (1852–1929), whose writing he had read. Johnson's description of his first meeting with Matthews leaves no doubt that it was a critical event in his literary career. Matthews received him cordially, and Johnson was flattered to discover that the professor was familiar with his work in musical comedy. The visit, Johnson states,

> was the beginning of a warm and lasting friendship between Brander Matthews and me. He talked a great deal about the musical comedy stage and the important people connected with it. In his lectures he frequently set me in an enviable light before the class.... I was fascinated with my work under him. I

was especially impressed with his catholicity, his freedom from pedantry, and his common sense in talking about the theater. I believe that he shocked most of us in the class when he declared that the best plays of Weber and Fields were the same sort of thing as the theater of Aristophanes.[1]

These comments, made after Matthews's death, indicate how deeply Johnson admired the professor, whose classes he attended for three years (1902–5) during a formative period in his literary career. In 1905, before leaving for a European musical tour with Rosamond and Cole, Johnson met with Matthews to discuss his "more serious work" and showed him the first two chapters of his novel. Matthews liked the chapters and the title, and he told Johnson that he was wise to write about what he knew best.[2] Though some attention has been paid to the Johnson-Matthews relationship, there is still a great deal to be learned about how Johnson's years of study under the Columbia professor shaped his literary views and influenced the development of *The Autobiography of an Ex-Colored Man* and later works. Johnson does not specify which of Matthews's numerous texts he read, and we do not know exactly what he heard in Matthews's classes or discussed in private conversations. However, by examining Matthews's major work on the writing and criticism of fiction and drama, we can infer what he taught Johnson about literary theory and the craft of fiction writing during and after his studies at Columbia.

Johnson was an accomplished musician, composer, and journalist before moving to New York City. But fiction writing was new to him. In this genre he was a novice. Matthews's lectures and critical writings provided him with knowledge, guidance, and advice about the craft of fiction that he needed in order to produce an international literary classic that, as Michael Nowlin argues elsewhere in this volume, would defy the white supremacist notion of African American "literary destitution." In *The Historical Novel and Other Essays* (1901), *Aspects of Fiction* (1896), and *Inquiries and Opinions* (published in 1907 but composed of essays and addresses dated 1903–5), Matthews explores a wide range of topics of interest to literary critics and fiction writers.[3] I believe that Matthews's writings and lectures, especially those that explore the problematic interconnections of race, nationalism, and cosmopolitanism, were as important to Johnson's conception and composition of *The Autobiography* as were works by Frederick Douglass, Booker T. Washington, and W. E. B. Du Bois, who provided Johnson with models and tropes relating to African American experiences. What Matthews contributed to Johnson's development as a fiction writer (and poet) was equally important: he presented Johnson with a series of theoretical and technical questions to think through and solve as he planned and drafted his novel.

Matthews was a political and social progressive, and like most white progressives, he believed that while African Americans were entitled to the benefits and protections of U.S. citizenship, they were essentially different; they were thus a part of yet separated from the dominant, white American culture. Matthews's racial ideology is clearly revealed in his introduction (which Johnson solicited) to Johnson's *Fifty Years and Other Poems*. Matthews praises the poetry and asserts that African Americans must be welcomed into the body politic as "American citizens, with the rights and the duties of other American citizens,"[4] a statement that Johnson would have appreciated. Yet Matthews also makes the confounding assertion that even if "they are not as we are," African Americans know "no language, no literature and no law other than those of their fellow citizens of Anglo-Saxon ancestry."[5] Johnson was an integrationist in his politics and aesthetics, but he certainly did not consider himself to be of Anglo-Saxon lineage, and he was fluent in Spanish as well as English. Thus Matthews's conflicted racial ideology, which permeates his critical writings, presented Johnson with a paradox as he was drafting *The Autobiography*.

Matthews's friendship and teaching, I believe, helped create in Johnson a productive tension that plays out in *The Autobiography* as well as in the theory of a modernist black poetics that he develops in his later works.[6] Though the book in many respects fulfills Matthews's criteria for the modern American novel, it also implicitly resists and subverts Matthews's theory of a cultural cosmopolitanism rooted in "Anglo-Saxon ideals."[7] If Matthews's theory of cosmopolitanism encouraged the cross-fertilization of art forms, it ignored the American reality—which Johnson knew all too well from his experience of nearly being lynched in Jacksonville in 1901—that any attempt or even suspicion of cross-fertilization of black and white bodies could mean brutal death. As Jeff Karem argues in his essay in this volume, white elites like Matthews might have had economic and class privilege, but they lacked "privileged knowledge of their own culture because they [did] not possess the [disturbing] truth about their nation in the way the narrator does."[8] One of Johnson's aims was to educate them about their own cultural blindness.

Brander Matthews and Columbia University

It is not difficult to understand why Johnson sought out Matthews when he moved to New York to pursue dual careers as a musical composer and literary artist. Matthews was one of the most prominent and influential scholars and critics of the Progressive Era on both sides of the Atlantic.[9] Though his scholarly interests were broad, drama was his major area of specialty. His numerous books include *French Dramatists of the Nineteenth Century* (1881) and *The Development of the Drama* (1903). Matthews was a regular contributor to the major literary magazines, and his textbook *An Introduction to American Literature* (1896) went through several editions and helped shape the American literary canon of the early twentieth century. Unlike most scholars at elite institutions during the period, Matthews had eclectic tastes and little patience with academics and critics who were "literary mandarins, dwellers in ivory towers, secure in their possession of the only key to all the arts."[10] He was as interested in popular culture as in elite culture, and in all the literary genres. Thus the Columbia professor appreciated and advocated for the western humor of Twain, the free verse of Whitman, the puppet shows performed in New York's Little Italy, the dramatic techniques of Molière and Shakespeare, and the black minstrels and vaudeville that Johnson was writing for and producing in New York City. Whereas the literary "mandarins" denigrated vaudeville and black minstrels, Matthews asserted in "The Importance of the Folk-Theatre" that these "humble forms of drama," which he compared to the French *opéra comique* and *comédie-française* that he enjoyed, were as essential to an understanding of the evolution of the drama as embryology is to a student of zoology.[11] Though that statement is well intentioned and supportive of the kind of work James and Rosamond Johnson were doing, it assigns black cultural production to a lower stage of development, which corresponds to the view that even the most progressive-minded whites had of black people at the time. Johnson would challenge that perspective implicitly in his novel and explicitly in his prefaces to his later anthologies.

Like Johnson, Matthews was a cultural diplomat and mediator who was respected by individuals representing diverse literary and political views, including anti-imperialists like Mark Twain, William Dean Howells, and Richard Watson Gilder, and imperialists such as Rudyard Kipling and Theodore Roosevelt. He was a founder or member of literary clubs in New York, London, and Paris; France awarded him the Legion of Honor in 1907 for his contributions to French literature. Matthews helped organize the American Academy of Arts and Letters, serving as its president during 1912–14, and he was elected as the president of the Modern Language Association in 1910. His personal friendship with Roosevelt, the embodiment of Progressive Era "manly Americanism," was especially close; the two corresponded for decades, often discussing literary and political matters, even while Roosevelt was in the White House.[12]

Literary "Technic"

When Johnson brought to Matthews the first two chapters of *The Autobiography* in 1905, he had already decided on the basic themes and form of his novel of racial passing, including W. E. B. Du Bois's tropes of the color line, double-consciousness, and the veil. However, although Du Bois's masterpiece *The Souls of Black Folk* (1903) inspired Johnson and helped clarify his views on race and black culture, it had little to offer in terms of crafting a modern novel—making decisions about plot, character, narrative technique (spelled "technic" by Matthews), and so on. Even if it had been possible for Johnson to read Du Bois's first novel, *The Quest of the Silver Fleece* (1911), before writing his own, he would have found it formally conventional, its style and narrative technique looking back to the realist and romantic traditions of the previous century. Du Bois had a poetic imagination, and his strength as a creative writer was the lyrical essay, which allowed him to express his own as well as black culture's soul. As he famously stated, the style of his hybrid work was "tropical—African. This needs no apology. The blood of my fathers spoke through me and cast off the English restraint of my training and surrounds."[13]

Johnson's popular musicals, like *Under the Bamboo Tree* ("if you lak-a me, lak I lak-a you") and *The Evolution of Rag-Time*, also may be said to reflect a tropical or African style. But in his novel exploring the psychic duality of a mulatto's experiences in a racist United States, he avoided the tropical style and black dialect, and instead exercised the English restraint of his training under Matthews. He used a "white" form to convey black culture to a racially mixed audience, in effect creating a novel that, like its protagonist, formally passes for white while being black in its essence. According to Matthews, by the end of the nineteenth century, fiction had deposed the competing genres to become the "Napoleon" of literary forms,[14] which is perhaps why Johnson, with his ambition to reach as wide an audience as possible, decided to compose a novel rather than an autobiography. As he states in *Along This Way*, writing fiction presented him with exciting new challenges and opportunities: "The use of prose as a creative medium was new to me; and its latitude, its flexibility, its comprehensiveness, the variety of approaches it afforded for *surmounting technical difficulties* gave me a feeling of exhilaration" (238, emphasis added).

Johnson was a student of form and technique since his childhood days, and he reveled in solving technical problems, whether in mathematics, music, or writing. In *Along This Way*, for example, he relates that when he returned to Stanton School as its principal, he was determined to build an "educational foundation" in higher mathematics, which became a "most fascinating pastime" for him (127). He was determined to discover and prove mathematical principles and to find "simpler and more understandable methods of solution," which "became an absorbing game" (127). As in his study of math, music, and the theater, Johnson was determined to establish the educational foundation that would allow him to understand and solve the technical problems of fiction writing. In Matthews, the epitome of the teacher-scholar, he found the ideal mentor for this type of education.

In his autobiography Matthews writes that during his many years as a professor at Columbia he strove to "make the history of literature alive by an incessant consideration of its ever-advancing technic."[15] In "An Apology for Technic" (1904) and other essays, Matthews offers observations and suggestions that could have helped Johnson surmount the technical difficulties of writing his novel of passing for both black and white audiences, who had conflicting perspectives on most issues involving race. Enduring works of art, Matthews argues in "An Apology for Technic," are the products of three factors: the author's "native gifts," technique, and character. The gifts and the author's character are largely beyond one's control, leaving technique as the one factor that the dedicated artist can improve and perfect. The writers that Matthews selects to support his arguments here and elsewhere are almost always white and male; there are rarely references to black authors, and there is scant attention to women. Great writers such as Shakespeare, Molière, Lope de Vega, Wordsworth, and Poe, he maintains, have always been willing to pay the price of mastering their craft—the "tricks of the trade"—through laborious study and experimentation.[16] All of them exhibit a "ravenous appetite for technic," and the solving of a technical problem has often led to the "ennobling enrichment of the original suggestion, with which the artist might have rested content if he had not been forced to the struggle" (*Inquiries*, 66). Indeed, the solving of technical challenges is the process by which all the arts advance or evolve. Matthews's contention that writing plays is more difficult than writing novels, because the latter are free of the practical constraints that limit playwrights, would have gotten Johnson's attention. So too the professor's quoting of Henry James's dictum that a work of art's moral message must stem organically from, and not be a capricious addition to, the work's inspiration (62).

Johnson of course drew on a wide variety of black and white texts as he constructed his novel, including Poe's mystery tales and perhaps Twain's *Pudd'nhead Wilson* (1894). There is no evidence that Johnson actually read *Pudd'nhead*, but he would have been introduced to that novel and *Huckleberry Finn* (1884) in Matthews's classes. Matthews was among the first academics to recognize that an emphasis on Twain's early humorous writings had obscured the serious and moral themes in his best novels, which to Matthews were *Tom Sawyer* (1876), *Huckleberry Finn*, and *Pudd'nhead Wilson*. Referring to the "great book" *Huckleberry Finn*, Matthews asserts in his introduction to a complete edition of Twain's works: "The influence of slavery, the prevalence of feuds, the conditions and the circumstances that make lynching possible—all these things are set before us clearly and without comment. It is for us to draw our own moral ... as we do when we see Shakespeare acted" (*Inquiries*, 158). To Matthews, *Pudd'nhead* was the most dramatic and "most ingenious" of Twain's novels (158). In "Poet and the Detective-Story," Matthews credits Edgar Allan Poe with being the inventor of the modern mystery/detective story because he shifted the focus of the mystery or horror story from the clever plot to the gradual elucidation of the character's psychological state.

His comments about Poe's psychological fictions apply equally well to Johnson's novel: "Attention is centered on the unraveling of the tangled skein rather than the knot itself" (120). Referring to "The Murders in the Rue Morgue," Matthews writes that the tale's ingenuity lies in the way Poe created a "secret" or problem that seemed to be absolutely hidden, though "all the facts needed to solve it were plainly presented to the reader" (132).

Surveying the development of the novel in his introduction to the 1908 edition of Clayton Hamilton's *The Art of Fiction*, Matthews asserts that the "doer-of-deeds" heroes of "romanticistic" or heroic idealistic fiction à la Walter Scott had become an anachronism, on the way to extinction in the evolution of the novel.[17] The novel's advantage over the drama was that it proved to be "a fit instrument for applied psychology"; thus the modern novelist's task was the "adjustment of character to its appropriate background" and the connection of his or her fiction to the "actual facts of life" (xxiii, xxxiii). In the concluding section of the introduction, Matthews provides a list of specific questions designed to "serve as a stimulus and a guide" for developing writers: "What is the best way to tell a story—in the third person, as in the epic—in the first person as in the autobiography—or in letters? Which is more important, character or incident or atmosphere? Is the novel-with-a-purpose legitimate? ... Ought a novelist to take sides with his characters and against them, or ought he to suppress his own opinions and remain impassive, as the dramatist must[?]" (xxxii).

In that essay and in "An Apology for Technic," Matthews expresses his opinions in response to these and other issues relating to writing fiction, and Johnson's novel is in accord with most of them. For example, Matthews states that any attempt to "require the artist to prove anything is necessarily cramping" (introduction to *The Art of Fiction*, xxv) and that the novel-with-a-purpose, the propagandistic novel, is "necessarily unartistic and unavoidably unsatisfactory" (xxvi). Technique is most effective when "its existence is least suspected" (*Inquiries*, 52). When a writer who is "overanxious" about conveying the moral of his tale makes it transparent for the reader, "he has failed to attain either of his ends, the ethical or the [a]esthetic" (62). One of the failings of fiction writers (including, ironically, Matthews himself) is that the moral message is usually "written so plain that all who run may read" (62). Unlike his preceptor, Johnson solves this problem by employing irony, ambiguity, and what Robert Stepto calls the "rhetoric of detachment"[18]—literary techniques that have compelled readers and critics for more than a hundred years to continue their debates over the ethical and aesthetic dimensions of the text and over placing the novel in the context of literary modernism.

Roughly a decade after leaving Columbia, Johnson repaid his former professor for his valuable lessons on technique: in his *New York Age* piece "About Poetry and Poetry Makers" (1915), he lectures novice poets that a poet "needs to learn his trade, to get the mastery of his tools, just the same as an artist or sculptor or a musician."[19] Of course they should read (but not copy) the great masters of English poetry, including Poe, but they must also learn the "mechanism of verse," which may be accomplished, he suggests, by reading Brander Matthews's *A Study of Versification* (1911).

Race, Nationalism, and Cosmopolitanism

Yet, despite the relentless focus on technique in his critical writings, Matthews warns that mere craftsmanship is insufficient if the work does not express ideas and emotions that flow from the artist's character, which is indelibly marked by the artist's race. The scientific study of race and racial differences was a Progressive Era obsession, and the Columbia University faculty included several of the most influential racialists of the day. Social scientists such as Franklin H. Giddings and John Burgess promoted the theory of Anglo-Saxon and Teutonic racial superiority and argued that the American ideals of democracy, individualism, family values, and even female chastity stemmed from what they proclaimed to be the two great world races. Matthews was initially influenced by his colleagues' scientific racism, but his views were altered by the anthropological research of another Columbia colleague, Franz Boas, and also, I suggest, by his relationship with Johnson.[20]

In Matthews's writings, race is an unstable term; it may refer to skin color but also to nation or culture; thus he refers to the Anglo-Saxon race, the French race, and the English-speaking race. Both Matthews and Theodore Roosevelt believed that U.S. culture was a "branch" of the English-speaking "race," whose ideals were rooted in Anglo-Saxon culture. Regarding the intersections of race and literature, Matthews was profoundly influenced by the French historian Hippolyte Taine's theory that cultures or nationalities could be explained in terms of "race, environment, and epoch."[21] According to Taine members of a particular race or culture exhibit distinct "dispositions of mind and soul" that in turn are reflected in the literature and art of that race or culture. This notion of art reflecting the soil and character of a given people or culture was one of Matthews's critical pillars, suffusing his criticism and scholarship. In his 1898 essay "The Study of Fiction," for example, he encouraged scholars to "test the fullness and the accuracy with which race characteristics are recorded in the fiction of a language—how the energy and the humor of the Anglo-Saxon stock dominate the novels of the English language."[22]

Johnson, Du Bois, and other black as well as white authors of the late nineteenth century who rejected biological racial inferiority nonetheless believed that distinct racial characteristics were inscribed in the formal aspects of music and literature; in other words, the formal aspects of the text functioned as an "analogical extension of the race."[23] Thus on the issue of a text's projection or embodiment of the writer's racial spirit, Matthews, Johnson, and Du Bois were in general agreement, even if they had differing conceptions of what "race" actually meant and what specific "gifts" each "race" possessed. Matthews took this theory a step further, however, by arguing that a racial or cultural heritage was transmitted through the particular language. In his 1896 essay "American Literature," for example, he avers that non-Anglos can assimilate "Anglo-Saxon ideals" through mastery of the English language, which he characterizes as possessing a "marvelous faculty for assimilating members of other allied stems, and . . . getting these newly received elements to accept its own hereditary ideals."[24] Thus language functions as an agent of assimilation, and anyone can, in theory, be assimilated or pass into a culture by learning its language. This theory, obviously, ignores white supremacy's often violent enforcement of the socially constructed color line, which Johnson would dramatize in his novel and in anti-lynching poems, such as "Brothers."

In 1904 Johnson met Du Bois, the author of *The Souls of Black Folk*, a critical event in the genesis and development of *The Autobiography of an Ex-Colored Man*. For Johnson, another important literary event that year was, I believe, Matthews's "Literature in the New Century," an address the professor delivered at the International Congress of the Arts and Sciences (held in St. Louis in 1904) and published as the first chapter of *Inquiries and Opinions*. If Johnson did not read the essay, he undoubtedly heard the major ideas in his classes or conversations with Matthews. Pulling together the threads of much of his earlier critical work, Matthews in many ways anticipated current literary and cultural debates over the intersections of race/ethnicity, nationalism, cosmopolitanism, and modernism, which are in turn reflected in much of the scholarship on Johnson since the late 1990s.[25] As the title implies, Matthews charts the literary trends of the twentieth century. Those trends, he asserts, are responsive to the environmental forces (social, political, and economic) that invariably shape cultural productions (*Inquiries*, 4).[26] Johnson would have been especially interested in his professor's view that literature of the new century, to which Johnson himself was contributing, would be shaped by four legacies or currents of the nineteenth-century culture—the scientific spirit, the spread of democracy, the accretion of nationality, and, finally, cosmopolitanism, "that stepping across the confines of language and race" (5). The cosmopolitan-minded Johnson was, of course, already stepping in that direction in his musical compositions, but Matthews articulates in "Literature in the New Century" a virtual blueprint for writers who wanted to make their mark on modern cosmopolitan literature, as Johnson did. I therefore want to examine the essay in some detail.

Matthews's perspective on the new century clearly reveals how his literary and political progressivism was rooted in a belief in racial or cultural difference. The first legacy, the scientific spirit, in essence requires writers to be literary realists, striving to examine life as it is and reporting accurately their perceptions in works that are characterized by "passionless proportion and moderation" (*Inquiries*, 8). He defines the second force, democracy, not only as a political system, but as a frame of mind that embraces the dignity of all humans, sympathy, tolerance, and a "rejoicing to learn how the other half lives" (12), an obvious reference to Progressive reformer Jacob Riis's book. All human history, Matthews continues, has been evolving toward national ideals. As noted above, he believed that racial or national ideals are embedded in and transmitted by language. Since a nation is composed of regions in which people speak different dialects, literary "local color" forms part of the national literary fabric. American writers ought therefore probe not only the "nooks and corners of our own nation," but also the literary productions of "other races," by which he means other national cultures. Quoting Tennyson's assertion that it is authors more than diplomats that "make nations love one another" (22), Matthews remarks that no tariff can prevent the masterpieces of foreign literature from crossing national boundaries and broadening human understanding, which implies that black literary works may enter cultural spaces closed off to black bodies. From there he segues into a call for cosmopolitanism, but it is a cosmopolitanism that is rooted in race/nationalism. Matthews believed that New York City was "really more cosmopolitan than Paris" because of its rich mixing of immigrant cultures, but he always privileged the national (American) over the international.[27]

In the essay, Matthews attempts to reconcile his seemingly conflicting embrace of both nationalism and cosmopolitanism by defining the former as a racial spirit or consciousness, which is not transferable, and the latter as the external forms of literature, which may be shared. Literary forms, he asserts, employing an evolutionary metaphor, may "cross-fertilize," and the "hybrids that result are ever struggling to revert each to its own species" (*Inquiries*, 8). Citing a list of titles by writers such as Goethe, Turgenev, Dumas, Miguel Piñero, and Gabriele D'Annunzio, Matthews states: "Similar as they are in structure, in their artistic formula, they are radically dissimilar in their essence, in the motives that move the characters and in their outlooks on life" (23), and these dissimilarities are due "chiefly to the nationality of each" (23). The essay concludes with a passage that summarizes his theory of cosmopolitanism: "It is the spirit of nationality which will help to supply needful idealism. It will allow a man of letters to frequent the past without becoming archaic and to travel abroad without becoming exotic, because it will supply him always with a good reason for remaining a citizen of his own country"(25). To be cosmopolitan, then, is to steep oneself in the literature and culture of other nations—or at least European nations and cultures—but then return patriotically home.

Johnson seems to have paid close attention to his mentor's ideas, for *The Autobiography* fulfills virtually all Matthews's requirements for a modern novel. However, it does so with a racial difference. Johnson echoes Matthews's "passionless proportion and moderation" dictum when he promises in the preface that his feigned autobiography will provide a "composite and proportionate" presentation of the African American race. We can hear Matthews's lectures on literary technique when the young narrator says, in the second chapter of *The Autobiography*, that he does not rely solely on the "mere brilliancy of technic" to astonish his audience, but always plays with feelings, expressing the "pathetic turns and cadences" that he absorbed through the "quaint songs" his mother sang when he was a boy (*The Autobiography*, 17). In other words, he uses universal forms to express his black racial heritage, producing multiracial "Siamese twins." Similarly, we are reminded of Matthews's condemnation of the academic mandarins and his defense of a democratic literature when the narrator—who is bestowed the title of "professor" of music while in the club—lectures the reader in defense of popular music after he has been dazzled by the masterly "technic" and "barbaric harmonies" of the ragtime pianist.[28] Referring to the elites' contemptuous dismissal of ragtime, the narrator asserts: "But that has always been the course of scholasticism in every branch of art. Whatever new thing the *people* like is poo-poohed; whatever is *popular* is spoken of as not worth the while." The best work, that with international appeal, stems not from the "brain of any master" but from the "hearts of the people" (61). *The Autobiography* also enacts Matthews's advice for novelists to explore not only the "nooks and corners" of the United States, but "those of other races," providing an international perspective. And if the picaresque structure that Johnson employs parallels that of the slave narrative, it also closely follows the evolutionary trajectory of Matthews's theory, from the local color of Jacksonville's Cuban community and of black bohemia in the Tenderloin, to the international setting of Europe. The novel, as Sarah Wilson has argued, exemplifies "melting pot modernism."[29]

For Matthews the true cosmopolitan artist must avoid the trap of becoming an "exotic" foreigner in another country and must, after experiencing that culture, return to the native soil that inspires idealism. The narrator starts on this path when he accompanies the unnamed millionaire to Europe. There he is initially charmed by the Old World and states that the carefree and pleasurable culture of Paris "appealed to me as an ideal" (*The Autobiography*, 78). His guide, of course, is the millionaire, who embodies that rootless form of cosmopolitanism that Matthews found pernicious. With no national or racial spirit to ground and inspire him, the millionaire has become a jaded, materialistic, self-indulgent "exotic" who devotes most of his time to observing the behavior of others. He has no sense of responsibility to others. One might say that he has elegant form but no moral center—like a novel that is technically sophisticated but soulless.

When the narrator makes the critical decision to leave the millionaire and Europe to return to the United States, with a determination to use his racial gifts to help African Americans in their struggle for justice and citizenship, he is on the verge of fulfilling Matthews's ideal of the true cosmopolite, who maintains the "spirit of nationality" that supplies the "idealism" necessary to produce great art—even if his motives are selfish, as he acknowledges (*The Autobiography*, 88). But at this critical juncture in the narrative, Johnson reverses the trajectory toward Matthews's cosmopolitan Americanism, for the rest of the novel demonstrates why an American of color has compelling reasons for not "remaining a citizen of his own country." As George Hutchinson has argued, the historical complexity of race can be best understood by examining those moments when the intertwined discourses of race, culture, and nation are exposed to skepticism and critique.[30] Such skepticism and critique, of course, infuse *The Autobiography*, beginning in chapter 2, when the young narrator discovers he is a "nigger" and from then on is forced to view everything "not from the viewpoint of a citizen, or a man, or even a human being, but from the viewpoint of a *colored* man" (*The Autobiography*, 13). Though the millionaire is a selfish, hedonistic character, the arguments he marshals to convince the narrator to remain in Europe are nonetheless persuasive, and they reflect Johnson's own conflicted feelings as he performed his diplomatic role for the country that nearly lynched him.[31]

The graphically depicted lynching that ultimately leads the narrator to become an *ex*-colored man, as well as the Texan's racial diatribe and ignorant championing of Anglo-Saxon racial supremacy on the train, dramatically challenge Matthews's Anglo-centered national ideology. Of course, the fact that the mulatto narrator is genetically both black and white poses a paradox for any racial ideology based on a stable color line. The narrator, like American culture, is an "impure" mixture of races, the skin colors of which, as he observes in Atlanta, range from "jet black to pure white" (*The Autobiography*, 39). He is part of (or separated from, depending on one's perspective) both black and white American culture. And if, as Matthews insisted, cultural ideals are transmitted through language, then it logically follows that the narrator, who becomes fluent in Spanish during his immersion in Jacksonville's Cuban community, has mixed Spanish ideals with Anglo-Saxon ones. Thus Johnson's novel subverts Matthews's theory of a linguistically transmitted American cosmopolitanism, even as it exemplifies his conviction, expressed in the second epigraph to this essay, that New Yorkers have to "make traditions for ourselves, as best we may, in the welter and vortex of conflicting influences." In *The Autobiography*, Johnson fashions his own tradition, an "Aframerican" one, to use his term.

Given that his novel so plainly and powerfully deconstructs the foundation of Matthews's Anglocentric literary and cultural theory, it is surprising that as Johnson struggled with the final section of the work in Venezuela in 1908, he sent the draft manuscript not to Du Bois, William Stanley Braithwaite, or one of his other African American supporters, but to Matthews. In the letter accompanying the manuscript, he confesses his doubts and expresses his hopes to his mentor. He worries that he has "lost the spirit of the story" and that the closing section is not up to the rest of the manuscript because he lacks the ability to write "convincingly" of love.[32] "I hope that the story will now get a chance," he writes, an implicit appeal for Matthews's assistance in getting the work in front of a publisher. But despite these concerns, Johnson has "found himself" in Venezuela, and he is now considering returning to New York with the "power to do better work than before."[33]

To his credit, Matthews remained completely supportive of Johnson and worked publicly and behind the scenes to promote the novel. When *The Autobiography* was first published in 1912, Matthews (who kept Johnson's secret about the work's authorship) sent copies to a number of influential white figures, including Felix Adler, Roosevelt, and Kipling.[34] When Roosevelt failed to respond after a year had passed, Matthews again encouraged him to read the work by the anonymous "colored man of letters," adding that it "is not exactly fact, but it is the truth! And it lets the light into some dark and curious places."[35] Roosevelt eventually replied that he read the "autobiography" and was "much impressed by it." Matthews passed those positive comments on to Johnson, but withheld Roosevelt's more troubling remarks: "There is not any more puzzling problem in this country than the problem of color. It is not as urgent, or as menacing, as other problems, but it seems more utterly insoluble. The trouble is that the conflict in many of its phases is not between right and wrong, but between two rights."[36]

Matthews also praised Johnson's novel in a review titled "American Character in American Fiction," published in *Munsey's Magazine* (1913). Subtitled "Three Books Which Depict the Actualities of Present-Day Life," the essay recommends Johnson's book along with Howells's *New Leaf Mills* (1913) and Robert Herrick's *One Woman's Life* (1913) as examples of literary art that explores the complexities of the human character and that demands repeated readings in order to be fully savored. *The Autobiography of an Ex-Colored Man* exemplifies, he says, Taine's principle that the fiction writer should be a "psychologist ... a transmitter of ideas and feelings," rather than a manufacturer of clever plots. Still pretending not to know the author or genre of the work, Matthews writes that *The Autobiography* "seems" to be fiction and that the "indisputable veracity" of the story convinces him that the author is indeed a black man. The book, he continues, "may not be a record of actual fact, but it contains what is higher than actual fact, the essential truth." And that truth, he asserts, "has significance for all of us who want to understand our fellow citizens of darker hue,"[37] as Matthews clearly did. Earlier in the essay, Matthews quotes Howells's remark that great novels "shame you" into at least wishing to be a better person. Perhaps Matthews felt shamed as he read the novel, which illuminates not only the cultural richness of black culture but also the sometimes savage injustices that blacks, including Johnson, are exposed to—and if so, he wanted Roosevelt, Kipling, and other white readers to feel that shame as well. Despite Matthews's positive review and behind-the-scenes lobbying, the novel did not sell well nor receive much critical attention until it was rediscovered by Carl Van Vechten, whose introduction to the 1927 reprinted edition echoes Matthews's 1913 review: Van Vechten describes the work as an "invaluable sourcebook for the study of Negro psychology."[38]

Johnson continued to correspond with and seek the assistance of Matthews into the mid-1920s, even after he had formed the friendships with H. L. Mencken and Van Vechten that have received so much critical attention.[39] In *Along This Way* he notes that he visited Matthews often after he returned to New York from Corinto, Nicaragua, in 1914, and in 1922 he asked Matthews to review *The Book of American Negro Poetry*.[40] Though Matthews's stature as a literary scholar and critic had faded, he was still well connected and influential, and Johnson no doubt hoped that a positive review by Matthews would promote sales of his book. Johnson's letter also reflects the genuine fondness for Matthews that he expresses in *Along This Way*, as well as a desire to impress his former mentor. Johnson urges Matthews to read the preface to the anthology, which, he says, discusses "some of the things which I have already talked to you about."[41] That remark indicates that Johnson's landmark preface was in part a continuation of the dialogue on race, nationalism, and cosmopolitanism that Johnson and Matthews had begun two decades earlier.

In the preface Johnson expresses his views with the power that he gained in Venezuela and that was reinforced by his relationship with Mencken, in effect using his former professor's theory of literary cosmopolitanism to make the case for the superiority of black cultural products. Now Johnson is the expert, and Matthews the undereducated student. The American Negro, Johnson famously proclaims in the preface, has created the "only things artistic that have sprung from American soil and been universally acknowledged as distinctive American products."[42] Echoing but transforming Matthews's ideas, Johnson states that blacks have "suck[ed] up the national spirit from the soil" to create art that has "universal appeal" because of their "remarkable racial gift of adaptability."[43] Three years later he sent Matthews a copy of *The Book of American Negro Spirituals* (1925). In the preface to that volume Johnson argued that the international appeal of the spirituals sprang from the melding of the "musical genius of Africa" with the experience of slavery and Christianity in America.[44] Matthews read this book with "profit and pleasure."[45] Like all exceptional students, Johnson built on his former professor's teachings to develop his own theory, which he presented in essays that are now canonical works of American and African American literature.

Thus Johnson's complex relationship with Matthews was reciprocal. Johnson broadened and deepened Matthews's perspective on African Americans by illuminating the beauties of black expressive culture and its contributions to world culture, as well as the subtle and blatant traumas of being black in a white supremacist country. Though Matthews's views on race and nationalism are by today's standards Eurocentric and conservative, the fact remains that he played a critical and, I believe, generally positive role in Johnson's development as a fiction writer and cultural critic. From *The Autobiography* through the anthologies, Johnson engaged in continuous conversation with Matthews, whose writings, lectures, and personal advice stimulated Johnson's thinking on literary technique and on the vexing interconnections of race, nationalism, and cosmopolitanism. The result was Johnson's enduring contributions to a "literature for the new century" that crosses the confines of language and race.

NOTES

1. *Along This Way: The Autobiography of James Weldon Johnson* (1933; rpt., New York: Penguin, 1990), 192–93. Future references to this edition are given parenthetically in the text.

2. Elsewhere in *Along This Way*, Johnson praises Matthews's teaching ability (93); he states that in 1904, "I applied myself with more diligence to my work at Columbia" and began planning "more literary work," evidently the novel (221); he sent his poem "Fifty Years" to Matthews, who saw to its publication in the *New York Times* on January 1, 1913 (290); and he visited Matthews often after he returned to New York from Corinto, Nicaragua, in 1914 (305). The James Weldon Johnson and Grace Nail Johnson Papers at the Beinecke Rare Book and Manuscript Library, Yale University (hereafter JWJ BRBL), JWJ Correspondence, ser. 1, box 13, folder 315, contain eighteen pieces of correspondence between Johnson and Matthews.

3. Matthews, *The Historical Novel and Other Essays* (New York: Scribner's, 1901); Matthews, *Aspects of Fiction and Other Ventures in Criticism* (1896; rpt., New York: Harper, 1902); Matthews, *Inquiries and Opinions* (1907; rpt., Freeport, N.Y.: Books for Libraries Press, 1968).

4. Johnson, *Fifty Years and Other Poems* (1917; rpt., New York: AMS Press, 1975), xi.

5. Ibid.

6. All page references are to *The Autobiography of an Ex-Colored Man*, ed. Noelle Morrissette (1912; rpt., New York: Fine Creative Media, Barnes and Noble Classics, 2007). I use the 1912 edition because it is the version that Matthews read and responded to.

7. See Ben Glaser's essay in this collection for an extensive reading of Johnson's subversive innovations in poetic meter and rhythm.

8. I find Karem's central thesis, that the novel's much-discussed "joke" is actually on white readers, intriguing. As Karem observes, throughout the novel Johnson "plays

upon assumptions of white privilege and authority." Since Matthews epitomized white privilege and authority, Johnson likely had him in mind as he developed the "joke"; meanwhile, Matthews was giving him the technical tools to pull it off, narratologically speaking.

9. For details of Matthews's career, writings, and influence, see Claudia Stokes, *Writers in Retrospect: The Rise of American Literary History, 1875–1910* (Chapel Hill: University of North Carolina Press, 2006), 33–74; Lawrence J. Oliver, *Brander Matthews, Theodore Roosevelt, and the Politics of American Literature, 1880–1920* (Knoxville: University of Tennessee Press, 1992).

10. Brander Matthews, "American Character in American Fiction," *Munsey's Magazine*, August 1913, 795.

11. Matthews, *Aspects of Fiction*, 106–8.

12. See Lawrence J. Oliver, ed., *The Letters of Theodore Roosevelt and Brander Matthews* (Knoxville: University of Tennessee Press, 1995).

13. Du Bois, "On *The Souls of Black Folk*," in *The Oxford W. E. B. Du Bois Reader*, ed. Eric J. Sundquist (New York: Oxford University Press, 1996), 305.

14. Matthews, *Historical Novel and Other Essays*, 80.

15. Brander Matthews, *These Many Years: Recollections of a New Yorker* (New York: Scribner's, 1917), 408.

16. Brander Matthews, "An Apology for Technic," in *Inquiries and Opinions*, 60. Future references to *Inquiries* are given parenthetically in the text.

17. Brander Matthews, introduction to *The Art of Fiction* by Clayton Hamilton (1908; rpt., New York: Doubleday, Doran, 1939), xxiii. Future references to this work are given parenthetically in the text.

18. Robert B. Stepto, "Lost in a Quest: James Weldon Johnson's *The Autobiography of an Ex-Coloured* Man," in *Critical Essays on James Weldon Johnson*, ed. Kenneth M. Price and Lawrence J. Oliver (New York: G. K. Hall, 1997), 54.

19. Johnson, "About Poetry and Poetry Makers" (1915), in James Weldon Johnson, *The Selected Writings of James Weldon Johnson*, ed. Sondra Kathryn Wilson (New York: Oxford University Press, 1995), 1:256–57. See also Ben Glaser's essay in this collection on Johnson's technical innovations in poetry.

20. In 1915 Matthews sent Boas's antiwar pamphlet *Race and Nationality* to Roosevelt (see Oliver, *Letters*, 207–8).

21. Oliver, *Brander Matthews, Theodore Roosevelt*, 9–10.

22. Brander Matthews, "The Study of Fiction" (1898), in his *Historical Novel and Other Essays*, 84.

23. John D. Kerkering, *The Poetics of National and Racial Identity in Nineteenth-Century American Literature* (Cambridge: Cambridge University Press), 8.

24. Matthews, *Aspects of Fiction*, 6, 9.

25. See, e.g., George Hutchinson, *The Harlem Renaissance in Black and White* (Cambridge, Mass.: Belknap, 1997); Kerkering, *Poetics*; Noelle Morrissette, *James Weldon Johnson's Modern Soundscapes* (Iowa City: University of Iowa Press, 2013); Amanda Page, "The Ever-Expanding South: James Weldon Johnson and the Rhetoric of the Global Color Line," *Southern Quarterly: A Journal of the Arts in the South* 46, no. 3 (Spring 2009): 26–46; Harilaos Stecopoulos, *Reconstructing the World: Southern Fictions and*

U.S. Imperialisms, 1898–1976 (Ithaca, N.Y.: Cornell University Press, 2008); and Sarah Wilson, *Melting Pot Modernism* (Ithaca, N.Y.: Cornell University Press, 2010).

26. In his presidential address to the Modern Language Association in 1910, "The Economic Interpretation of Literary History" (rpt., *PMLA* 115, no. 7 [December 2000]: 1762–69), Matthews sounds quite modern when he encourages literary critics and historians to move beyond the "great man" approach to literary studies and instead explore the influences of the economic and political contexts—including copyright law, trade unions, and government support for the arts—that shape literary production. It is especially important, he argues, that creative writers in a democratic society be fairly rewarded for their work so that they can appeal to the common people.

27. Brander Matthews, "More American Stories," *Cosmopolitan*, September 1892, 626.

28. See Lori Brooks's essay in this collection for a full discussion of the ragtime "perfessor."

29. Wilson writes that Johnson "approached integration as melting-pot thinkers approached assimilation: that is, he understood cultural merging to take place at a formal level. Johnson's melting-pot modernism is most distinctly registered in his decision to advance his political and cultural agendas through sustained experimentation at the level of expressive form" (*Melting Pot Modernism*, 92). As Noelle Morrissette, *James Weldon Johnson's Modern Soundscapes* (Iowa City: University of Iowa Press, 2013), has shown, Johnson employs the musical technique of interpolation—the insertion of foreign or unrelated material into a musical or literary work—to dissolve binaries and boundaries and to illuminate cultural heterogeneity.

30. George Hutchinson, *The Harlem Renaissance in Black and White* (Cambridge, Mass.: Belknap, 1997), 26.

31. For good discussions of Johnson's complicated and often conflicted feelings toward U.S. imperialism during this period, see Stecopoulos, *Reconstructing the World*, 53–76; Page, "The Ever-Expanding South."

32. Johnson to Matthews, November 1908, JWJ Correspondence, ser. 1, box 13, folder 315, JWJ BRBL.

33. Ibid.

34. Kipling apparently did not read the book, and he continued to express his racist, imperialist views in his letters to Matthews.

35. Oliver, *Letters*, 199.

36. Ibid., 200.

37. "American Character in American Fiction," 798.

38. Van Vechten, introduction, reprinted in Price and Oliver, *Critical Essays*, 26–27. Ironically, Van Vechten singles out the passage in the novel in which Johnson criticizes "scholasticism in every branch of art," which, as noted above, was one of Matthews's refrains.

39. See, for example, Charles Scruggs, *The Sage in Harlem: H. L. Mencken and the Black Writers of the 1920s* (Baltimore, Md.: Johns Hopkins University Press, 1984); Emily Bernard, introduction to *Remember Me to Harlem: The Letters of Langston Hughes and Carl Van Vechten, 1925–64* (New York: Knopf, 2001).

40. Matthews declined Johnson's request to review *The Book of American Negro Poetry*, stating that it was not the "kind of book I can review to advantage; and I want to see it well reviewed." Matthews to Johnson, March 23, 1922, JWJ Correspondence, ser. 1, box 13, folder 315, JWJ BRBL. He also declined to review *The Book of American Negro Spirituals* for the same reason.

41. Johnson to Matthews, March 20, 1922, ibid.

42. Johnson, preface, *The Book of American Negro Poetry* (1922), in his *Writings*, ed. William L. Andrews (New York: Library of America, 2004), 688–89.

43. Ibid., 697.

44. Johnson, preface, *The Books of American Negro Spirituals: Two Volumes in One*, ed. James Weldon Johnson and J. Rosamond Johnson (1925, 1926; rpt., New York: Da Capo, 1969), 18–20.

45. Matthews to Johnson, October 14, 1925, JWJ Correspondence, ser. 1, box 13, folder 315, JWJ BRBL.

How *The Autobiography of an Ex-Colored Man* Became an Unlikely Literary Classic

MICHAEL NOWLIN

In the first major interview he gave after winning the National Book Award for *Invisible Man*, Ralph Ellison was asked whether he thought his novel would still be around in twenty years. "I doubt it," he answered. "It's not an important novel. I failed of eloquence, and many of the immediate issues are rapidly fading away. If it does last, it will be simply because there are things going on in its depth that are of more permanent interest than on its surface. I hope so, anyway."[1] The humility rings a bit false here, even with the benefit of hindsight. Still, the complex literary fate in store for Ellison was likely far different from what he had in mind in 1954. On the one hand, the book his interviewers referred to as typical of "first novels" would prove to be his only completed novel, even though he would continue writing as a novelist for another forty years; on the other, over the course of his career he would see it consecrated as one of the major achievements in American fiction, even as indeed "many of the immediate issues" it dealt with more or less rapidly faded away.

Ellison had good reason to feel he could not bask too much in his success at becoming the most recent "Negro American" literary star. He knew that important African American novels tended to become historical curiosities or at best milestones marking the progress of a separate-but-unequal Negro literature on the road toward full literary equality with (white) American literature. In 1954, *Invisible Man* was already promising to have that effect on *Native Son*, Richard Wright's 1940 bestseller, which in the eyes of most critics at the time eclipsed all African American literary achievements before it. But rather than recalling the example of Wright, whose literary output was fertile if uneven during the eight years between the appearance of *Invisible Man* and his death in 1960, Ellison's career invites a more striking comparison with that of a relatively unacknowledged earlier precursor, James Weldon Johnson, who also began his literary career with the publication of a novel he could pretend was not terribly important. That first and only novel was meant to pave the way for his higher calling as a poet, but it proved to be the book on which his claim to literary immortality primarily would rest.

We can more easily imagine Johnson being genuinely surprised by the "classic" status *The Autobiography of an Ex-Colored Man* still enjoys more than a century after its initial publication than we can wholly accept Ellison's claim—"thirty astounding years" after the publication of *Invisible Man*—that his "highest hope for the novel was that it would sell enough copies to prevent [his] publishers from losing on their investment and [his] editor from having wasted his time."[2] There were crucial differences in their literary situations that reflect worse and better moments in African Americans' struggle against segregation. *Invisible Man* appeared on the cusp of Jim Crow's legal demise, *The Autobiography of an Ex-Colored Man* in the midst of Jim Crow's "nadir" period.[3] *Invisible Man* was published by a major New York firm (Random House), enjoyed good sales and laudatory reviews, and was given the National Book Award: it became something of an instant classic and won its author a literary celebrity that he managed to sustain. *The Autobiography of an Ex-Colored Man* was published by a small Boston house (Sherman, French and Company) to negligible sales and few notices; it was soon out of print, and Johnson was asked to help sell the remaining copies. And because, for reasons inseparable from the meaning of the work, Johnson chose to publish it anonymously, any celebrity he hoped to garner from it was deferred (though in the meantime he signaled his literary arrival with the publication of "Fifty Years," his poem commemorating emancipation, in the *New York Times* on New Year's Day 1913). *The Autobiography* reappeared with Johnson's name on it in 1927, during the heyday of the Harlem Renaissance, and only then was it touted as a "classic of Negro literature" by his publisher, Alfred A. Knopf. As such it remained in print until 1961, bolstered by a cheap paperback edition issued by the New American Library in 1948. Knopf's marketing gimmick undoubtedly helped the novel resurface in the 1965 Avon paperback *Three Negro Classics* (alongside Booker T. Washington's *Up from Slavery* [1900] and W. E. B. Du Bois's *The Souls of Black Folk* [1903]), but it never led to big sales or, more important, gave Johnson's work the force of a classic. Virtually no subsequent black writer, let alone most of his or her white American counterparts, could ignore *Invisible Man*. Neither Ellison, Wright, nor even Zora Neale Hurston ever felt compelled to mention *The Autobiography of an Ex-Colored Man* as an influence.[4] And one would be hard pressed to find much evidence of its existence for white American or European writers throughout the rest of the century.[5]

Nonetheless, James Weldon Johnson once harbored literary ambitions almost as lofty as Ellison's, and their achievements are to some degree commensurate. Aspiring to literary seriousness, they had no choice but to accept the circumstances of having to write within and against the culture of Jim

Crow to the ultimate political end of defeating legal segregation and the fictions of white supremacy. The most fundamental of these circumstances, I would argue, was the perceived condition of black literary destitution, which defined any African American literary aspirant's relation to the literary field. That is, both Johnson and Ellison sought to make their mark under a widespread assumption (which they shared) that African American authors still had little to show the nation, let alone the world. And this mattered precisely because they felt the truth of the concomitant assumption, repeatedly voiced by Johnson, that "no race that produced a great literature has ever been looked upon by the world as distinctly inferior."[6] The entrenchment of Jim Crow wrought by *Plessy v. Ferguson* in 1896 imposed a peculiar double burden on the aspiring African American writer that was more fundamental than the problem of how to reach both white and black readers. To recall Kenneth Warren's succinct summary of that burden, African American literature had to be largely instrumental, a means of combating more or less indirectly the injustices of American racism, while also being inescapably indexical, a measure of the race's growing capacity to produce genuine art.[7] Given that tendentiousness was increasingly assumed to be at odds with aesthetic integrity in high literary circles, the African American writer's situation was paradoxical indeed. I am most concerned here with the effect of *Plessy v. Ferguson* on African Americans' sense of the indexical value of "literature." The further impetus it gave African Americans to think of themselves as a distinct "people" or "race" or "nation" made the problem of literary destitution suddenly loom larger, and the imperative to produce internationally recognized literary "classics" all the more urgent. It is surely no coincidence that the 1890s witnessed seminal calls for a "race literature" by Anna Julia Cooper and Victoria Earle Matthews, among others, one that might establish itself in what Matthews calls "the broader field of universal literature."[8]

The initial successes of Paul Laurence Dunbar and Charles Chesnutt around the turn of the twentieth century—pioneering figures in virtually every early and mid-twentieth-century account of African American literature—should suggest that the sense of literary destitution could be as productive as it could be debilitating. I mean to demonstrate here that the virtues and staying power of *The Autobiography of an Ex-Colored Man*, let alone *Invisible Man*, owe much to that productive awareness. I begin making this case by recovering the moment when Johnson gradually discovered his literary vocation, an experience coinciding with the long gestation of his novel, begun early in 1905 and published in 1912. Given the care with which he worked on the book, his decision to publish it anonymously seems at first glance perverse, since in the interests of the "practical joke on society" he was playing by launching a fake autobiography of a black man living as white,[9] he risked losing any literary reputation he stood to gain as its author. And Johnson was indeed after a reputation as a serious literary artist in these years—but in 1912 he was confident that he would win it through his poetry.

Johnson makes for a unique case of literary ambition not because his efforts emerged in the wake of discarded bourgeois career paths—school principal, lawyer—but because his ambition arose in the wake of his considerable success at the turn of the century as a popular songwriter for Broadway shows. That success established him, along with his brother, J. Rosamond Johnson, and Bob Cole, in New York City and in the cosmopolitan milieu in which he remained forever at home. Johnson's conception of "serious" literature (like "legitimate" theater) no doubt owed much to his upbringing and formal education, but it gained traction from his early achievements in Tin Pan Alley and on Broadway. He may have tasted a modest fame and fortune, the good will of white audiences, and even momentary freedom from racism (as he remembered feeling during their European tour). But that success was founded on a form of entertainment with deep roots in minstrelsy, one that sat relatively comfortably with white expectations of black cultural capacities. Johnson's subsequent, lifelong effort to erect a racial literature on the foundation of popular expressive forms—which he thought of as vital, yet of a lower order—correlates neatly with his graduation from show business to the higher calling of literary writing. The very "dearth of Afro-American writers," to recall the title of an April 20, 1905, editorial by his friend T. Thomas Fortune for the *New York Age*, suggests how risky a trajectory Johnson was taking, but he minimized that risk by accepting the consulate positions opened up for him (first in Venezuela, then in Nicaragua) by his work for Theodore Roosevelt and the Republican Party in 1904, and by upgrading his literary education under the tutelage of the critic and Columbia University English professor Brander Matthews. Despite Matthews's flattering familiarity with Johnson's "work in musical comedy" and his shocking declaration to his students that the theater of Weber and Fields was comparable to that of Aristophanes, it was not work in this vein about which Johnson approached Matthews for advice before embarking on the 1905 European tour, but rather the "more serious work" represented by a draft of the opening chapters of *The Autobiography of an Ex-Colored Man* and a couple of poems he subsequently placed with the *Bookman*.[10]

Encouraged by Matthews, Johnson set out to make his mark as a writer, and he surely saw the diplomatic career as more conducive to serious literary work than was the sociable hustle of show business. "I have lots of leisure for reading and thinking," he wrote to his friend George Towns from Puerto Cabello in October 1906.[11] His first important poem, "O Black and Unknown Bards," appeared two years later in the prestigious, genteel *Century* magazine. In late 1908 he sent a fresh draft of the last part of *The Autobiography* to Matthews, describing the work he had put into it as "fearful." Johnson seems to have thought the novel readier to go than it was. He asked Matthews to "have the whole book made into a clean, typewritten copy in duplicate" and hoped it would "now get a chance" to appear, given the currency of passing stories and the articles on lynching and segregation in the South by Ray Stannard Baker, which had been collected in *Following the Color Line* (1908).[12] But the novel clearly underwent substantial revision before finally appearing in 1912, the last full year of Johnson's consulship. After "Fifty Years" appeared at the beginning of January 1913, his friend J. Douglas Wetmore could hardly believe that Johnson was ready to give up such a good situation: "If you can turn out this kind of stuff while you are receiving a good salary from Uncle Sam, I think you would be foolish to resign. You ought to stay in the Consular service and devote most of your time to writing."[13]

Despite Johnson's frustration with Uncle Sam—especially in the wake of Woodrow Wilson's presidential victory, which dashed his already withering hopes for promotion to a European post—the fact remains that he emerged from his government posts with the works he hoped would launch a significant literary career. He first publicly signaled his aspirations by changing his middle name from William to Weldon for the appearance of his poem "Father, Father Abraham" in the February 1913 *Crisis*. To Towns, he confided that this was done "for purely literary advantages.... The Weldon gives it a little distinctiveness, and makes it a good deal more of a literary 'trade mark.'"[14] To his wife, Grace Nail Johnson, he had confided his literary ambition more tellingly in the summer of 1912, just after completing "Fifty Years":

> To-night I have finished 15 verses of the greatest race poem that has yet been written, and it made me feel like chatting with you about my work—it would be no posing to say, my art, for I know that I am a poet, and with the power to be the first great poet that the race has produced in America. I say this with a full recognition of Dunbar's position. But Dunbar, though he was a master of his art, had great technic and a mastery of pathos, humor and delicacy, he lacked depth, comprehensive broadness, prophetic vision and consecrated seriousness, and so he falls short of being the first *great* poet of the race in America. In a good measure I know that I possess these very qualities which Dunbar lacked.[15]

He had written her another letter earlier that day, this one reveling in the positive review of *The Autobiography* by the *New York Times*, "the highest and most authoritative of any daily paper in the United States." Especially pleasing to him was the *Times* critic's avowed uncertainty about whether or not the story were true, which proved for Johnson "that I am sufficiently a master of the technical art of writing." His course was clear:

> I have been plugging away at several things, but I shall now concentrate on my poems. I must follow this book up as soon as possible with another

from S.F. & C. [Sherman, French and Company].... If I get my poems properly launched I believe they will make a reputation for me, the kind of reputation that I really want, the reputation of a writer and thinker. Don't doubt I'll win it. It's hard, slow work, but I know I'll succeed. You see, for so many years I've divided my efforts and energies that I haven't done in any one line as much as I could have done by concentration.[16]

These letters shed some light on what seems a most paradoxical gambit: Johnson's decision to publish *The Autobiography of an Ex-Colored Man* anonymously while aiming for a major literary reputation. They suggest above all that Johnson was not staking that reputation on the novel he had intermittently worked on for years. *The Autobiography* was conceived of primarily in instrumental terms: that is, in terms of the political ends it might serve through its effect on contemporary readers. The technical artistry Johnson brought to it mainly served to disguise the book's true nature so that it could successfully "pass" as a true autobiography, and anonymity was essential to the trick. Counting on friends like Towns to distribute the book in Atlanta University circles and on his brother, Rosamond, to "do an enormous amount of advertising" for it while touring, Johnson underscored for his wife that "the absolute secrecy of authorship must be maintained—you can see the importance of this from the *Times*'s review; as soon as it is known that the author is a colored man who could not be the character in the book, interest in it will fall. There must always be in the reader's mind the thought that, at least, it may be true."[17]

Johnson's evident commercial hopes for the novel were inseparable from the goal of changing as many hearts and minds as possible. "There are no present prospects of its being a 'best seller,'" he wrote to Towns, "but I have hopes that it will finally reach a large number of the people who ought to see it. One thing against its popular success is that it is being handled by an ultra conservative publishing house."[18] As Jacqueline Goldsby has persuasively argued, even the choice of that "ultra conservative" house—Boston's Sherman, French and Company, a throwback to the waning era of the "gentleman publisher"—was strategic and served to enhance the plausibility of the hoax.[19] The purpose of the work was spelled out clearly enough in the preface attributed to the publishers but written by Johnson: to give the (white) reader "a view of the inner life of the Negro" and to "reveal the unsuspected fact that prejudice against the Negro is exerting a pressure which ... is actually and constantly forcing an unascertainable number of fair-complexioned colored people into the white race" (*The Autobiography*, xxxiv). But to facilitate that goal by presenting his book as a "document ... stranger than fiction,"[20] in the same register as Ray Stannard Baker's journalism, Johnson had to suppress not only his name but his book's literariness: the stylistic ingenuity and irony that potentially gave it indexical value as a measure of black artistic ability. "The great majority of books on the race question have been written in a dry, a complaining, a bombastic or an angry tone," he wrote to his publisher. "Not yet has the entire question been treated in an interesting story form."[21] Johnson seems to have banked on revealing his responsibility for the aesthetic distinctiveness of the book after it had made its short-term political impact as a *succès de scandale*. "If the book succeeds I shall claim it later," he wrote to Towns in August 1912, "if it doesn't there won't be anything lost."[22]

Johnson's rather cavalier attitude here—uncannily anticipating Ellison's claim that *Invisible Man* "is not an important novel"—stems from greater confidence in his artistic capacities than the future would bear out. As already mentioned, by August 1912, mainly on the basis of "Fifty Years," Johnson aimed to be "the first great" African American poet. Johnson clearly thought he could claim *The Autobiography of an Ex-Colored Man* from his superior position as a nationally recognized poet, which suggests he thought of *The Autobiography* as a relatively minor work, the recoverable "first book" of a writer who would go on to do something grander. Instead, ironically, his first steps toward reclaiming the novel were motivated by its failure rather than success,[23] a disappointment aggravated by diminishing expectations for his poetry. By late 1914 he was apologizing to Towns for the trouble he had "got into by striving to establish my reputation as a poet; I'm afraid I can do but little, as, and I say it regretfully, I have published nothing at all lately." His last poems "of importance"—Johnson listed but five—were "Father, Father Abraham" and "Fifty Years," and at this point his best hope still lay in publishing a collection in which those poems would be the highlight.[24]

Fifty Years and Other Poems did not appear until 1917 in a slim volume published by Cornhill, another genteel Boston firm, with a little help from his friend William Stanley Braithwaite.[25] Its literary impact was negligible. In the meantime the authorship and genre of *The Autobiography of an Ex-Colored Man* became public knowledge. Matthews's *Munsey's Magazine* review in the summer of 1913 half betrayed the hoax by treating the book as an instance of literary realism; alongside novels by William Dean Howells and Robert Herrick, it was described as one of "three serious studies of American character in the form of fiction."[26] Twenty-five hundred copies of that review were printed and circulated by Sherman, French to help sell the remaining copies of the first (and, at the time, only) edition, which seems to have been no easy feat.[27] With the book going out of print, Johnson finally announced in a December 23, 1915, editorial for the *New York Age*, "A couple of years ago the writer of these columns wrote and published anonymously a novel entitled, 'The Autobiography of an Ex-Colored Man.'"[28] Johnson's authorship of the novel was then duly recorded in Benjamin Brawley's landmark *The Negro in Literature and Art* (1918), but by that time it seemed destined for the historian's archive.

In sum, within a few years of *The Autobiography of an Ex-Colored Man*'s initial publication, Johnson would have been hard pressed to imagine its future destiny as a literary classic. This was not only because the book by common measures flopped, but because it was not primarily written to be the great work on which Johnson was staking the literary reputation he clearly coveted. It served a kind of preparatory function, paving the way not just for Johnson's career as a poet,[29] but for higher artistic achievements from black Americans in general. Johnson shared his Ex-Colored Man's assumption that an African American higher culture—measured by achievements in literature, classical music, and plastic arts—lay largely in a state of potential stymied by the injustices and prejudices of Jim Crow. The best evidence for this, paradoxically, was the rich character of the lower, vernacular performative arts—spirituals, sermons, ragtime, the cakewalk—that black Americans invented and perfected under such adverse conditions. The Ex-Colored Man pays serious tribute to these while making it his life's ambition to draw on and translate their virtues into a lasting, classical form. But Johnson distances himself from the Ex-Colored Man by having him abandon this project as the price for becoming white, and the "fast yellowing manuscripts" become an emblem in the novel of the high cultural achievement that might have been. As such they seemed to haunt Johnson as much as the guilt-ridden narrator, as Kenneth Warren has shrewdly suggested: "more illustrative than the case that Johnson's novel makes for culture is the case that it proves itself unable to make for the classic possibilities lying within black culture. That is, Johnson's novel reveals itself as a text that was written only because the quest to create a text of 'classic' expression had to be abandoned along the way."[30] Johnson's novel, like *The Souls of Black Folk* to which it owes much, was founded on a premise of black literary destitution that the exigencies of political activism made only more difficult to overcome, exigencies reflected in Johnson's willingness to sacrifice recognition for his accomplishment in the short run in the interests of maximizing its social impact.[31] By 1916, when Johnson was committed full time to writing editorials for the *New York Age* and working for the NAACP, *The Autobiography* itself threatened to become like its antihero's "fast yellowing manuscripts, the only tangible remnants of a vanished dream, a dead ambition, a sacrificed talent" (*The Autobiography*, 154).

Not until the heyday of the Harlem Renaissance, more than a decade after *The Autobiography of an Ex-Colored Man* went out of print, was Johnson's novel resurrected as "a text of 'classic' expression," to recall Warren's phrase. The logic behind this recovery becomes most apparent when we understand the so-called Renaissance in part as a concerted effort to overcome the condition of African American literary destitution. To this effort Johnson began directing his energies well before they converged in the 1920s with the work of Alain Locke, Charles S. Johnson, Jessie Fauset, W. E. B. Du Bois, Carl Van Vechten, and various white liberal sponsors and well-wishers. He began this work, that is, soon after experiencing the disappointment of his individual literary ambition, first through his literary editorials and the establishment of a "Poetry Corner" in the *New York Age*, and then through his plans for what would prove to be the first anthology of African American poetry.

Between the publication of *The Autobiography of an Ex-Colored Man* in 1912 and the poetry sequence *God's Trombones* in 1927 (which he had begun as early as 1916), Johnson's most important literary work was *The Book of American Negro Poetry* (1922), the lengthy preface to which remains a foundational essay in African American poetics (alongside those he wrote for two collections of American Negro spirituals he edited with his brother in the mid-1920s). *The Book of American Negro Poetry*, whose second edition in 1931 would be much enriched by the poetry of the Harlem Renaissance, was hardly an anthology of "classics" but rather a showcase of literary competencies, "effective in following up the work of making America at large aware," Johnson retrospectively wrote in *Black Manhattan*.[32] "It may be said that none of these poets strike a deep native strain or sound a distinctly original note, either in matter or form," Johnson conceded of the poets prior to Dunbar. To which he responded that "the same thing may be said of all the American poets down to the writers of the present generation, with the exception of Poe and Walt Whitman. The thing in which these black poets are mostly excelled by their contemporaries is mere technique."[33] Countering the assumption of black America's literary shortcomings with the common charge of *American* literary destitution, Johnson also emphasizes a crucial difference: white America's Poe and Whitman, its world-acknowledged "classics." It is thus not surprising that he then turns to Dunbar "as the first poet from the Negro race in the United States ... to reveal innate literary distinction in what he wrote,"[34] a phrase echoing William Dean Howells's judgment of 1896. One of the functions of the anthology, in effect, was to enable the selective emergence of the singular, classic author and text(s) from the run-of-the-mill, from the vast bulk of "normal" literature that African Americans were presumed so incapable of producing that any Negro-authored book was cause for taking notice. The Harlem Renaissance was meant to function much like Johnson's anthology: to enable and advertise as much literary work as possible in order to bring forth a few literary classics that future black writers could proudly take for granted and experimentally build upon.[35]

It thus seems in hindsight inevitable that *The Autobiography of an Ex-Coloured Man* would resurface by 1927 (now with British spelling), marketed precisely as "a classic in Negro literature" by Knopf in its Blue Jade series, which was "designed to cover," according to the publisher's catalog, "the field of semi-classic, semi-curious books—books which for one reason or another have enjoyed great celebrity but little actual distribution."[36] According to

Goldsby, Johnson had begun trying to interest prominent critics in his novel as early as 1922, just after *The Book of American Negro Poetry* appeared, though Carl Van Vechten did not read it until March 1925.[37] Van Vechten presumably brought the novel to the attention of Blanche Knopf, who sent Johnson a contract for it in early 1926 and whose enthusiasm for the book's potential likely swayed Johnson away from rival publisher Liveright.[38] Its reemergence during the high point of the Harlem Renaissance is no accident, those years being less notable for the number of new novels, stories, and poems that appeared, including the landmark *New Negro* anthology,[39] than for the emergence of a healthy critical struggle to discover what might distinguish truly good, even great African American literature from literature that just happened to be written by black Americans. It was no longer a perceived dearth of African American writing so much as a dearth of African American "classics"—works destined to stand the test of time as great—that underlay the fruitful antagonisms of 1926–27, signaled most notably by various manifestos and polemical essays (Langston Hughes's "The Negro Artist and the Racial Mountain"; Du Bois's "Criteria of Negro Art"; George Schuyler's "The Negro-Art Hokum"), the conflict over Van Vechten's novel *Nigger Heaven*, the *Crisis* symposium "The Negro in Art," and the announcement through *Fire!* of a new literary generation bent on repudiating the old. This provided a crucial context for the discovery of forgotten classics and the criteria by which they might be distinguished, and Van Vechten arguably led the way by promoting first Charles Chesnutt (whose *Conjure Woman* [1899] alone, however, would get reprinted during the Renaissance), then Johnson.

Witness the experience of Van Vechten's thwarted writer Byron Kasson midway through *Nigger Heaven* (1926). Comparing his own inability to overcome a self-consciousness about the race problem that taints everything he writes with "propaganda," Byron recalls the example of Chesnutt, "an author strangely unfamiliar to most of the new generation."[40] Conveniently ignoring the political protest of Chesnutt's *The Marrow of Tradition* (1901) in favor of such stories as "The Wife of His Youth," Van Vechten has Byron admiring "the cool deliberation of its style, the sense of form, but more than all the civilized mind of this man who had surveyed the problems of his race from an Olympian height and had turned them into living and artistic drama.... Chesnutt had surveyed the entire field, calmly setting down what he saw, what he thought and felt about it."[41] The terms are strikingly similar to those with which Van Vechten introduced Johnson's resurrected novel a year later and distinguished it from its otherwise notable precursors: Washington's *Up from Slavery*, Du Bois's *The Souls of Black Folk*, Chesnutt's *The House behind the Cedars* (1900), and Dunbar's *The Sport of the Gods* (1902). The "limitations of his subject matter," for example, "made it impossible for Dr. Washington to survey the field as broadly as Mr. Johnson, setting himself no limitations, could." Du Bois does, on the other hand, "explore a wide territory," but without Johnson's "calm, dispassionate tone."[42] This was another term for "the gentle irony which informs the pages from beginning to end" for which he privately praised Johnson after first reading the novel; he thought it the book's most remarkable quality.[43] It was what he declared in his introduction "an unself-conscious manner, totally novel in Negro writing at the time this book originally appeared."[44] And here I think is the most crucial critical justification for the novel's resurrection as a "classic in Negro literature." It had hardly enjoyed the "great celebrity" that the "semi-classic, semi-curious" books in the Blue Jade series were advertised as having had. Rather, from an expert's point of view—and whatever one thinks of *Nigger Heaven*, Van Vechten could claim expertise in African American literature in 1927—the book introduced an innovation that marked a decisive formal step forward. But *The Autobiography of an Ex-Colored Man* was a step forward that promised to bring African American writing closer to a condition taken for granted by white writers like Van Vechten: a condition of literary freedom wherein gentle irony, a playful disinterestedness, and a lack of self-consciousness about one's racial identity are aesthetic norms. (Van Vechten admits to the influence of *The Autobiography* on *Nigger Heaven*—but as "an invaluable source book for the study of Negro psychology.")[45] In effect, what Van Vechten's terms of praise describe is an aesthetic advance during Jim Crow that underscores more than anything else the separate but unequal literary situation of aspiring black and white authors.

Has *The Autobiography of an Ex-Colored Man* lived on as a literary classic on grounds fundamentally different from those in play when it was given a second chance in 1927? Or, to put this another way, in continuing to make explicit or implicit claims for its greatness are we, on whatever side of the color line, belying a kind of condescension whose roots go back to the Harlem Renaissance project of making African American literary "parity," in Johnson's term,[46] a precondition of, if not substitute for, full political and economic equality? Van Vechten could declare it "surprising how little the book has dated in fifteen years," but that is because Jim Crow with its taboos against miscegenation and its pervasive prejudice was still fully entrenched.[47] Indeed, what would "date" the book, according to Van Vechten's logic, would be more "cheering" evidence of "how much has been accomplished by the race in New York alone since the book was originally published."[48]

In the 1951 reprint of the novel, Knopf conceded that "most" of the other "minor classics" in the Blue Jade series "had passed again into obscurity"; but with *Invisible Man* and *Brown v. Board of Education* still on the horizon, he could assume that *The Autobiography*, which had been reissued as a New American Library paperback in 1948, was still "finding new readers."[49] (Yet after *Invisible Man* appeared in 1952, one veteran reader, Alain Locke, could recall only two works of African American fiction of comparable significance: Jean Toomer's *Cane* [1923] and Wright's *Native Son*.)⁵⁰ *The Autobiography*'s reappearance in 1965 in an Avon paperback as one of "three Negro classics" was clearly meant to help white and black readers navigate the troubled times wrought in part by the beginning of the end of Jim Crow. If each work could still reveal "the deep apprehension and troubling dilemmas that virtually every sensitive Negro American has experienced," according to the book's editor, John Hope Franklin,⁵¹ the title of the omnibus volume looked forward to the more widespread establishment of black studies programs and African American literature courses in universities, with its reassuring news or reminder that there were "Negro classics." Only the eradication of racism altogether, or at least the dismantling of the Jim Crow culture of enforced segregation, to which Johnson dedicated his life, would presumably make the novel into the curious historical document it originally passed for, and lessen the need for specifically Negro literary classics.

I would argue that the novel's now classic stature owes much, despite American multiculturalist orthodoxy, to the separate but unequal conception of African American literature nurtured under Jim Crow, and to the understandable condition of literary destitution that such a conception of African American literature was designed to redress. Under that condition—inescapably comparative, since the very value of "literature" was in part a product of competing have and have-not nations—every formal step toward "universality" was to be cherished as evidence of a people's capacity to rank as great within the global republic of letters. (Johnson stated in his preface to *The Book of American Negro Poetry* that "the sooner they are able to write *American* poetry spontaneously, the better.")⁵² Van Vechten's introduction emphasized such a formal step in noting *The Autobiography*'s stylistic and tonal distinction from its precursors, and thus shaped the tenor of what little scholarly notice *The Autobiography* received until the late 1960s.⁵³ Hugh Gloster emphasized Johnson's "calm, dispassionate treatment" of his subject in his *Negro Voices in American Fiction* (1948), describing *The Autobiography* as "more impartial and more comprehensive than any earlier novel of American Negro life," "a milestone because of its forthright presentation of racial thought."⁵⁴ Robert Bone went further in *The Negro Novel in America* (1958): "Johnson is the only true artist among the early Negro novelists"; "*The Autobiography of an Ex-Colored Man*, simply by virtue of its form, demanded a discipline and restraint hitherto unknown in the Negro novel"; and finally, "compared to the typical propaganda tract of the period, *The Autobiography of an Ex-Colored Man* is a model of artistic detachment."⁵⁵ Bone still commented that Johnson "cannot wholly repress a desire to educate the white folks," an understandable failing that Sterling Brown and Van Vechten noted and forgave.⁵⁶

But the drift of the praise is clear: epoch making, a milestone, groundbreaking *as far as African American writing goes*. All such claims anticipate more recent orthodoxy to the effect of its being the first work of African American "modernism." In his introduction to the 1989 Vintage Books edition of the novel, for example, Henry Louis Gates Jr. draws on modernism's rhetoric to describe *The Autobiography* as "the bridge between nineteenth- and twentieth-century black literature."[57] Gates mainly bases his claim on Johnson's use of an ambiguously drawn first-person narrator and his exploration of the theme of spiritual alienation under capitalism,[58] both staples of late nineteenth-century European fiction. Thus through another spatial metaphor Gates emphasizes the novel's temporal advancement of a literature still lagging behind, still struggling to come to full literariness, still struggling to be recognized as art in an interracial, international literary field impacted to no small degree by the "modernist" imperative to be modern.[59]

The persistent force of that imperative—especially in its effects on the academic study of literature—becomes startlingly evident in Jacqueline Goldsby's introduction to the 2015 Norton critical edition of the novel, wherein her explicit argument for approaching *The Autobiography* as "an early experiment in literary modernism" is inextricable from her more implicit argument that it should no longer be regarded as affected by the unequal conditions within the American or global literary fields.[60] Goldsby goes so far as to recast the book in the quasi-mythical terms of modernist avant-gardism: "Johnson wrote a novel that so thoroughly transformed the depiction of character, consciousness, time, and plot that the American reading public was utterly confounded when [*The Autobiography*] was released in 1912."[61] This claim is unverifiable, and it is largely undermined by the critical materials and supplementary documentation Goldsby has so helpfully gathered for the edition.[62] Too much hinges in her introduction on what she tellingly refers to as *The Autobiography*'s "status as a modern novel,"[63] where the adjective "modern," which she uses interchangeably with "modernist," confers status. Its publication as a Norton critical edition would seem to make its literary value more stable than ever. Does its status become more precarious if we are not persuaded by Goldsby's claims for the radical innovativeness of its narrative technique, or her statement that it "swam in the stream of consciousness that defined Anglo-American modernism," or her argument that the novel's "history as a book make[s] it modernist"?[64] One of her oddest suggestions is that Johnson did not find the "critical discourse" to discover how "modern" his novel was until he read E. M. Forster's *Aspects of the Novel* (1927) in the early 1930s, since there Forster famously eschewed "modern" as an evaluative category.[65] Working to undo the effects of a Jim Crow literary field, Goldsby cannot let go of modernism's legacy of literary timekeeping, which left most African American literature from the early twentieth century looking relatively conventional if not old-fashioned (the way Forster's fiction looked to his friend Virginia Woolf). And so it is not enough for her to have *The Autobiography of an Ex-Colored Man* recognized, as it is, as a "modern" classic in the sense used for most serious fiction written in the early twentieth century; she must promote it in terms that suggest *Ulysses* or William Faulkner's *The Sound and the Fury* (1929), the effect of which is ironically to reconfirm *modernist* works as the measure of literary greatness and legitimacy.[66]

The 1927 reissue of Johnson's novel as a "classic" of "Negro literature" did not entail such terms of comparison. The reprint automatically bestowed on the book an indexical value, and it would be gauged not merely for what it had anticipated and supposedly already enabled in Negro writing—Harlem Renaissance fiction like Toomer's *Cane*, Walter White's *Flight* (1926), Claude McKay's *Home to Harlem* (1928), and Nella Larsen's *Passing* (1929)—but more speculatively for the literarily richer African American future that it *might* enable, the future that would eventually bring books on the order of *Invisible Man* and Toni Morrison's *Beloved* (1987). It also better assured the novel the place in the schools it eventually came to have by the mid-1970s. Though it is not an "avant-garde" work, it accidentally shares with such work the fact of having sacrificially served higher interests (in Johnson's case, political first, then artistic) rather than those of short-term commercial success. It thus survived thanks to the anti-economic logic structuring the modern literary field's persistent opposition—fundamental to the success of high modernist literature—between common readers/consumers and their educated and expert counterparts. Like many a modernist classic, *The Autobiography of an Ex-Colored Man*, from its 1927 reincarnation to its 2015 publication as a Norton critical edition, benefited from the social process by which long-term success depends initially, in Pierre Bourdieu's description, on "a few 'talent-spotters'"—in this case, Van Vechten and Blanche Knopf—and eventually on "the educational system, which alone is capable of offering, in time, a converted public."[67] The difference, though, is that the educated public created for Johnson's novel since the 1970s has had to be converted less to an appreciation of what were once wildly innovative literary possibilities than to an acceptance of African American literary value on largely separatist terms.[68]

For Johnson, *The Autobiography of an Ex-Colored Man* was a work that, from both a personal and collective standpoint, promised more than he was ever able to deliver. Goldsby rightly insists in an earlier work that "it was not the literary achievement Johnson wanted to be remembered for," because that achievement was finally subordinate to, and an instrument of, the lifelong political crusade he took up against lynching.[69] Indeed Johnson describes his "literary efforts" in his real autobiography, *Along This Way* (1933), as "mere excursions; my main activity was all the while the work of the [NAACP]," and he dedicates but two pages to the genesis and nature of his novel.[70] But we also know from Johnson's correspondence during his Latin American years that he harbored relatively grand literary aspirations, and with these in mind we might shift the emphasis of Goldsby's assertion to insist that *The Autobiography* was not "*the* literary achievement" he wanted to be remembered for. He thought he was launching a literary career with it, not marking its pinnacle; he thought he might become a great poet who wrote fiction and essays on the side, not mainly the "Maker-of-Beautiful-Prefaces," as Anne Spencer once fondly called him,[71] who had to salvage his forgotten first book in order to have much hope for a posthumous literary reputation at all.

As a result of his successes of 1927—the publication year of *God's Trombones* and the reissue of *The Autobiography of an Ex-Coloured Man*—Blanche Knopf and others continued to assume that Johnson would write another novel.[72] But with the relative freedom from political activism that he won in his later years, he wrote but one poem and no other novel, becoming instead an important chronicler and professor of black literary achievement to date. The capstone book of his career—as measured by publicity (a profile in the *New Yorker*), acclaim, and sales—was in fact *Along This Way*, to which he gave a novelistic tinge by shadowing his own success story with the tragic passing figure of D, based on his friend J. Douglas Wetmore, who committed suicide in 1930.[73] Though Van Vechten thought it stood "with the GREAT autobiographies" and Johnson himself believed it had "a good chance of becoming one of the standard American autobiographies,"[74] it has remained a remarkably neglected book—even by academic critics and teachers since the advent of black studies—in comparison with *The Autobiography of an Ex-Colored Man* of twenty years earlier. It is as though after he had playfully appropriated one of the key genres to which African American literature had been accidentally confined, Johnson's recourse to that genre toward the end of his life could only be, from a literary standpoint, regressive.

The Autobiography of an Ex-Colored Man should be read, in effect, with a recovered appreciation for Johnson's sense of the relatively scant literary resources he had to draw on in his bid to make a name for himself as a "racial" artist in an almost exclusively white, "American" literary field. Taking the condition of black American literary destitution for granted was paradoxically one of the enabling assumptions of his career, and accounts for the greater instructive value that late nineteenth-century literature by white writers probably had for him.[75] It emboldened him to write his pseudo-autobiographical and pseudo-documentary novel (thus bringing fictive impartiality and multilayered irony to the success story recently modeled by Washington and the didactic, poetic, and essayistic excursions of Du Bois) and to find his way beyond the dialect tradition epitomized by Dunbar to a small but respectable oeuvre of race poetry that might resonate universally. But beyond that it left him mainly burdened with the task of facilitating more African American literary production in the interest of making it more possible in the long run to discover black works of lasting aesthetic distinction—"classics" broadly recognized as such by that audience he referred to as "the world."[76] In addition to reading the 1912 novel as testimony to the great literature that could not yet be written, as Warren would have us do, I suggest reading the 1927 reprint as testimony to what had to serve as "classic" African American literature at that point in time, with all the signs pointing to a better day ahead.

NOTES

1. Ralph Ellison, "The Art of Fiction: An Interview," in *The Collected Essays of Ralph Ellison*, ed. John Callahan (New York: Modern Library, 1995), 217.

2. Ralph Ellison, introduction to *Invisible Man* (1952; rpt., New York: Vintage, 1995), xxiii.

3. Though the extent of this nadir period remains debatable, I am referring to the era from the end of Reconstruction to World War I, as originally described by historian Rayford W. Logan, *The Negro in American Life and Thought: The Nadir, 1877–1901* (New York: Dial, 1954), and summarized by Dickson D. Bruce, *Black American Writing from the Nadir: The Evolution of a Literary Tradition, 1877–1915* (Baton Rouge: Louisiana State University Press, 1989), 1–4.

4. "For a work to become a source of tradition," Richard Brodhead writes with Nathaniel Hawthorne's fiction in mind, "a later worker must locate it as a significant model; must find—by which we really mean invent or construct—what its significance as a model might really consist of (we forget that the exemplary nature of past works is not necessarily obvious, when a tradition is still forming); then must devise a way to imitate what he has isolated, or to reactivate its powers in his own making" (Brodhead, *The School of Hawthorne* [New York: Oxford University Press, 1986], 83–84). That *The Autobiography of an Ex-Colored Man* became a source for *Invisible Man* in this way has been most compellingly made, though not until the 1970s, by Houston Baker Jr. and by Robert Stepto in his still standard argument for a specifically African American prose tradition. For Baker, see "A Forgotten Prototype: *The Autobiography of an Ex-Colored Man* and *Invisible Man*," in *Critical Essays on James Weldon Johnson*, ed. Kenneth M. Price and Lawrence J. Oliver (New York: G. K. Hall, 1997), 31–42; for Stepto, see *From behind the Veil: A Study of Afro-American Narrative*, 2nd ed. (Urbana: University of Illinois Press, 1991). The claim for Johnson's novel's influence on Hurston's *Their Eyes Were Watching God* (1937), twice authoritatively asserted in Henry Louis Gates Jr.'s introduction to a 1989 edition of *The Autobiography* (New York: Vintage) (see xvi, xxi), seems to me overstated, however likely it was that Hurston read it and echoed at least one key scene from it (the protagonist's discovery that he is black). The impact of *God's Trombones* (1927) (on *Jonah's Gourd Vine* [1933]) and perhaps even *Along This Way* (1933) (on *Dust Tracks on a Road* [1942]) is easier to substantiate.

Ellison must have become familiar with Johnson's novel either as a result of reading African American writing in the 1930s and 1940s or through his wife, Fanny McConnell, who worked for Johnson at Fisk University. His refusal to acknowledge it publicly as an influence or source of power might be explained by the relatively low cultural capital still attached to the work of his "relatives" (apart from Richard Wright)—a lingering effect of the ongoing perception of African American literary destitution—in comparison to the high cultural capital attached to the American Renaissance authors and modernists, like T. S. Eliot and James Joyce, he ostentatiously claimed as "ancestors." On the other hand, academic scholars committed from the 1960s onward to creating a specifically black literary tradition/canon and a theory of black literature surely had a large stake in forging the relations they claimed to uncover. For Ellison's distinction between relatives and ancestors, a distinction Hurston also might have drawn, see "The World and the Jug," in Callahan, *Collected Essays*, 185.

5. In her extensive introduction to the Norton critical edition of the novel (2015), xxxiii–xxxix, Jacqueline Goldsby is at pains to draw correlations, some of them highly strained, between Johnson's novel and the work of various white "modernists." Goldsby suggests lines of comparison—between Johnson's novel and Virginia Woolf's *Jacob's Room* (1922), and F. Scott Fitzgerald's *The Great Gatsby* (1925), and Gertrude Stein's *The Autobiography of Alice B. Toklas* (1933)—while avoiding the argument that the later writers were influenced by Johnson. And for good reason. There is no evidence that Woolf or Fitzgerald, both of whom left ample documentation of their reading, had ever heard of the novel, though they may plausibly have learned of it after 1927 (after the novels in question were written). Stein received a copy of *God's Trombones* when it came out in 1927 and probably learned of Johnson's novel from Carl Van Vechten. Whether she read it, or read it with much care, is impossible to determine. But it seems highly unlikely that someone as established and stubborn in her artistic ways as Stein was by the early 1930s took formal lessons from Johnson's novel. The more plausible of the correlations Goldsby draws, those between Johnson and Fitzgerald, can be explained by common fictional influences, resources, techniques, and preoccupations available to the two writers, both of whom were well read in both nineteenth-century and early twentieth-century fiction.

6. Johnson, "Some New Books of Poetry and Their Makers," in *The Selected Writings of James Weldon Johnson*, ed. Sondra Kathryn Wilson (New York: Oxford University Press, 1995), 1:272. On the nature of "literary destitution" as I am using it here, see Pascale Casanova, *The World Republic of Letters*, trans. M. B. DeBevoise (Cambridge, Mass.: Harvard University Press, 2004), 177–85. Scholars of nineteenth-century African American literature, about which we have learned a great deal more over the past few decades, will likely take issue with such an understanding on the grounds that it is counterfactual. But I would insist on distinguishing between the views of the field held by contemporary specialists and those of most of black America's most ambitious and successful writers during the first half of the twentieth century, including Johnson, Charles Chesnutt, Jean Toomer, Nella Larsen, Wallace Thurman, Wright, and Ellison. As I argue below, the *perception* of African American literary destitution was clearly an enabling one.

7. See Kenneth Warren, *What Was African American Literature?* (Cambridge, Mass.: Harvard University Press, 2011), 9–10.

8. Victoria Earle Matthews, "The Value of Race Literature," in *The New Negro: Readings on Race, Representation, and African American Culture, 1892–1938*, ed. Henry Louis

Gates Jr. and Gene Andrew Jarrett (Princeton, N.J.: Princeton University Press, 2007), 288. See also Anna Julia Cooper, "One Phase of American Literature," in Gates and Jarrett, *The New Negro*, 157–72. For a more detailed elaboration of this argument, see Nowlin, "'The First Negro Novelist': Charles Chesnutt's Point of View and the Emergence of African American Literature," *Studies in American Fiction* 39 (2012): 147–51.

9. James Weldon Johnson, *The Autobiography of an Ex-Colored Man* (1912; rpt., New York: Penguin, 1990), 1. Future references to this edition are given parenthetically in the text.

10. James Weldon Johnson, *Along This Way: The Autobiography of James Weldon Johnson* (1933; rpt., New York: Penguin, 1990), 192–93.

11. Miles M. Jackson, "Letters to a Friend: Correspondence from James Weldon Johnson to George A. Towns," *Phylon* 29 (1968): 184.

12. Johnson, letter to Brander Matthews, n.d. [ca. November 1908], JWJ Correspondence, ser. 1, box 13, folder 315, James Weldon Johnson and Grace Nail Johnson Papers, Beinecke Rare Book and Manuscript Library, Collection of American Literature, Yale University (hereafter JWJ BRBL); Ray Stannard Baker, *Following the Color Line: American Negro Citizenship in the Progressive Era* (New York: Doubleday, Page, 1908).

13. Wetmore, letter to Johnson, June 26, 1913, JWJ Correspondence, ser. 1, box 23, folder 535, JWJ BRBL.

14. Jackson, "Letters to a Friend," 191.

15. Johnson, letter to Grace Nail Johnson, June 26, 1912[b], JWJ Correspondence, ser. 1, box 41, folder 22, JWJ BRBL.

16. Johnson, letter to Grace Nail Johnson, June 26, 1912[a], JWJ Correspondence, ser. 1, box 41, folder 22, JWJ BRBL.

17. Ibid.

18. Jackson, "Letters to a Friend," 191.

19. See Jacqueline Goldsby, "Keeping the 'Secret of Authorship': A Critical Look at the 1912 Publication of James Weldon Johnson's *Autobiography of an Ex-Colored Man*," in *Print Culture in a Diverse America*, ed. James P. Danky and Wayne A. Wiegand (Urbana: University of Illinois Press, 1998), 254–55.

20. The phrase comes from the draft introduction that Johnson enclosed in a letter to his publisher (from which the original preface was drawn). See letter from Johnson to Sherman, French and Company, February 17, 1912, JWJ Correspondence, ser. 1, box 18, folder 435, JWJ BRBL.

21. Ibid.

22. Jackson, "Letters to a Friend," 189.

23. Goldsby's collection of the twenty-two reviews of the 1912 book for the 2015 Norton critical edition (273–302), which indicates that *The Autobiography* was more widely reviewed across the country than has been generally assumed, does not make it any less of a "failure" in the conventional sense I am describing: disappointing sales, going quickly out of print. Most of the notices are anonymous newspaper reviews. Brander Matthews was the only established name to trumpet the novel in public; Jessie Fauset was yet unknown. "The book fell flat more or less," Johnson wrote to Carl Van Doren on December 28, 1922, when he began entertaining the possibility of republishing it (quoted in Goldsby, *The Autobiography*, 235). Alice Dunbar Nelson's claim in 1927 that

"in 1912 ... the reading public among Negroes and friends of Negroes was shaken to its inner core" by the book's appearance may tell us something about its reception in her circles, but also sounds like the kind of hyperbole enthusiastic book reviewers are famous for ("Our Book Shelf," quoted in Goldsby, *The Autobiography*, 324). It is one of those difficult to verify claims, but despite little corroborating evidence, Goldsby gives remarkable weight to it.

24. Jackson, "Letters to a Friend," 194–95.

25. That Johnson's first volume of poems met with possibly several rejections might be inferred from the fact that he had a version of it ready in the spring of 1913. Matthews read it, offered some constructive criticism, and encouraged him to send it to Scribner's. Letter from Matthews to Johnson, May 21, 1913, JWJ Correspondence, ser. 1, box 13, folder 315, JWJ BRBL.

26. Brander Matthews, "American Character in American Fiction," *Munsey's Magazine*, August 1913, 798.

27. An April 24, 1914, letter from Sherman, French and Company gives some clue as to how poorly the novel sold: fifty-nine copies since the last report (presumably six months previous). Johnson's royalty check was for $12.53 (JWJ Correspondence, ser. 1, box 18, folder 435, JWJ BRBL). According to Goldsby, the firm was eager to get the novel off their hands by 1915, and it was out of print by 1916. Goldsby, "Keeping the 'Secret of Authorship,'" 263, 271n61.

28. Johnson, "Stranger than Fiction," in Wilson, *Selected Writings*, 2:258.

29. "[A] man must write prose now if he wishes to get an audience," he wrote to Towns at the beginning of his stay in Venezuela, referring to his novel in progress (Jackson, "Letters to a Friend," 182–83).

30. Kenneth Warren, *So Black and Blue: Ralph Ellison and the Occasion of Criticism* (Chicago: University of Chicago Press, 2003), 35–36.

31. I do not mean to discount here a more immediate motive for anonymous authorship, which was Johnson's ultimately futile struggle to get a promotion in the consular service. His white "superiors" were among the original target audience for his hoax, since it was the hearts and minds of that type of man that most immediately required changing. See Brian Russell Roberts, "Passing into Diplomacy: U.S. Consul James Weldon Johnson and *The Autobiography of an Ex-Colored Man*," *Modern Fiction Studies* 56 (Summer 2010): 305–8; and Goldsby, "Keeping the 'Secret of Authorship,'" 259–62.

32. James Weldon Johnson, *Black Manhattan* (New York: Knopf, 1930), 266.

33. James Weldon Johnson, "Preface to the First Edition," in *The Book of American Negro Poetry*, ed. Johnson, rev. ed. (New York: Harcourt, Brace, 1969), 34.

34. Ibid.

35. Certainly throughout the Harlem Renaissance, Kenneth Warren's assertion holds true: "Despite the attention given to the folk past and the artistic achievements of past greats whose work had gone unacknowledged, African American literature was prospective rather than retrospective.... In the main, writers and critics tended to speak as if the best work had not been written but was yet to come, and the shape of that work was yet to be determined" (*What Was African American Literature?* 42–43). For a fuller elaboration of the argument in the text, particularly its ramifications for

an understanding of African American modernism, see Michael Nowlin, "Race Literature, Modernism, and Normal Literature: James Weldon Johnson's Groundwork for an African American Literary Renaissance, 1912–20," *Modernism/Modernity* 20 (2013): 503–18. I draw the term "normal" literature from Franco Moretti, *Graphs, Maps, Trees* (New York: Verso, 2005), 17–29.

36. *Borzoi Books Catalogue* (New York: Knopf, Autumn 1927), 25–26; see also Amy Root Clements, *The Art of Prestige: The Formative Years at Knopf, 1915–1929* (Amherst: University of Massachusetts Press, 2014), 73, 87.

37. Goldsby, "Keeping the 'Secret of Authorship,'" 246; Van Vechten, letter to James Weldon Johnson, March 23, 1925, JWJ Correspondence, ser. 1, box 21, folder 497, JWJ BRBL.

38. See Claire Hoertz Badaracco, "*The Autobiography of an Ex-Coloured Man* by James Weldon Johnson: The 1927 Knopf Edition," *Papers of the Bibliographical Society of America* 96 (2002): 283–84.

39. Arnold Rampersad, ed., *The New Negro: Voices of the Harlem Renaissance* (1925; rpt., New York: Touchstone, 1997).

40. Carl Van Vechten, *Nigger Heaven* (1926; rpt., Urbana: University of Illinois Press, 2000), 176.

41. Ibid.

42. Carl Van Vechten, "Introduction to Mr. Knopf's New Edition," in *The Autobiography of an Ex-Coloured Man* by James Weldon Johnson (1927; rpt., New York: Knopf, 1951), vii.

43. Van Vechten, letter to Johnson.

44. Van Vechten, "Introduction," viii.

45. Ibid., vii.

46. Johnson, "Preface to the First Edition," 9.

47. Van Vechten, "Introduction," vi. Similarly, Benjamin Brawley described *The Autobiography* in 1929 as "as fresh to-day as when it was written" (*The Negro in Literature and Art in the United States* [New York: Duffield, 1929], 100), and John Chamberlain called it "epoch-making" for anticipating the jazz age while exploring "problems that remain as portentous today as they were in 1912" (Chamberlain, "The Negro as Writer," *Bookman* 70 [February 1930]: 607).

48. Van Vechten, "Introduction," vi.

49. Publisher's note in *The Autobiography of an Ex-Coloured Man* by James Weldon Johnson (1927; rpt., New York: Knopf, 1951), x.

50. Alain Locke, "From *Native Son* to *Invisible Man*: A Review of the Literature of the Negro for 1952," *Phylon* 14 (1953): 34.

51. John Hope Franklin, introduction to *Three Negro Classics* (New York: Avon, 1965), xx.

52. Johnson, "Preface to the First Edition," 42.

53. Johnson's 1912 version of the novel was clearly unknown to John Herbert Nelson when he wrote *The Negro Character in American Literature* (Lawrence, Kans.: Department of Journalism Press, 1926). More inexplicably, the 1927 version seems to have been unknown to Nick Aaron Ford, who published in 1936 *The Contemporary Negro*

Novel: A Study in Race Relations (rpt., College Park, Md.: McGrath, 1968). In *The Negro in American Fiction* (1937; rpt., Port Washington, N.Y.: Kennikat, 1968), Sterling Brown dedicated but a paragraph to the novel, which he thought "ground-breaking" mainly in terms of its content, that is, the breadth of the field it surveyed, and especially its cosmopolitan aspects (105).

54. Hugh M. Gloster, *Negro Voices in American Fiction* (Chapel Hill: University of North Carolina Press, 1948), 80.

55. Robert Bone, *The Negro Novel in America* (New Haven, Conn.: Yale University Press, 1958), 48.

56. Ibid., 48–49. Brown admired the "complex and interesting" protagonist, but noted that the novel "seems to exist primarily for the long discussions of race, and the showing of the Negro in different milieus" (*Negro in American Fiction*, 105). He uncannily echoed Van Vechten's private reservations about the novel, communicated in the March 1925 letter to Johnson cited above: "The book lacks, I think, sufficient narrative interest . . . , but after all you were chiefly concerned with presenting facts about Negro life in an agreeable form, through the eyes of a witness who had no reason personally to be particularly disturbed."

57. Gates, introduction, xvi.

58. Ibid., xvi, xviii–xix.

59. See Pascale Casanova's insightful remarks on this subject in *The World Republic of Letters*, trans. M. B. DeBevoise (Cambridge, Mass.: Harvard University Press, 2004), 87–94.

60. Goldsby, introduction to *The Autobiography*, xiv.

61. Ibid.

62. Unless Goldsby is illogically suggesting that "the American reading public" was "utterly confounded" by what most members of it did not read, we have mainly the twenty-two reviews she has reprinted as evidence of a collective reading response. And those reviews do not suggest bafflement (in the vein, say, of the initial reviews of Stein's *Three Lives* [1909], or T. S. Eliot's *The Waste Land* [1922], or James Joyce's *Ulysses* [1922]), only some uncertainty about whether the book is factual or fictional. The review by Johnson's friend and mentor Brander Matthews, who as Goldsby stresses taught the first "modern novel course" in an American university, puts Johnson's novel squarely in line with post-Howellsian realism ("American Character in American Fiction"). Alice Dunbar Nelson's 1927 review, which Goldsby thinks is the most perceptive ever, sees it as resembling but going beyond Washington's *Up from Slavery* and finds antecedents for it in works by Daniel Defoe and Jonathan Swift ("Our Book Shelf," in Goldsby, *The Autobiography*, 325). Wallace Thurman, who was aggressively committed—at least in theory—to modernism in African American writing, thought the novel passé by 1927, and "little more than just a well-written book" when it appeared in 1912 ("Nephews of Uncle Remus," in Goldsby, *The Autobiography*, 319). And the scholar Nick Aaron Ford listed it in 1948 as the fourth best African American novel—an odd choice for a critic hostile to modernism ("Here Are the Ten Best Novels by and about Colored People," in Goldsby, *The Autobiography*, 334).

63. Goldsby, introduction to *The Autobiography*, xiv.

64. Ibid., xxxv, xiv.

65. Ibid., lvi. "This idea of a period of a development in time, with its consequent emphasis on influences and schools," writes Forster, "happens to be exactly what I am hoping to avoid during our brief survey.... Time, all the way through, is to be our enemy" (*Aspects of the Novel* [New York: Harcourt, Brace, 1927], 21).

66. Lawrence Oliver's essay in this collection helpfully reminds us of some standard tenets of "modern" fiction passed on by Johnson's friend and mentor Brander Matthews, which likely influenced Johnson at the time of writing. In his 1904 essay "Literature in the New Century," Matthews set out, Oliver tells us, to "chart the literary trends of the twentieth century," and I would add that these literary trends still stemmed from the battle on behalf of "realism" led in the 1890s by Howells, whose latest novel was reviewed by Matthews alongside Johnson's. Oliver concedes that by the early 1920s "Matthews's stature as a literary scholar and critic had faded": this surely had something to do with the modernist revolution of the previous decade, which brought about far more radical aesthetic innovations than Matthews could have anticipated in 1904.

67. Pierre Bourdieu, *The Rules of Art: Genesis and Structure of the Literary Field*, trans. Susan Emanuel (Stanford, Calif.: Stanford University Press, 1996), 146–47.

68. I acknowledge that as a result of the relative success of the separatist paradigm, at least in the universities, *The Autobiography of an Ex-Colored Man* has more readily entered the canon of a more pluralistically construed "American literature" or "modernism" in a way Johnson might have applauded. Thus Gates ends his introduction to the Vintage edition by proclaiming the novel "a classic of American literature" (xxiii), despite the lack of virtually any evidence for its artistic impact on nonblack American literature, especially of "classic" stature. Thus Goldsby promotes it as "an early experiment in literary modernism" (introduction to *The Autobiography*, xiv) despite its failure to be recognized as such in the era of Stein's *Tender Buttons* (1914), Joyce's *Ulysses*, and Eliot's early poetry, let alone in 1927. I acknowledge as well that my emphasis on artistic influence may be considered irrelevant by some readers: for if the new multiculturalist canon was undoubtedly abetted by the politics of group affirmation, it was perhaps more lastingly abetted by a general turn toward cultural-historical approaches to literature that made a given work's documentary value as or even more important than a disputable aesthetic value. As a document about the sociological possibilities and psychological tolls of racial passing, as well as the rich history of African American popular culture and its bohemian enclaves around the turn of the twentieth century, Johnson's novel has few peers.

69. Jacqueline Goldsby, *A Spectacular Secret: Lynching in American Life and Literature* (Chicago: University of Chicago Press, 2006),165.

70. Johnson, *Along This Way*, 382, 238–39.

71. Letter from Anne Spencer to Johnson, ca. 1927. The undated letter refers to a recent debate between Alain Locke and Lothrop Stoddard, which was published in the October 1927 *Forum*, and Spencer clearly has in mind Johnson's prefaces to the two collections of American Negro spirituals (JWJ Correspondence, ser. 1, box 19, folder 449, JWJ BRBL).

72. Blanche Knopf, letters to Johnson, October 21, 1927, and August 27, 1930, JWJ Correspondence, ser. 1, box 12, folder 267, JWJ BRBL.

73. See Joseph T. Skerrett Jr., "Irony and Symbolic Action in James Weldon Johnson's *The Autobiography of an Ex-Coloured Man*," in Price and Oliver, *Critical Essays*, 70–87.

74. Letter from Van Vechten to Johnson, October 11, 1933, JWJ Correspondence, ser. 1, box 21, folder 501; letter from Johnson to Marshall Best, February 22, 1937, JWJ Correspondence, ser. 1, box 22, folder 511, JWJ BRBL.

75. See Goldsby, introduction to *The Autobiography*, xxxiii–xxxiv.

76. Johnson, "Preface to the First Edition," 42.

Authenticity and Transparency in *The Autobiography of an Ex-Colored Man*

JEFF KAREM

Critical discussions of authenticity in *The Autobiography of an Ex-Colored Man* have been curiously bounded by either the text's complex provenance or the putative cultural (in)authenticity of the title character. The novel's initial reception as a genuine autobiography has made the text a touchstone for debates about African American authorship, genre, and social change at the dawn of the twentieth century. Robert Stepto and William Andrews were among the first to note that Johnson's text appears to join the historical tradition of African American self-authorship, only to break from it by constructing a "false" self and a "false" text in multiple dimensions: (1) *The Autobiography of an Ex-Colored Man* is not an autobiography but a novel masquerading as one; (2) the Ex-Colored Man is manifestly not Johnson, as was clarified in later editions of the text; and (3) the antiheroic Ex-Colored Man breaks from the pattern of socially conscious ascent and uplift articulated by the text's precursors in the nineteenth century, including autobiographies by Frederick Douglass and Booker T. Washington and post-Reconstruction novels by Charles Chesnutt and Frances Harper. It is no wonder, then, that scholars have described *The Autobiography of an Ex-Colored Man* as "Janus-faced," for the text offers a dizzying genre-bending achievement: it simultaneously joins and rebuts multiple literary tropes and traditions, while nonetheless preserving a sufficiently seamless surface to be received, at first, as a straightforward autobiography, with the actual identity of the author veiled in mystery.[1] As Michael Nowlin notes in his essay in this volume, the success of this endeavor depended on a crucial authorial paradox: "Johnson had to suppress not only his name but his book's literariness: the stylistic ingenuity and irony that potentially gave it indexical value as a measure of black artistic ability." In this respect, one might argue that the most skillful and subversive "passing" in the novel is not that of the Ex-Colored Man, but that of Johnson's text itself, as it manages to move in and among conflicting literary categories.[2]

Ironically, Johnson's craft in smoothing these discursive edges has ensured that many audiences have read the text as a historical or sociological document, even after the 1927 edition revealed Johnson's authorship and the text's fictive nature. Indeed, the history of the novel's reception confirms Nowlin's assertion in his essay here that "the technical artistry Johnson brought to it mainly served to disguise the book's true nature so that it could successfully 'pass' as a true autobiography." One might add that the text was *too* fictionally authentic for its own good, if by "good" one means provoking attention to the text's complexities beyond its cultural reportage. Giulia Fabi notes, "Although Johnson originally intended it [the presentation of the book as an autobiography] as a way of creating interest in the novel, this autobiographical misconception encouraged literal readings of the text, and the author eventually came to regret it."[3] Daphne Lamothe aptly observes that such literal readings of the text are especially likely because of its "sociological tone" and its appearing to be "a kind of ethnography that promise[s] to reveal the secrets of Black culture to its White readership."[4] For Fabi, Lamothe, and many others, these responses reveal a problematic relationship between the text and its audience, a "misreading" of Johnson's aspirations, which critics ought to correct.[5] In most of these scholars' arguments, the fabricated authenticity Johnson achieves in the text is either a lure or a red herring, a textual phenomenon that merits notice but must be transcended to explicate the author's deeper literary or cultural agenda, whether parodying previous genres, critiquing Western ethnography, or advancing an ideology of "self-sacrifice" using the Ex-Colored Man as a negative example.[6] But what if the fabrication of authenticity was a desired end in itself for Johnson?

Ample evidence makes clear that maintaining an aura of genuineness for the text's first publication in 1912 was not an accident or a by-product, but a central aspect of Johnson's design. Most notably, extensive archival research by Jacqueline Goldsby has revealed the careful steps Johnson took to ensure his anonymity so as to preserve a "fiction of authenticity" as a literary and publication strategy.[7] Johnson eschewed using an African American publisher (such as Atlanta University) because of his keen awareness that the contours of the manuscript, as well as his general reputation among the African American intelligentsia, might have linked the volume back to him and spoiled its debut. According to Goldsby, in choosing a relatively obscure white publishing house (Sherman, French and Company) Johnson also could exert more authorial control than he would have had in working with a dominant New York publishing house. Goldsby discovered that "Johnson made mutual confidentiality a stipulation in his contract"—an insistence that reveals the centrality of anonymity to his original design.[8] Indeed, writing to his wife, Grace, Johnson shows a keen awareness of the complex reception accorded to the work and its paradoxical dependence on his fiction of authenticity: "I wrote the book to be taken as a true story.... But in it all, the absolute secrecy of the authorship must be maintained. You can see the importance of this from the *Times* review; as soon it is know[n] that the author is a colored man who could not be the character in the book, interest in it will fall."[9] In his contribution to this volume, Nowlin astutely observes that this secrecy was a risky gambit: "Given the care with which he worked on the book, his decision to publish it anonymously seems at first glance perverse, since in the interests of the 'practical joke on society' he was playing by launching a fake autobiography of a black man living as white ... he risked losing any literary reputation he stood to gain as its author." The natural question, then, is what made this gambit worth such a risk?

Goldsby's answer is that Johnson was especially concerned to maintain "interest" because of his need for a literary success as he was moving away from a stalled diplomatic career. After serving in Venezuela and Nicaragua, a change in administration (Wilson's replacing Harding) ensured that he was headed not toward a desired promotion to a post in Europe, but to the Azores, so it was all the more urgent for him to reinvigorate his career as an artist.[10] While I concur with Goldsby that withholding his identity was a crucial strategy of Johnson for generating enthusiasm in the book and gaining a new foothold in American publishing, I argue that this secrecy also advanced intratextual strategies that are equally important for appreciating the text's tricky design. In particular, Johnson used the fiction of an authoritative autobiography to promise his white readers a tempting initiation into racial secrets, only to confront those same readers with their inability to fathom those secrets, ultimately challenging their understanding of whiteness as a privileged American identity. Indeed, the Ex-Colored Man himself makes clear that trickery will be central to his narrative by professing a "diabolical desire to gather up all the little tragedies of my life, and turn them into a practical joke on society."[11] Following both the narrator's cue and Johnson's elusive authorial pose, most critics see some variety of trickery as vital to the novel, but they disagree considerably as to how to map it.

In *The Autobiography of an Ex-Colored Man*, who is the trickster, who is the mark, and what is the trick? For Goldsby, the "literary trickster" is Johnson himself and the mark the reading public writ large, with Johnson's "charade" aimed primarily at an extratextual purpose: "to prolong debate—and to stimulate sales of his book."[12] For Fabi and many others, the joke is on the Ex-Colored Man, who is an "unreliable first-person narrator" and a failed "interpreter of black culture."[13] Critics focused on identity construction and race argue that the object of the trickery is the discourse of racial difference; Johnson's text exposes the absurdities and contradictions of racism, revealing, ultimately, "racial identity as a social and historical construct."[14] In the most fully developed reading of *The Autobiography of an Ex-Colored Man* as a trickster text, Heather Russell skillfully reframes Johnson as an African American Legba (the West African trickster who manifests in the Caribbean by the same name and also more colloquially as the Signifying Monkey). For Russell, Johnson's trickery is narratological, since he succeeds in creating a hybrid text from a "tight space"; while the text appears at first to be a smooth, antiheroic autobiography, it smuggles in trenchant sociocultural critique: Johnson "appropriates another character's voice to extend his own ideological position."[15]

Despite their persuasiveness, all of these readings underestimate the scope of the trickery at work in *The Autobiography of an Ex-Colored Man*. By compartmentalizing its effects to discrete discursive or narrative phenomena, they effectively close the loop of trickery, usually at the narrator's expense. Fabi, for example, asserts that the deficiencies Johnson implants in the Ex-Colored Man empower the reader, "prompt[ing] the reader to assume the inquisitive critical pose that the protagonist himself lacks."[16] Similarly, Russell finds that Johnson's structures lead his readers to "decipher narrative truth" from the book, in spite of its flawed narrator.[17] I argue that it is a mistake both to quarantine the reader from the trickery and to figure the reader as the implicit hero/critic of the text. Such stabilizing interpretations of the reader are only fully persuasive for a very specific audience (which Johnson sought to reach beyond by turning to a white publisher), that is, Johnson's fellow "race men" and "race women" who were already familiar with the social criticism embedded in *The Autobiography* and the program of social uplift and responsibility that the narrator abandons at the end. As Stepto has aptly noted, in the light of narratives of ascent and Reconstruction fiction aimed at uplift, the Ex-Colored Man functions powerfully as a "negative example" for the racially conscious reader.[18] But what are the implications of the book for a white reader in Johnson's context, particularly one seeking to penetrate the "freemasonry of race"? Evidence both internal and external to *The Autobiography of an Ex-Colored Man* suggests that Johnson aimed to establish via this text a much more challenging relationship with white readers than with African American readers. Masami Sugimori convincingly argues that "Johnson foregrounds the Ex-Colored Man's consciousness of an imagined white audience," but claims that he does so in order to highlight the Ex-Colored Man's subservience to that audience, evoking an ongoing master-slave dialectic.[19]

I argue, in contrast, that instead of affirming the privilege and authority of white readers, Johnson's publishing strategy for the first edition depended on his assumption that most of his white readers would be reliably unreliable, that is, they would be unable to fathom his narrative deception. While within the novel, key scenes and gestures may provide plausible evidence of the Ex-Colored Man's deference to the white reader, I see this as only an apparent deference and merely one layer of the narrator's multiple performances. Expanding on Stepto's influential concept of "distrust of the reader" in African American literature, one can argue that Johnson uses the Ex-Colored Man subtly to undermine the imagined white reader's hope to gain authoritative cultural knowledge via this text, thus inverting the expected power dynamic of the narrator as subservient informant to an authoritative white reader. In this reader-narrator relationship, I find a textual correlative inside the novel to the "productive tension" Lawrence Oliver observes in his essay in this volume between Johnson's literary ideals and those of white mentors like Brander Matthews. Across the novel, Johnson plays upon assumptions of white privilege and authority and, by the end, inverts them with respect to crucial questions of racial legibility, interpretation, and cultural inheritance.

What if, much as his narrator has a "joke" on society (*The Autobiography*, 1), Johnson is having a "joke" on his readers, particularly white readers who expect the text to be their legible guide to navigating blackness, to be the key to the "freemasonry of the race," as the author's 1912 preface promises? If so, then autobiographical or ethnographic misreadings of the text are evidence of its success, and the textual map producing such misreadings ought to be traced. Put another way, if scholars wish fully to understand Johnson's achievement, they ought to probe more deeply into the contradictory logic of what that "freemasonry" actually offers the reader by the end of the text. In spite of its promise of initiation to racial outsiders, Johnson's book simultaneously asserts to white readers that there is much that they do not—and *cannot*—know about African Americans, their culture, and the legacy of discrimination in the United States. By this skillfully paradoxical movement between revelation and opacity, the novel suggests that the landscape of race in the United States is not fully legible for whites, who, in spite of their power and claims to authority, do not really understand the color line and American culture in the way that African Americans do. By offering this vision, Johnson indeed reveals "racial identity as a social and historical construct,"[20] but he also offers a much more resistant challenge: that this is a construct that whites cannot reliably navigate, in spite of their other privileges, even after their passing through the world of the Ex-Colored Man, who promises such a revelation. Most broadly, this motion serves to undermine, as Oliver describes in his contribution to this volume, the "Anglocentric literary and cultural theory" against which Johnson's work was likely to be judged. More pointedly, it is the white readers themselves, rather than the Ex-Colored Man, who are finally subject to the most resonant irony and critique at the end of *The Autobiography*.

The Promise of the Preface

The publisher's preface to the 1912 edition (which has been proven to have been written by Johnson) seeks to establish a strong and reliable relationship with the reader, claiming a bracing representative power for the volume: "Not before has a composite and proportionate presentation of the entire race, embracing all of its various groups and elements, showing their relations with each other and to the whites, been made" (*The Autobiography*, xxxiii). Although most critics would dispute that any text could actually accomplish such a representative stance, it is vital to note that the text aims to or, rather, claims to offer that to the reader. Lest this promise seem too sociological or scientific, the preface quickly offers an even more intimate connection with the reader, famously asserting, "In these pages it is as though a veil had been drawn aside; the reader is given a view of the inner life of the Negro in America, is initiated into the 'freemasonry,' as it were, of the race" (xxxiv). As seductive as this promise of the "inner life" revealed may be, Johnson's vehicle for this claim is also provocative. As a secret society, the Freemasons have occupied a complex niche in American life, ranging from an object of fascination, to an object of suspicion, to the subject of conspiracy theories. By comparing *The Autobiography* to a Masonic rite, the preface draws the reader into a realm of forbidden ceremonies hidden from the public view. Johnson offers a subtle temptation and challenge in describing this process as an "initiation," rather than merely a revelation or exposé. The reader of his text is promised the chance not merely to "see" the other, but virtually to "pass" into this society by reading this book.

Robert Stepto has observed that the preface serves as a species of "authenticating text" in the tradition of the slave narrative, but with the "focus . . . removed from the author."[21] I would add that the preface does not serve to shore up the narrator's individual authenticity, but claims a narrative authenticity for the text on the basis of its authority to provide unprecedented access to the reader. This offer has a powerful double valence, however. While no doubt many white readers (to whom the preface seems to be addressed) desired knowledge of "the Negro," it is far less likely that they sought initiation into African American life in a culture of Jim Crow and the penumbra of *Plessy v. Ferguson*. Thus the preface provides the prospect not only of knowledge, but also of fraternization or even (depending on the reader's assumptions) contamination. From the standpoint of drawing readers into the text, this preface makes a powerful and provocative gesture; whether Johnson actually believes that any such initiation is possible is highly debatable, that is, he may be offering a promise in the preface that cannot but be disappointed by the end of the book. Put another way, the preface may be Johnson's first play as a trickster with the white reader.

The Ex-Colored Man quickly hooks the reader, though with little of the sociological framework promised in the preface. Instead, the narrator focuses on crimes and secrets, as if he were drawing the reader into a conspiracy. Whatever one thinks of the Ex-Colored Man's ultimate (un)reliability as a narrator, he speaks in the opening paragraphs with confidence and intimacy, though also with a peculiar sense of abstraction that serves to heighten the text's suspense. Although he is relatively open about his secret—his first sentence avows, "in writing the following pages I am divulging the great secret of my life"—he is remarkably coy about the nature of that secret. As the narrator continues his introduction, he teases the reader by simultaneously escalating the stakes of his secret, while assiduously avoiding further detail. Following his opening declaration, the Ex-Colored Man cannot settle on a coherent figuration to elucidate what he is hiding. He compares himself to "the un-found-out criminal" who cannot help but "take somebody into his confidence," but then reframes that impulse as a "savage and diabolical desire to gather up all the little tragedies of my life, and turn them into a practical joke on society" (*The Autobiography*, 1). Although these famous passages have been well analyzed by generations of critics, few have noted the imagistic trajectory and its progressive impingement on the reader. The reader begins as a confidant, evolves into the recipient of a criminal confession, and finishes as an implicit target of a practical joke (the reader, after all, is part of society). The mixture of intimacy and danger here is striking, as the Ex-Colored Man mixes confession and aggression to place the reader in a decidedly vexed, but exciting position.

In tandem with this complex relationship with the reader, the narrator also charts, in miniature, his tumultuous relationship with himself, speaking of his "unsatisfaction," "regret," and "remorse" (*The Autobiography*, 1–2). The narrator explicitly denies any ready elucidation or closure to the reader, ending the opening paragraphs with the further confession that he seeks "relief" from these feelings, "of which I shall speak in the last paragraph of this account" (2). In the two opening paragraphs, the Ex-Colored Man's narrative framing is striking for what it obscures even as it purports to reveal. Even with the preface and the title in mind, there is very little the reader can do to develop a reliable prediction as to the nature of the secret, the crime, or the source of regret—and the narrator makes clear that only at the very end of the narrative will he return to these concerns. This self-conscious deferral of the reader's narrative satisfaction shows a highly skilled literary design on the part of both Johnson and his Ex-Colored Man. Whatever deficiencies or inconsistencies one ultimately attributes to the Ex-Colored Man, he exerts a sophisticated and manipulative pull on the reader at the outset, withholding knowledge while simultaneously claiming to reveal all (eventually). While the Ex-Colored Man may be a famously unreliable narrator, he appears aware of his complexities at the outset of his tale, even avowing his role as a secret-keeper, criminal, and joker (though with the implicit promise to transcend these roles as the text unfolds). Alongside Johnson's preface, these two frames lure the reader with the promise of legibility and authenticity of both cultural practice (promised by the preface) and personal history (promised by the Ex-Colored Man). Whether the narrative lives up to those promises is the crux of the trickery facing the reader.

Epistemologies of Transparency and Opacity

Both the preface and the Ex-Colored Man's narrative frame establish a pattern that repeats throughout *The Autobiography of an Ex-Colored Man*: namely, a dialogic relationship between a seemingly authoritative African American speaker and a reader or interlocutor deficient in knowledge of African American culture. That relationship will reach a particularly fevered pitch in the Ex-Colored Man's relationship with his white musical patron, and with white society and the reader at the end of the novel, but there are ample moments of cultural representation or personal confession that seem to open a window between the authoritative figure and the "initiate" into the Ex-Colored Man's life and/or African American culture. In assessing this evolving relationship, I focus specifically on scenes of self-conscious secrecy and revelation between narrator and reader, but I tread lightly on some of the sociological issues already well explored by many critics: specifically, the question of whether or not the various set pieces describing African American life are sufficiently "representative" or "authentic." As I have argued elsewhere, "authenticity" is a moving target in American literary history, dependent not on a stable cultural or ontological essence, but on a transaction or negotiation among author, text, and audience (and their expectations) that establishes what is deemed authentic and what is not.[22]

For readers familiar with Johnson's milieu, most of the Ex-Colored Man's comments about music or folk culture resonate not as stereotypical or essentializing in their context, but as musicological or aesthetic commentary comparable to what Johnson writes in the decidedly nonironic critical prefaces to his collections of spirituals and poetry.[23] Consequently, I do not agree with Lamothe and Fabi that Johnson uses these sociological or ethnographic passages ironically either to undermine the narrative authority of the Ex-Colored Man or to problematize the discourse of cultural reportage.[24] Instead, I agree with Russell's argument that such passages serve a transactional function; they provide a reliable discourse to draw in the reader, which builds the narrator's authority and gives him the opportunity to make bolder political assertions elsewhere in the text, based on that authority and trust.[25] Whether twenty-first-century critics agree with the accuracy of Johnson's representations is a distinct matter and not the subject of this essay. For assessing questions of putative *cultural* representativeness or authenticity in its context, one might note that Johnson aimed his book to be taken as such (as his letters to his wife, Grace, indicate) and that it was received as such by the press (as evident in the reviews),[26] so the question of whether its cultural portraiture was understood as authentic in Johnson's context has already been answered.

I would also argue that it is a case of curiously misplaced concreteness to look to those quasi-ethnographic scenes as a source of unreliability or irony when there are so many other moments in the text that are ripe for analysis in terms of legibility and transparency (or the lack thereof) between the text and the reader. Valerie Smith accurately notes that there are numerous "lapses in logic, in interpretation, and in clarity" in the Ex-Colored Man's account,[27] and I would add that there are also significant moments when the narrator foregrounds those problems, in effect emphasizing the periodic opacity of the text. In counterpoint to clear sociological descriptions or intimate familial confessions, these moments point out problems of ambiguity or unfathomability, which threaten to undermine the confidence that readers may have regarding the degree of knowledge of the "other" that they are obtaining from the text. While I agree with Lamothe's apt characterization of Johnson's work as balancing a dynamic tension between "mak[ing] and withhold[ing] the promise to unveil a Negro subculture,"[28] I believe that the trick runs deeper, as the book questions whether the white reader, even after absorbing all that the novel discloses, can achieve the knowledge of race and identity promised by the preface's trope of "initiation."

The Autobiography unfolds its problematic epistemology gradually, through a series of interruptions that step away from the narrator's developmental trajectory or cultural commentary and provide metareflections on the nature of perception. The broadest example of such a phenomenon is the text's early silence with regard to race. Though the title and preface invoke the African American experience, the narrator does not discover his "blackness" until the end of the opening chapter, during the famous school sorting scene, when his "colored" identity is effectively thrust on him by the teacher's declaration, "I wish all the white scholars to stand for a moment.... You sit down, and rise with the others" (*The Autobiography*, 11). As many critics have noted, this scene depicts the relative and contingent nature of race in the United States: the narrator's "true" racial identity emerges here not from any essential inheritance or cultural characteristic, but via imposition by an authority figure.[29] In addition, the Ex-Colored Man, in eschewing references to race until that moment, places the reader in an epistemological space that doubles the narrator's experience as a young boy. For the first ten pages, neither the narrator nor the reader can fully fathom the nature of the protagonist's identity. This silence may have edifying humanist implications (his early narrative consciousness could be that of any precocious young boy in a similar class position), but the sorting scene also shows the dramatic consequences of not knowing how to navigate the racial landscape of the United States. Being innocent of the categories of race—however contradictory and arbitrary they may be—does not provide protection from them and may make their revelation all the more intense in effect.

At the start of the narrative, those costs accrue primarily to the narrator, but the issue of race has implications for whites as well, although they are held in abeyance. Although the father's identity is shielded, the narrator's mother confides to her son that "the best blood of the South is in you" (*The Autobiography*, 12), which implants a latent threat of exposure of another secret. To be sure, the effects of these mysteries are not symmetrical: the Ex-Colored Man is "exposed" at school and loses privilege, while his white father maintains his secret and his esteemed position. The fact that both the Ex-Colored Man and his mother know the father's identity, while his white family does not know theirs, produces a distinctive asymmetry that will extend throughout the book. While whites maintain their privilege via the legal system and strict categorization, it is African Americans who have superior knowledge of the secrets and contradictions within that system.

In tandem with the narrator's unanticipated discovery of his "true" identity in school, the first chapter has several moments that suggest the difficulty for him in accessing other crucial knowledge—a problem that will, by extension, also afflict the reader. Reflecting on his mother, the Ex-Colored Man remembers her in an essential pose of impenetrability: "I can see her now, her great dark eyes looking into the fire, to where? No one knew but her" (*The Autobiography*, 5). Although the absent father is often understood as an emblem of distance, this reflection shows the possibility of absence coterminous with presence, as his loving mother nonetheless maintains a core privacy with respect to her history, knowledge, and experience.

For his own part, the narrator acknowledges that his early methods of learning were as dependent on fancy and conjecture as they were on decoding a text or symbol: "whenever I came to words that were difficult or unfamiliar, I was prone to bring my imagination to the rescue and read from the picture.... I would sometimes substitute whole sentences and even paragraphs from what meaning I thought the illustrations conveyed" (6). Although this statement could certainly foreshadow the narrator's unreliability, one might also take it to be a prediction of his creative talent as an improviser and his skill at succeeding via unusual methods (he does, after all, get good grades through this approach). In the context of questions of knowledge, this moment also offers a metacomment on the nature of interpretation, posing two competing visions of how to decode a scene—reading the words or taking cues from appearances. If one considers the book's words to be the logos or textual authority, then the narrator's choice to focus on appearances denotes his development as a trickster who subverts the strict categories of written authority. Significantly, the narrator does not give any specific details of this creative reading, so this narrative methodology is kept essentially private, and the reader is not granted the privilege of learning either how to mimic or how to counter the Ex-Colored Man's avowed tendency to improvise upon a scene rather than transmit it verbatim.

Performance, Adaptation, and Dialectics of Knowledge

The Ex-Colored Man's skill as an improviser is doubled in the habits he observes in African Americans, who shift their behavior to adapt to the stringencies of their position in white society. Much as the reader never learns the details of the Ex-Colored Man's creative reading, the narrator explains that whites will likely never understand the complexities of the interiority of African Americans:

> It is a difficult thing for a white man to learn what a colored man really thinks; because, generally, with the latter an additional and different light must be brought to bear on what he thinks; and his thoughts are often influenced by considerations so delicate and subtle that it would be impossible for him to confess or explain them to one of the opposite race. This gives to every colored man, in proportion to his intellectuality, a sort of dual personality; there is one phase of him which is disclosed only in the freemasonry of his race. (*The Autobiography*, 14)

As many critics have noted, this passage echoes the theory of double-consciousness articulated by W. E. B. Du Bois in *The Souls of Black Folk*, but Johnson inflects his words with a subtle polemicism distinct from Du Bois's original vision. Du Bois treats double-consciousness as a divisive force challenging African Americans: "It is a peculiar sensation, this double-consciousness, this sense of always looking at one's soul by the tape of a world that looks on in amused contempt and pity. One ever feels his twoness,—an American, a Negro; two souls, two thoughts, two unreconciled strivings; two warring ideals in one dark body."[30] Johnson's narrator reframes this as a "diffi-cult[y]" for whites. His mention of black people's "dual personality" may imply a model of unstable or fractured identity, but the Ex-Colored Man does not represent this duality in the tortured terms of Du Bois. Instead, the passage reframes double-consciousness as an epistemological problem facing whites: they cannot know the "other" in their midst. The final sentence quoted above, in the context of the preface, seems an ironic jab at the reader's own expectation; Johnson invokes "freemasonry" not to invite the white reader in, but to keep him or her out. This passage undermines the preface's claim that the book will "initiate" the white reader into the "inner life" of African Americans.

As a corollary to this proposition regarding white access to African American interiority, the Ex-Colored Man observes that the need to maintain dual personalities has put African Americans in a superior position of knowledge with respect to whites: "I believe it to be a fact that the colored people of this country know and understand the white people better than white people know and understand them" (*The Autobiography*, 14). There is a telling bit of grammatical ambiguity at the end of this sentence. At first glance, there is a simple parallel of discrepant knowledge: African Americans understand whites better than whites understand African Americans. This claim clearly challenges white privilege, but the potentially vague pronoun "them" (it could refer to whites as well) may imply an even broader challenge: that African Americans understand whites better than white people understand themselves. Taken together, these statements constitute a tricky power play for Johnson and the Ex-Colored Man: they position African Americans, in spite of (or because of) their subordinate legal position, as the masters of identity in the United States, in terms of both performing and interpreting it.[31]

This alternating dialectic of knowledge and ignorance effectively demands of the reader ascent or coming to enlightenment, but the narrator comments on the perpetual difficulty for whites in doing so, even as he purports to guide them. In contrast, the Ex-Colored Man, in spite of his original class position, succeeds throughout his narrative in moving from one African American community to another, deepening his own initiation into those cultures while learning how to position himself appropriately in these milieus. Throughout, he benefits from the "freemasonry of race," as he is consistently guided and educated by his brethren. Indeed, it is a porter who advises him of his capacity to pass: "Of course, you could go in any place in the city; they wouldn't know you from white" (*The Autobiography*, 41). That the porter, who is too dark to pass himself, would advise the narrator how to do so shows both the depth and the sophistication of the community greeting the narrator in Atlanta. The Ex-Colored Man depends on the porter and other colleagues to initiate him into his own race and to teach him how to adapt to white society when it is advantageous. As the narrator enriches himself through these experiences, the reader does gain access to new cultural material as well and may feel the benefit of a parallel sense of cultural education, but the narrator's own trajectory, along with his reflections on acculturation and performance, challenges the reader's capacity to enter into this "freemasonry." Paradoxically, the Ex-Colored Man, who is defined early in his narrative as "Negro," does not even start to understand himself as culturally competent within black communities until his time in Jacksonville: "This was really my entrance into the race. It was my initiation into what I have termed the freemasonry of the race. I had formulated a theory of what it was to be colored; now I was getting the practice" (54). If the African American narrator must pass through a series of initiations, be led by numerous guides, and "practice" in order to acquire an understanding of his own race, then how could readers ever hope to experience the promise of the preface and be "initiated" themselves?

As the narrator develops his observations regarding various classes of African Americans, he offers numerous windows onto new venues for the reader, but simultaneously he reminds the reader of how little whites really know about African Americans. This gap emerges partly because of the condescension and class expectations of whites—the Ex-Colored Man notes that a white southern lady who feels comfortable visiting "Aunt Mary" in her cabin "would no more think of crossing the threshold of Eliza's cottage than ... of going into a bar-room for a drink" (*The Autobiography*, 57)—but also because African Americans have learned to develop a protective distance from whites. Specifically, the Ex-Colored Man avers that the most well-educated and cultured African Americans are the most inaccessible: "this class of colored people is the least known. ... One who is on the outside will often find it a difficult matter to get in" (59). Ironically, after notifying the reader of this desired and remote cultural milieu—specifically, the balls and parties of educated black people—the Ex-Colored Man effectively denies the reader access to it. He mentions the presence of heady and exclusive social events, but does not describe them with details comparable to his other observations (a striking contrast to his incisive observations of high New York society later in the narrative). In fact, he uses the issue of African American society events to comment on the reader's own expectations: "the reader will make a mistake to confound these entertainments with the 'Bellman's Balls' and 'Whitewashers' Picnics' and 'Lime-kiln Clubs' with which the humorous press of the country illustrates 'Cullud Sassiety'" (60). Besides critiquing the reader for a presumably limited point of view, the Ex-Colored Man summarizes the white opinion via heavy dialect. This gesture not only indicts the ignorance of stereotypical media depictions, but puts the dialect in the mouth of the white press and white reader, effectively isolating them not only from black society events, but from standard English as well.

Culture, Violence, and National Legitimacy

By withholding portraits of these social events, the narrator maintains a zone of privacy and privilege, tantalizing white readers by notifying them of an exclusive culture to which they will never have an invitation. In contrast, the Ex-Colored Man, after moving to New York to pursue his musical career, gains access to the most exclusive circles of New York society, not by passing as white, but because of whites' desire for his distinctive cultural production, specifically ragtime and the cakewalk. In his description of the role of African American music in the United States and Europe, Johnson makes another incursion into the citadel of white cultural supremacy, offering another level of challenge. The Ex-Colored Man informs the reader that "in Europe the United States is popularly known better by ragtime than by anything else it has produced in a generation. In Paris they call it American music" (*The Autobiography*, 63). The first sentence stakes a clear claim for the exceptional role of African American music as a cultural ambassador; the second makes an even bolder assertion with its careful choice of words. By shifting the reader's perspective to what Paris (arguably the most celebrated cultural metropole for Americans in Johnson's context) says about the United States, Johnson reflects back a new image of "American" culture to the reader—and that image is a black one.[32] In this formulation, African American music does not assimilate or "pass" into American forms, but the reverse: ragtime and the cakewalk become synecdoches for all of American music. Indeed, the Ex-Colored Man observes that the music has become so desirable that "I have learned also that they have a large number of white imitators and adulterators" (73). This statement offers a clear critique of cultural appropriation, and the word choice is stinging: white musicians are positioned as, at best, mimics or attenuators of cultural forms that they cannot master, thus mirroring to the reader a traditional critique historically leveled at African Americans by white supremacists in the United States.[33]

With these reversals of the expected location of cultural power and "American" privilege, the Ex-Colored Man's relationships with his wealthy patron and audiences take on a new light and bear startling implications for the white reader. As many critics have noted, the white patron's "ownership" of the Ex-Colored Man—disturbingly distilled in the statement that "occasionally he 'loaned' me to some of his friends" (*The Autobiography*, 88)—is a chilling echo of slavery and a reversal of the rise to masculinity typical of prior narratives of ascent. Several scholars also have observed strong homoerotic strains in the patron's fascination and virtual intimacy with the Ex-Colored Man.[34] I would add that, in the context of other discussions of privilege and cultural appropriation in *The Autobiography*, the patron seems to have the goal of not merely acquiring exclusive access to the Ex-Colored Man, but owning the music itself. Indeed, more than the narrator's company, the patron is obsessed with listening to the music: "He would sometimes sit for three or four hours hearing me play, his eyes almost closed, making scarcely a motion except to light a fresh cigarette.... The stopping of the music always aroused him enough to tell me to play this or that.... The man's powers of endurance in listening often exceeded mine in performing" (88). Beyond the strong sexual undertones, there is a discourse of obsession or addiction, suggesting that the patron needs this music to fill a personal, spiritual, or cultural void. Indeed, the trajectory of the narrator's relationship with the patron reveals that this white man, for all of his wealth and privilege, is profoundly rootless and decentered. Like an updated Rasselas, he travels from country to country in pursuit of stimulation or fulfillment but is perpetually dissatisfied. Significantly, the glories of Paris and London do not satisfy the patron: it is through the narrator alone that he finds centering, and the patron appears willing to pay any price to "keep" him. Although the dynamics of this relationship (which is ultimately rejected by the narrator) are demeaning to the Ex-Colored Man, the implications of it are demeaning for the patron and for white culture in general. The patron, in spite of his wealth, has no birthright or pottage (in terms of cultural inheritance or legacy) of his own, so he must depend on the Ex-Colored Man and his music to provide a supplement.

Along with its depiction of American culture as dependent on African Americans for its best global cultural capital, *The Autobiography* reveals that white Americans need to listen to African Americans like the narrator if they want to acquire a full portrait of American culture. Indeed, much as the Ex-Colored Man had to be "initiated" into his own race by fellow African Americans in the South, white readers are initiated into the knowledge of harsh truths about the United States of which they would be ignorant were it not for the Ex-Colored Man. In several crucial set pieces, the narrator exposes the tarnish and stains on the country's reputation, giving the reader a privileged perspective on the national destiny very different from the preface's promise. Most powerfully, he effects this critique by revealing the damaged and scarred bodies created by U.S. racial violence. This confrontation is most painfully evident in the gruesome lynching scene, which threatens the narrator personally and shocks him into flight: "A great wave of humiliation and shame swept over me. Shame that I belonged to a race that could be so dealt with; and shame for my country, that it, the great example of democracy to the world, should be the only civilized [state], if not the only state on earth, where a human being would be burned alive" (*The Autobiography*, 137).

Most critics have addressed the shame of the Ex-Colored Man over his racial membership by interrogating whether his subsequent passing after witnessing this scene is a rational strategic response or a cowardly retreat from racial responsibility, but I would argue that the more important impact for the reader in Johnson's context is the national shame revealed by the Ex-Colored Man, regardless of his personal response. This scene reveals the savagery lurking beneath U.S. "civilization," and the narrator subsequently questions whether that term can even be applied to the South: "The Southern whites are not yet living quite in the present age; many of their general ideas hark back to a former century, some of them to the Dark Ages" (*The Autobiography*, 138). More broadly, the Ex-Colored Man reframes American exceptionalism with a horrifying twist: "the great example of democracy" proves to be "the only civilized, if not the only state on earth, where a human being would be burned alive." Indeed, this scene provides a terrifying and personal complement to the Ex-Colored Man's discussions of the United States with Europeans during his travels, where even those sympathetic to the nation ask the narrator, "did they really burn a man alive in the United States?" (99). With this exposure of racial violence, the Ex-Colored Man draws the reader not into the Masonic rituals of his race, but into the secret rites of violence that define the nation, especially in the eyes of the world.

Beyond this direct indictment, the Ex-Colored Man offers other interpretations of American bodies, symbolic or actual, that reveal the textures of violence undergirding U.S. life. One of the most polemical moments in *The Autobiography* emerges when the narrator travels north to New York City, entering what has long been framed as the place of refuge for African Americans. Rather than affirming the trope of the North as the "promised land," Johnson's narrator reveals America's broken promises of succor and opportunity for migrants inside and outside its borders, and he does so by confronting the Statue of Liberty herself: "She sits like a great witch at the gate of the country, showing her alluring white face and hiding her crooked hands and feet under the folds of her wide garments—constantly enticing thousands from far within, and tempting those who come from across the seas to go no farther. And all these become victims of her caprice" (*The Autobiography*, 65). In exposing the failures of Lady Liberty, the narrator figures her as a temptress who preys on innocent newcomers. By framing an opposition between an "alluring white face" and the "crooked hands and feet" below, the narrator reveals the deformities of a powerful national symbol and enacts another dynamic of secrecy and revelation. This image demonstrates that he (and perhaps other migrants, by extension) can penetrate the secrets hidden by this tarnished lady and see her failures.

While successful white people may have economic and class privilege, they lack privileged knowledge of their own culture because they do not possess the truth about their nation in the way the narrator does. This confrontation with the reader plays out in a more visceral register when the Ex-Colored Man faces the gruesome murder of the white woman visiting the New York club. Reflecting on the violence inflicted on her by a jealous lover, the narrator recalls: "I could still see that beautiful white throat with the ugly wound. The jet of blood pulsing from it had placed an indelible red stain on my memory" (*The Autobiography*, 91). Significantly, it is this scene that prompts him to flee New York and escape the tensions of interracial desire and hostility. Many critics have noted that this scene suggests that the Ex-Colored Man is a coward or disloyal to his community because he ran or felt such transformative sympathy for a white woman, but I would argue that Johnson is being bold in asserting this image of stained and violated white femininity—precisely the iconic figure on behalf of whom the racial violence in the South was so often committed. In this light, Johnson has established a northern double to the lynching scene that the Ex-Colored Man witnesses in the South, suggesting a disturbing logic of symmetrical violence in the nation.

The White Reader's Birthright in *The Autobiography of an Ex-Colored Man*

In addressing the novel's concluding chapters, many scholars gravitate toward a discussion of the narrator's marriage, his final "passing," and his loss of birthright, demonstrating that the "joke" promised at the beginning may not be on society but on the narrator himself. Without disputing that Johnson sets up the Ex-Colored Man for a tragic whimper of an ending, I would argue that the white reader is left in an even more ironized and compromised position and thus the final "joke" may be on white society, in several respects. The question of whose culture and civilization will prove enduring in the United States haunts the final chapters of the narrative—and makes the narrator's passing all the more poignant. He is turning his back on what he believes to be the most truly "American" of cultures. In a highly polyphonic discussion on a train, one of the narrator's interlocutors interrogates the superiority of white culture, reminding his listeners that Euro-Americans are latecomers to the history of world civilizations and may not remain on top for long: "we ought to remember that we are standing on a pile of past races, and enjoy our position with a little less show of arrogance. We are simply having our turn at the game, and we were a long time getting to it. After all, racial supremacy is merely a matter of dates in history" (*The Autobiography*, 119). The narrator reparses this discussion as a matter of cosmology, comparing white claims of racial superiority to the geocentric model of the solar system—an analogy that skillfully parallels white supremacists with the eclipsed scientists from the Dark Ages.

Beyond these abstract comparisons, the Ex-Colored Man offers anecdotes and personal experiences that make "the problem of the color line" even more immediate for his white readers. On the subject of racial misreadings, he reminds readers that the illegibility and instability of racial identification goes in both directions: "Yet it cannot be so embarrassing for a colored man to be taken for white as for a white man to be taken for colored; and I have heard of several cases of the latter kind" (*The Autobiography*, 126). Whatever ontological truth his reader imputes to racial categories, the fact that whites have been misidentified as African Americans offers an equivalence that should terrify his readers. Crucially, the Ex-Colored Man offers this observation immediately before his return to the South, where he views a lynching. While it would be an exaggeration to suggest that white readers would see themselves as the victim in the lynching scene (and they would certainly not want to identify with the perpetrators), the illegibility of race as a stable category for identification produces the possibility that a white man could be a potential victim of lynching—in which case the "mistake" would go far beyond the "embarrassing" situations alluded to in the prior anecdotes. More broadly, the mysteries of racial categorization (and the inability of whites to navigate them), in tandem with the culture of violence in the United States, suggests the potential for anti–African American violence to expand in new directions, even against whites themselves.

More subtly, the Ex-Colored Man confides to the reader that, after passing into white society, his narrative of economic ascent has continued: "Today I am the owner and part owner of several flat-houses. I have changed my place of employment four times since returning to New York, and each change has been a decided advancement. Concerning the position which I now hold I shall say nothing except that it pays extremely well" (*The Autobiography*, 143). For a narrative that began with the promise of induction and unveiling, this is a most cryptic point of arrival. The narrator's "place" in New York society is ultimately withheld, but it is described with hints of economic and class privilege. Moreover, the Ex-Colored Man owns rental property and exhibits social mobility (changing employment four times). Although most readers are not likely to view this economic exchange as worthy of the Ex-Colored Man's sacrifice of his culture and ancestry, his paradoxically secret prominence is intact at the end, however melancholy it may be, and the novel confronts white readers with the startling fact that the Ex-Colored Man is not only hidden among them, but may be hidden "above" them. Beyond the metaphor of Conrad's "secret sharer," the Ex-Colored Man may be the readers' "secret landlord" or "secret boss"—a discomfiting destabilization of white privilege itself.

The reader who began the novel with the expectation of gaining a map for understanding African American life has been confronted, systematically, by scenes that demonstrate the illegibility of African American culture and of racial categories in general to white Americans, as well as white Americans' ignorance about the secret truths of their own culture. By the time the narrator confides his regret that "I have chosen the lesser part, that I have sold my birthright for a mess of pottage" (*The Autobiography*, 154), a final "joke" may arise for the white reader: in comparison with what the Ex-Colored Man has observed of African American culture, does the white reader have a true "part" or "birthright" in this nation at all? Perhaps the most challenging revelation of the novel is not the narrator's exposing the "freemasonry" of black culture, but his confronting white readers with their utter inability ever truly to fathom that culture. Simultaneously, they have learned that the promises of white civilization, when unveiled by the Ex-Colored Man, reveal only an empty space. Which is the more melancholy conclusion: trading one's culture and birthright at a cheap rate, or not having a birthright in the first place?

NOTES

1. For "Janus-faced," see M. Giulia Fabi, *Passing and the Rise of the African American Novel* (Urbana: University of Illinois Press, 2001). Johnson is, of course, not the first African American author to veil crucial aspects of his or her identity: Harriet Wilson published *Our Nig* anonymously in 1859; Harriet Jacobs used the pseudonymous character of Linda Brent in *Incidents in the Life of a Slave Girl* (1861) to shield her friends and family still in the bonds of slavery; Charles Chesnutt did not advertise himself as an African American author in the first edition of *The Conjure Woman* (1899). Johnson, however, innovated dramatically on this tradition by using veiling not merely as a technique for extratextual purposes—such as political protection or authorial positioning—but as a foundational structure in his text's narrative and in its relation to the reader.

2. See Lawrence Oliver's detailed discussion in his essay in this volume of the multiple literary influences on, and resulting hybridity of, Johnson's text.

3. Fabi, *Passing*, 91.

4. Daphne Lamothe, *Inventing the New Negro: Narrative, Culture, and Ethnography* (Philadelphia: University of Pennsylvania Press, 2008), 71.

5. Ibid. See also Lamothe's chapter in this collection, which reframes Johnson's novel in twenty-first-century discussions of race, cosmopolitanism, and belonging.

6. Fabi, *Passing*, 92; Lamothe, *Inventing the New Negro*, 73; Heather Russell, *Legba's Crossing: Narratology in the African Atlantic* (Athens: University of Georgia Press, 2009), 44.

7. Jacqueline Goldsby, "Keeping the 'Secret of Authorship': A Critical Look at the 1912 Publication of James Weldon Johnson's *Autobiography of an Ex-Colored Man*," in *Print Culture in a Diverse America*, ed. James P. Danky and Wayne A. Wiegand (Urbana: University of Illinois Press, 1998), 255–56.

8. Ibid., 254.

9. Johnson to Grace Johnson, June 26, 1912, quoted in Goldsby, "Keeping the 'Secret of Authorship,'" 257.

10. Goldsby, "Keeping the 'Secret of Authorship,'" 264–65.

11. Because my essay is concerned with the complex relationship between Johnson's text and readers who did not (at first) know of his authorship, I use the original, anonymous edition of *The Autobiography of an Ex-Colored Man* (1912), including the publisher's preface (written by Johnson), which, in my analysis, further enriches and complicates the reader's relationship to *The Autobiography*. This original text is reproduced in *The Autobiography of an Ex-Colored Man and Other Writings*, ed. Noelle Morrissette (New York: Fine Creative Media, Barnes and Noble Classics, 2007). Future references to this work are given parenthetically in the text.

12. Goldsby, "Keeping the 'Secret of Authorship,'" 259.

13. Fabi, *Passing*, 92, 95. The number of scholars who argue that the "joke" is on the narrator is too great to address, but it indicates a critical consensus that the governing irony of the novel must be at the expense of the narrator, and this judgment has remained relatively constant for decades. Prior to Fabi's assertion, crucial analysis from the 1970s to the 1990s reached similar conclusions. Robert Fleming, one of the

first critics to discuss irony in the novel, observes, "The reader who turns to the end of the book at this point finds the key to one of the central ironies of the novel: the practical joke may, after all, be on the narrator" (Fleming, "Irony as a Key to Johnson's *The Autobiography of an Ex-Colored Man*," *American Literature* 43, no. 1 [March 1971]: 85). Donald Goellnicht considers the parodic/ironic discourse of the novel to be more destabilizing ("we worry that a joke is being played on us that we cannot quite get"), but ultimately he finds the irony directed back to the Ex-Colored Man because "the joke rebounds upon him" (Goellnicht, "Passing as Autobiography: James Weldon Johnson's *The Autobiography of an Ex-Colored Man*," *African American Review* 30, no. 1 [1996]: 14, 15).

14. Lamothe, *Inventing the New Negro*, 69.

15. Russell, *Legba's Crossing*, 35, 47.

16. Fabi, *Passing*, 97.

17. Russell, *Legba's Crossing*, 30.

18. Robert B. Stepto, *From behind the Veil: A Study of Afro-American Narrative*, 2nd ed. (Urbana: University of Illinois Press, 1991), 104.

19. Masami Sugimori, "Narrative Order, Racial Hierarchy, and 'White' Discourse in James Weldon Johnson's *The Autobiography of an Ex-Colored Man* and *Along This Way*," *MELUS* 36, no. 3 (Fall 2011): 41.

20. Lamothe, *Inventing the New Negro*, 69.

21. Stepto, *From behind the Veil*, 98.

22. See Jeff Karem, *The Romance of Authenticity: The Cultural Politics of Regional and Ethnic Literatures* (Charlottesville: University of Virginia Press, 2004).

23. For an illustrative example, compare the observations in Johnson's preface to *The Second Book of American Negro Spirituals* to the Ex-Colored Man's reflections on African American music. After hearing spirituals sung at a camp revival, Johnson's narrator comments, "I doubt that there is a stronger theme ["Go down, Moses"] in the whole musical literature of the world. And so many of these songs contain more than mere melody; there is sounded in them that elusive undertone, the note in music which is not heard with the ears" (*The Autobiography*, 132). Although today's reader may find the mystical or essentializing nature of these remarks problematic, they are consistent with Johnson's writings on the subject. In one preface Johnson observes, "A further explanation of the variety of the Spirituals lies in the Negro's many-mooded nature; his sensitiveness and quick response to the whole gamut of human emotions. And what a range he has. I do not believe there is any other people in the world that can be so lugubriously sad as the Negro, or so genuinely gay" (Preface to *The Second Book of American Negro Spirituals* [1926], in James Weldon Johnson, *Writings*, ed. William L. Andrews [New York: Library of America, 2004], 732). My point here is not to evaluate whether either claim is accurate, but to suggest that this discourse of the Ex-Colored Man, because of its congruence with Johnson's own observations, is not meant to be taken ironically. Instead, in these quasi-ethnographic passages the Ex-Colored Man gathers narrative authority (and the trust of the white reader)—which enhances the power of his ultimate trickery at the end.

24. Fabi, *Passing*, 95; Lamothe, *Inventing the New Negro*, 72.

25. Russell, *Legba's Crossing*, 46–47.

26. As Noelle Morrissette demonstrates in the appendixes of her edition of the novel, multiple publications accepted the text as authentic, including the *New York Times* ("there is nothing in it that violates probability, and the book carries the publisher's assurance of good faith"; May 26, 1912) and the *Crisis* (it "is indeed an epitome of the race situation in the United States told in the form of an autobiography"; November 1912).

27. Valerie Smith, *Self-Discovery and Authority in Afro-American Narrative* (Cambridge, Mass.: Harvard University Press, 1987), 59.

28. Lamothe, *Inventing the New Negro*, 72.

29. See Robert Stepto's close reading of this passage and its importance to American autobiography in his essay in this collection.

30. W. E. B. Du Bois, *The Souls of Black Folk* (New York: Signet, 1969), 45.

31. The narrator extends this observation beyond the United States to other contact zones between Africans and Europeans (and Asians): "It is remarkable, after all, what an adaptable creature the Negro is. I have seen the black West Indian gentleman in London, and he is in speech and manners a perfect Englishman. I have seen natives of Haiti and Martinique in Paris, and they are more Frenchy than a Frenchman. I have no doubt that the Negro would make a good Chinaman, with exception of the pigtail" (*The Autobiography*, 112). While it is certainly possible to read this passage as merely an expression of the Ex-Colored Man's assimilationist tendencies, it is also possible to see it as a testament to the capacity of members of the African diaspora to adapt and thrive in many cultural settings. This observation has a double-edged rhetorical thrust, however: while it implicitly praises European cultures by setting them up as the benchmark to which Africans aspire, it destabilizes the boundaries of cultural supremacy by arguing that "the Negro" can equal and exceed the competence of Europeans within their own cultures.

32. See Lawrence Oliver's discussion in this volume of Johnson's cosmopolitanism and his appropriation of his mentor Brander Matthews's concepts of race and nation.

33. In order to see the persistence of this racist truism, consider the following analysis of African American music: "Blacks were able to mimic white music harmonically to some degree, and to exceed white music rhythmically (in some sense), altering its feel by incorporating into it their sense of rhythm.... But blacks were much less able to imitate whites melodically (again, this is relative to their success in other areas of music). I'm not sure why this is so, but it may be that the composition of melody is somehow creative in the sense of originating something new, and is therefore less susceptible of imitation." This commentary was not made in the nineteenth century or even in the twentieth, but in an online discussion in 2012. "What Have Blacks Contributed to Our Civilization?" *Journal of the Lawrence Auster Society* (April 24, 2012), http://www.amnation.com/vfr/archives/022271.html.

34. See, for example, Jeffrey Q. McCune Jr., *Sexual Discretion: Black Masculinity and the Politics of Passing* (Chicago: University of Chicago Press, 2014); Siobhan B. Somerville, *Queering the Color Line: Race and the Invention of Homosexuality in American Culture* (Durham, N.C.: Duke University Press, 2000); and Cheryl Clarke, "Race, Homosocial Desire, and 'Mammon' in *Autobiography of an Ex-Coloured Man*," in *Professions of Desire: Lesbian and Gay Studies in Literature*, ed. George E. Haggerty and Bonnie Zimmerman (New York: Modern Language Association, 1995), 84–97.

PART TWO

Relational Tropes

Transnationalism, Futurity, and the Ex-Colored Man

The Futurity of Miscegenation
James Weldon Johnson's *The Autobiography of an Ex-Colored Man* and Pauline Hopkins's *Of One Blood*

DIANA PAULIN

Although both Hopkins's *Of One Blood* (1902–3) and Johnson's *The Autobiography of an Ex-Colored Man* (1912) are now considered canonical African American literary texts, they have been examined most extensively in terms of their contributions to African American literary representation, including their excavations of the undocumented past and their complex depictions of self-discovery, interiority, passing, and racial hybridity.[1] Interdisciplinary scholarship has added to current understandings of the interactivity of these texts with diverse forms of African American, black diasporic, and transnational cultural production, like Susan Gillman's work on Hopkins and the occult and Siobhan Somerville's queer readings of both Hopkins's and Johnson's cultural production.[2] These examinations, including my own, also take into account the collective political and social engagement of "black" intellectuals, artists, and activists that helped shape cultural production during the transitional and unsettled postbellum, Progressive, and pre–World War I eras.

In this essay I investigate Hopkins's and Johnson's staging of miscegenation's transnational and diasporic contours in roughly the first decade of the twentieth century. Creatively reconceptualizing the black-white binary, their works emphasize the elastic cultural definitions that organize the messy intersections of race, nation, gender, and class. Hopkins and Johnson illuminate racial-ethnic hybridization: their work demonstrates how interracial intimacies and intermixture possess powerful representational potential. They also suggest the national and global implications that the overriding black-white divide so often subsumed by radically staging miscegenation, which legitimized a diverse black population and documented the black diaspora's vital historical and contemporaneous societal contributions. By reading Johnson's *The Autobiography of an Ex-Colored Man* and Hopkins's *Of One Blood* relationally, in this essay I illuminate the transnational concerns embedded in both works' stagings of miscegenation. I demonstrate how *The Autobiography* not only interacts with the global concerns of the people of color of his generation but also engages a concept of racial futurity, anticipating the transnational and diasporic concerns of Johnson's literary descendants.

Hopkins and Johnson deploy miscegenation as a performative trope in their fiction. Miscegenation is a taboo that enables them to create characters that transcend the confines of local and national belonging. Hopkins's strategic use of the miscegenation trope allows her to intervene in other cultural bifurcations, particularly the divisions between performance and writing, domesticity and transnationalism, and citizen and alien. Johnson's representation of miscegenation also addresses the divisions of domestic and international, and spectator and participant, and is informed by his position as an international agent for the U.S. government and as a spokesperson for domestic African Americans. Both authors enact miscegenation in their writing and life in multivalent ways. A close comparative reading of their texts and the contexts in which they were produced reveals both the convergence and the distinction of their creative visions. Unlike nineteenth-century drama and fiction writers, Hopkins and Johnson utilize the performative trope of miscegenation to suggest how intermixture might revolutionize the meanings of race in the twentieth century.[3]

Of One Blood; or, The Hidden Self appeared serially in the *Colored American Magazine* shortly after Hopkins's *Winona* (1902). Her literary romance incorporates pan-Africanism and miscegenation, presenting the complexity of black diasporic identity and various forms of whiteness. Foregrounding the intercultural, multiracial, and transnational contributions that helped build civilization, Hopkins's love story interrogates and revises historical understandings of Western Europe's central role in formulating these ideals of race, culture, and nation. Published a decade after *Of One Blood*, Johnson's *The Autobiography of an Ex-Colored Man* documents how a fictional mixed-race protagonist moves among various racial and ethnic communities because he can pass as both white and nonwhite. While foregrounding the black-white divide, Johnson illuminates the early twentieth-century racial and national matrix that informed identity. In his portrait of an "ex-colored" man he showcases various scenes of productive black life that lynching and racial violence upstaged. Through a story of racial mobility and a lasting black-white marriage, Johnson revises the problematic ideologies associated with miscegenation. Like Hopkins, Johnson uses his work as a platform to reevaluate the miscegenated roots of the American diasporic family tree.[4]

Hopkins and Johnson both develop the miscegenation trope by emphasizing how it serves as a multidimensional representational concept. Strikingly they both employ the form of the novel rather than the play, rejecting the familiar, prescribed genre. Yet Hopkins and Johnson use strategies from multiple genres as they test miscegenation's diverse potential meanings. Drawing from their experiences as performers, historians, orators, writers, and critics, Hopkins and Johnson blend nineteenth-century genre conventions to enhance their works' modern impact and their own influence as black cultural producers and activists.[5] Through this approach, they reevaluate the cultural fascination with miscegenation and its taboo status during the Civil War era, even surpassing the decentering of the black-white binary in their earlier work on Afro-Indian relations. Their playful yet representationally powerful experiments with varied forms and hybridized identities, as opposed to adherence to monolithic voices and belief systems, gestures toward the future rather than the past.

Hopkins's *Of One Blood* and Johnson's *The Autobiography of an Ex-Colored Man* offer responses to the historical residue of slavery and miscegenation, but they do so in ways that underscore the performance of race and nationhood more self-consciously and explicitly than earlier works by American authors. Dramatizing miscegenation, Hopkins and Johnson reveal how its innumerable manifestations—in private and public, both domestically and transnationally—might be read as productive, even productively disruptive, formulations of identity and subjectivity. Not only do they expose the reductivity of the black-white color line, they refigure America's restrictive structures of identification and classification. In the context of an increasingly varied white population, each segment of which insists on the purity and superiority of whiteness, they respond with representations and enactments of equally varied "blackness." In their works, performance displaces the "real" and the "authentic," disrupting persistent stereotypes prevalent both onstage and in real life. Their novels exhibit nonwhite racialized performances that were desirable at the time to mainstream white audiences, such as the tragic octoroon, staging the miscegenation process through which white audiences and readers consumed "black" cultural production. However, they also include the possibility of black pleasure and agency,[6] critiquing the reductive discourse of miscegenation as a contaminating and destructive force.

Transnationality in Black and White

For Hopkins and Johnson, the trope of miscegenation provided a performative site for playing out the dynamic, contradictory ways that the transgression of racial boundaries exposed the bifurcation's mutual contingency. Miscegenation functioned as an emblem of intermingling and hybridity while also offering an imagined alternative to polarized nationalisms, such as black versus white supremacist, which were pitted against each other as *the* solution to racialized oppositions. It could help in the reimagination of conventional transnational and cross-racial formulations that did not rely solely on the bifurcated model, such as empire-colony. Taking full advantage of this trope in their works, Hopkins and Johnson address more rigid formulations of race and reference the extension of the black-white polarity to other populations, such as the increasing hostility toward Chinese citizenship and national identity (the "yellow peril") and military acts against indigenous nations.[7] Both authors reimagined and resisted the overwhelming resiliency of racial binaries in favor of a rich and multivalent diasporic vision.

Of One Blood, Hopkins's intensely racialized manifestation of miscegenation, sets the stage for a radical reimagination of interracial relations in which agency and authority are always in play. By highlighting this process of interplay in the performative praxis of miscegenation, Hopkins creates space to envision more elastic formations of racial, gendered, national, and sexual interrelations, as well as the complex desires and repulsions that inform them.[8] Hopkins emphasizes the fluidity of the lines that distinguish not only race but also forms of cultural and aesthetic expression.[9] Like her heroine, Dianthe, Hopkins's text blends intercultural, trans-hemispheric, cross-genre, intertextual, and interracial conventions.[10]

Of One Blood is unlike any other text. Critics have focused on the significance of the occult and of passing in this piece as they pertain to Hopkins's reframing of black identity. The work has also been characterized as part sentimental, part melodrama, part science fiction, and part "New Negro" rhetoric, to name a few interpretations.[11] It is a strange blend that consistently confounds the reader's expectations with uncanny plot twists, hauntings and interventions from dead ancestors, mysterious disappearances, and spectral visitations, not to mention the exposure of a convoluted lineage that crosses national, racial, cultural, and class boundaries. Travel, too, defies the laws of science, allowing ancient Ethiopians to interact with their twentieth-century diasporic heirs in the United States and allowing modern-day explorers to enter hidden ancestral and mystical cities thought to be no longer in existence or mythological fictions. Every aspect of Hopkins's fantastic spectacle—plot, characters, setting, genre, subject, conclusion—resists reductive readings. The intersections cannot be easily untangled, segregated, or self-contained. Instead, Hopkins's work stresses the hybridity of racial identity, history, civilization, and nationhood.

Throughout her book, Hopkins deliberately fuses seemingly distinct traditions of "white" Western and "black" African cultures. In *Of One Blood*'s staging of miscegenation, Hopkins demonstrates how ancient Ethiopian cultures are appropriated, absorbed, and thereby presented as unique aspects of white Western heritage. Hopkins's narrative suggests that not only are seemingly diverse cultures and traditions interconnected through intermixture, but that it is also the long history of miscegenation, rather than its prohibition or absence, that created the need to promote "white" cultural supremacy and pure lineages. By connecting the interrelated fates of her main characters,

Reuel, Dianthe, and Aubrey, to the origins of African civilization, Hopkins's text destabilizes conventional views of both blackness and whiteness by redefining them in terms of intersecting African and Western (Greek) cultures.[12]

According to Hopkins, part of her task as a writer was to "*portray the inmost thoughts and feelings of the Negro with all the fire and romance which lie dormant in our history*" (emphasis in original).[13] *Of One Blood*'s serialized publication in the *Colored American Magazine* placed her writing in conversation with contemporaneous texts, reinforcing its issues.[14] For instance, Hopkins wrote an editorial to address criticisms of her portrayals of interracial love, and in articles like "Venus and the Apollo, Modeled on Ethiopians," she asserted her theories about the advancement of ancient black cultures, such as her contention that black Ethiopian slaves were the physiological models for classical art.[15] It has been argued that Hopkins used fantastic and melodramatic forms to avoid facing the realities of social problems directly.[16] I believe, however, that she deliberately placed the serial novel alongside her discussions of relevant debates and concerns about race and identity in the United States and abroad.[17] Her imaginative novels and short stories echoed issues that she raised in her nonfiction essays, such as miscegenation history and black America's cultural ties to African civilizations. Combining biography, history, and even science fiction, Hopkins challenged the unquestioned legitimacy of "facts" about race, culture, and civilization (re)produced in mainstream authorized sources, such as science and Western history.[18]

Of One Blood's triad of central characters immediately disrupts the binary of race implied by miscegenation in their complex enactment of interracial intimacies. Because of their intersecting familial, diasporic, and interracial ancestry, Aubrey, Dianthe, and Reuel's triangular relationship serves as a microcosm for the broader concept that all "races" are linked through intersecting and mutually informative histories.[19] The careful policing of racialized, familial, and national borders does not remove the erotic appeal of interracial or incestuous sex, Hopkins shows. Rather, the suppression and denial of the intersecting histories of racial, familial, and transnational relations have led to much more violent and destructive crossings of those boundaries. The familial and incestuous bond shared by Aubrey, Reuel, and Dianthe exposes the history of the displacement and exploitation of black slaves, which was built on the violent rupture of familial, cultural, and kinship ties. All three characters appear white, but they inhabit different roles: Reuel is passing as white; Dianthe is living as black; and Aubrey is living as white, unaware of his African ancestry. Reuel discovers that Dianthe and Aubrey are his sister and brother, while Dianthe learns independently that she, Reuel (whom she married), and Aubrey (who forced her to marry him after claiming that Reuel was dead) are siblings. They are all the children of Aubrey's father and his slave Mira, but Aubrey was taken at birth and raised as a "free" white man.

Yet Hopkins also suggests that their "incestuous" relations lead to a powerful discovery of the ancestral and diasporic bond that unites Reuel and Dianthe and reanimates Reuel's pan-African destiny. The lines drawn to distinguish among race, family, and nation, Hopkins shows, are always in the process of being reformulated at different moments in history in order to enforce different ideological imperatives.

By staging her characters' dynamic and multivalent relationship as a type of miscegenation, Hopkins also displays the gendered and eroticized power dynamics that inform the discourse surrounding interracial intimacies. For example, both Reuel and Aubrey exert power over Dianthe, recalling the illicit, mixed-race relations that occurred on slave plantations and that were part of imperialist practices and domination in transnational sites. Rather than valuing her independent agency, both Aubrey and Reuel consider Dianthe an object to be possessed and protected. Dianthe, then, serves as the vehicle through which both Reuel and Aubrey express their manhood. By allowing both Aubrey and Reuel to marry Dianthe, Hopkins actualizes the incestuous valence of the relationship, which was merely suggested in earlier textual representations of miscegenation (and is implied in Johnson's *The Autobiography* as well). Hopkins's bold reconfiguration of miscegenation produces explicit meanings that amplify the muted implications of earlier representations.

Through these embodied and ethereal figures, Hopkins represents the past, present, and potential future of miscegenation. The racialized black diasporic female figures that reemerge in multiple sites and forms throughout the narrative remind us of our miscegenated past—overlapping histories, diasporic ancestry, tangled racial and national lineages—and signify the potential of our uncharted future. Hopkins indicates that the black woman's body remains integral to her revision of the trope of miscegenation as productive and even procreative rather than destructive.

Toward the novel's end, the narrator asks—in no uncertain terms—the story's most fundamental question:

> Who is clear enough in vision to decide who hath black blood and who hath not? Can any one tell? No, no one; for in His own mysterious way He has united the white race and the black race in this new continent. By the transgression of the law He proves His own infallibility: "Of one blood have I made all nations of men to dwell upon the whole face of the earth," is as true today as when given to the inspired writers to be recorded. No man can draw the dividing line between the two races, for they are both of one blood![20]

Hopkins's exposure of the intermingled bloodlines that supposedly polarize black and white reinforces her representation of miscegenation as a performed reiteration of cultural and juridical beliefs rather than an actual violation of legitimate racialized boundaries. The focus on corrupt blood, associated with the conflation of incest and miscegenation in the public imagination, supports segregationist assertions that the races are biologically distinct and should remain separate. At the same time, however, the notion of shared blood invokes the humanistic belief that all people, regardless of color, creed, or class, share common (human) blood. The extension of this belief is that all races should be treated equally because they are part of the same human species.

In the context of Hopkins's commitment to racial uplift and her striving to create what Hazel Carby refers to as a "black literary renaissance" in Boston twenty years before Harlem's Renaissance was in the spotlight,[21] her story of miscegenation offers a new way of narrating the past and using it productively for the future. Hopkins's work announces a commitment to displacing the black-white binary, divesting it of its power, and embracing the multiple lineages and histories that constituted black diasporic identity at the beginning of the twentieth century.

Johnson, like Hopkins, was intensely involved in the political, racial, and social environment in which he worked and lived; he was active in politics and the NAACP, campaigning against lynching, against the U.S. occupation of Haiti, and for the promotion of black culture.[22] Working and traveling in Central and South America for almost a decade—as a representative of the United States—imbued him with a unique understanding of race, nation, and imperialism. Unlike most of his fellow black artists, he occupied a somewhat ambiguous position: he was both an official promoter of U.S. political and economic interests in Venezuela and Nicaragua, and he still did not possess equal rights at home.[23] Johnson's own body, along with the representations he created in multiple genres, staged miscegenation at the very moment when the stakes of maintaining binary oppositions were increasing. His mixed Haitian-European-Bahamian lineage could be traced explicitly to interracial and transnational intimacies born out of imperialist conquest and the slave trade linking Europe to the Caribbean and the Americas.[24]

Scholars have read *The Autobiography* as an extended representation of a man torn between "domestic struggle" and "imperial reward," informed by Johnson's relationship to Latin America.[25] In *The Autobiography*, Johnson employs performances of miscegenation and passing to navigate complexities with which he was very familiar. Through the musing and mobility of his protagonist, Johnson contests the hierarchical and reductive binaries that structure race, class, and transnational relations. Illustrating this dynamic, his protagonist not only transgresses the black-white divide, occupying each category at different points, but also circumvents the binary's restrictions by passing as Cuban, something Johnson experienced as a young man traveling to Atlanta with a longtime Cuban friend who spoke Spanish. They were spared from being ejected from the first-class car because the conductor believed that they were not black Americans and presumably were just passing through Florida.²⁶

The Autobiography, similar to Hopkins's serialized novel, interrogates genre conventions in its literary staging of miscegenation. The narrative first shows the protagonist's experiences as a young boy unaware of his black ancestry. Readers witness the process through which the unnamed narrator's racial classification is employed as a performative device and then witness his metamorphosis: from a man who is not visibly black but who attempts to connect with the "black" community to a man who discards his black ancestry altogether and passes into the white world permanently, although uneasily.

Noted critics such as Robert Stepto and Valerie Smith have detailed Johnson's strategic fusing, appropriation, and revision of canonical Afro-American narrative tropes, such as the rhetoric of omission, which highlights his protagonist's (failed) attempt to come to terms with his own racially hybridized identity. Stepto argues that the narrator in *The Autobiography of an Ex-Colored Man* does not possess the racial literacy to learn from his experiences; instead, he stagnates in a superficial performance of noncommittal racial indeterminacy, resisting the deep communal connection and illumination forged by the literary ancestry that his narrative recalls, such as Du Bois's *The Souls of Black Folk* (1903) and Booker T. Washington's *Up from Slavery* (1900).²⁷

However, as Samira Kawash contends, the Ex-Colored Man's "failure" to embody or name his racialized identity effectively challenges Stepto's and other critics' underlying assumption that a "knowable" or "stable" underlying racial identity, to which the narrator must align himself, exists at all.²⁸ In fact, the question of whether or not he successfully chooses one side or the other of the color line also relies on the bifurcated racialized model that the narrator's liminal position simultaneously invokes and resists. In his refusal to occupy the empty signifier of race, the narrator's story reinforces the arbitrariness of racial classifications, as in Hopkins's work. Yet the social and legal structures that police bodies that resist or violate the norms of race remain firmly in place.

Even though the narrator in *The Autobiography of an Ex-Colored Man* plays a racially liminal role, the legibility and cultural implications of his performance come into view only in the context of its relationship to the static black-white binary. The narrator's mobility relies on the consistently oppositional categories of black and white, which he alternately resists and enacts. Part of the power of Johnson's narrative rests in the continual staging of miscegenation as a disruption of these binaries. Miscegenation, not racial passing, is the book's central trope. It is through miscegenation that the social, legal, and embodied realities of racial classification put pressure on the narrator's resistance to the seemingly arbitrary imposition of explicit racial markers. Johnson's text is therefore best understood as a narrative performance, an extended staging of miscegenation.

The Ex-Colored Man performs distinct identities based on physical and social contexts. Similar to the theatrical dynamic that brings together actors, a script, and an audience, which are then activated collaboratively in the experience of the performance, the narrator's performance of race and his embodied contestation of the black-white binary are legible because of his mobility and instability as he navigates bifurcated identities.

Johnson's narrative insists on the Ex-Colored Man's embodied and racialized performance. The narrator acknowledges his own role as a racial performance—an uneasy balance between lived experience and theatricality—when he meets the white woman he wants to marry. He claims that in the past he had "assumed and played" his "role as a white man with a certain degree of nonchalance." When he believes that he may lose the woman he loves, he begins to doubt his "ability to play the part" and fears she might detect something that makes him "differ from the other men she knew."[29] His uncertainty about how she will interpret his performance highlights the intersecting roles of the viewer, the actor, and the act. The narrator fears that her scrutiny or disapproval of his performance may reveal some inconsistency, a mark of difference, or indisputable evidence that will position them on opposite sides of the black-white binary, create an impenetrable divide, and terminate their union.

Along these same lines, Johnson's narrative staging of miscegenation highlights the powerful process through which racial difference is enunciated—rather than focusing on the narrator's in-between status or passing performance. Ultimately, the narrator cannot completely transcend the strictly polarized formulations of black and white and their mutual constitution of his rogue status; instead, he comes dangerously close to reenacting the restrictive "cover story" of miscegenation, which reproduces the binary and promotes limited visions of the individual, the community, the nation, and the globe. His choices also seem to limit the productive possibilities of his own imagination and position in society. However, through the Ex-Colored Man's discomfort with his "present position" (*The Autobiography*, 126) at the end of the narrative—a "privileged spectator" (126) rather than a participant, who neither "disclaim[s] the black race nor claim[s] the white race" (115)—Johnson reminds his readers of other routes to success that do not involve sacrificing one's self. The narrator's regret plays a pedagogical role, illustrating the damage that one-dimensional languages and reductive (hi)stories can produce, even when they provide temporary comfort or simplicity in a complicated world.

Johnson's staging of miscegenation invokes a multilayered reading of the genre of autobiography. The narrator continually performs a kind of intermixing—culturally, geographically, sexually, racially, and aesthetically—in his travels throughout the United States and Europe. Even his roles as both outside observer and undetected performer blur the line between actor and spectator. He does not fully occupy whiteness or blackness, despite his elitist enactments of both categories. Instead, Johnson offers his readers a bifurcated view of race without ever fully committing his narrator to either role. Moreover, even the act of reading this autobiographical fiction enacts a type of miscegenated reading practice, because the text does not privilege any one perspective. Instead, it invites a diverse yet unnamed readership that is compelled to both participate and observe along with the protagonist-narrator, releasing both readers and *The Autobiography*'s performer from any obligation to pledge allegiance to any racial category.[30]

Both reader and narrator can rehearse interracial intimacies without directly experiencing the violent consequences imposed on those who engage in interracial sex. If the narrator can play out his autobiography and his interracial intimacies, then other narratives might be implicated as mere performances rather than "authentic" forms of knowledge, such as pseudoscientific discourses that deem racial intermixture degenerate and "pure" blacks inferior. This unsettling effect approximates Hopkins's challenge to claims about the supremacy and origins of white Western culture in *Of One Blood*; it also recalls the romanticized depictions of indigenous cultures in *Winona*, which can be read as strategic performances designed to unsettle reductive or essentialized portraits of Indianness.

Like Hopkins's work, this counterfeit autobiography "exceeds the limits" of the form,[31] approximating it through repetition and revision. This allows Johnson to counter the claims of legitimacy offered in conventional narratives. If, as the Ex-Colored Man's story demonstrates, certain formulations of blackness can be enacted through performance, rather than imposed on particular bodies because of inherent qualities or biological facts, then whiteness can also be read as a similarly constructed category with an equally unsettled (and unsettling) foundation. In addition, Johnson's work calls into question the notion that miscegenation is always a transgressive violation of the color line and, especially when occurring between a black man and a white woman, always a form of rape. Regardless of Johnson's challenge to mainstream rhetoric about the criminality of interracial intimacy, no matter what the circumstances, his fictional narrative does not shy away from the violent responses that miscegenation generates; instead, his work acknowledges the palpability of the punishment, including the lynchings of black men and the social or legal castigation of white women.[32] In his life, Johnson negotiated both the real bodily repercussions of "crimes" of miscegenation and the artificiality of the rigid black-white binary. *The Autobiography* follows suit, crossing genres, mixing audiences, and hybridizing identities. Johnson's generative staging of miscegenation invites a critical reassessment of historical racial performances and encourages an examination of just who benefits from the strategic opposition of black and white.

Johnson's fictional account of successful enactments of whiteness, blackness, and even Cubanness reinforces his representation of racial performance. Through the narrator's racially hybrid body, Johnson stages miscegenation as a disruptive and potentially productive process. He exposes how his narrator's embodied performances resist the color line while simultaneously relying on its powerful resilience.

Like *Of One Blood*'s Reuel, the narrator of *The Autobiography* moves in and out of various racial classifications at different points in his life. Ultimately, however, he distances himself from the African heritage that Reuel embraces. The two experiences that solidify the narrator's reevaluation of his identity and strategic repositioning of himself as distinct from both black and white rehearse the cultural, juridical, and violent prohibition of miscegenation.

The first scene is the teacher's reclassification of him as part of the black student body. His blackness suddenly materializes through its distinction from whiteness. This moment initiates the narrator's resistance to the magnetic pull of the polarized positions of black and white: "I had a very strong aversion to being classed with them [the black students]. So I became something of a solitary" (*The Autobiography*, 17). His reaction reveals an inability to identify with blacks, as well as an increasing awareness of his difference from whites. He thus refuses to settle with either group. Another consequence of this revelatory scene, in which he is "raced" by his teacher, is his identification of particular characteristics that both distinguish him from and associate him with the white students.[33] The "liquid darkness" of his eyes, the "long lashes that fringed and shaded them," and the "glossiness of [his] dark hair" exoticize and sexualize his "dusky," nonwhite facial features (*The Autobiography*, 13). Yet these same characteristics reemphasize his proximity to whiteness, because they are simultaneously framed by and contrasted with the "ivory whiteness of [his] skin" (13).

The narrator's bodily self-inspection invokes the powerful performative trope of miscegenation because it highlights the opposition between black and white along with other binaries. His feminized eyelashes and hair recall other literary representations in which white-looking characters are marked as racially liminal because of their appealing and vulnerable traits, which suggest availability and erotic difference, such as Zoe in Dion Boucicault's *The Octoroon* (1859) and Reuel in Hopkins's *Of One Blood*. Johnson carefully blends various narrative strategies, allowing him to foreground the complexity of representing and embodying racial subjectivity.

Once he is named as black, everything changes for Johnson's protagonist. Looking back, he says: "And so I have often lived through that hour, that day, that week, in which was wrought the miracle of my transition from one world into another; for I did indeed pass into another world. From that time I looked out through other eyes, my thoughts were colored, my words dictated, my actions limited by one dominating, all-pervading ideal which constantly increased in force and weight" (*The Autobiography*, 15). His move from an unmarked and normative (read: white) racial performance to an identifiably "colored" role restructures his life and provides him with a transformative understanding of the world. Although he detests the inferiority associated with his new racial role, he considers it an opportunity to explore communities that he never identified with while growing up in Connecticut. His mobility, however, compared with others assigned to the black racial class, gives him a distinct observer's distance.

The second event that cements the Ex-Colored Man's decision to inhabit whiteness occurs after he witnesses the horror of a lynching in the South. Once again, miscegenation takes center stage: it serves as the rationale for the lynching and reiterates the hierarchized positions of black and white.[34] Through the lynching and the narrator's visceral reaction, Johnson highlights how the racialized brutality incited by miscegenation (or the fear of it) relies on the ongoing fortification of racialized divides.

In response to this torturous murder, the narrator determines that he can no longer endure the shame of identifying with a race that whites treat so savagely. Ironically, as Eugenia Collier notes in her analysis of the text, the narrator feels no shame about aligning himself with those who carry out the horrific lynchings he witnesses.[35] His unease leads the narrator to reason that "to forsake one's race to better one's condition was no less worthy an action than to forsake one's country for the same reasons" and that "it was not necessary for [one] to go about with a label of inferiority pasted across [one's] forehead" (*The Autobiography*, 115). Conflating blackness with complete abjection, the Ex-Colored Man chooses what he positions as the exact opposite. For him, success in the white world means obtaining wealth and status and receiving the treatment he experienced while traveling abroad with the white millionaire. He considers his swift achievement of this objective a direct challenge to white supremacist beliefs. At times, he says, he wishes he could assert: "I am a colored man. Do I not disprove the theory that one drop of Negro blood renders a man unfit?" (119). However, his continued silence indicates that he is not completely confident that his performance is infallible or undetectable.

Still, the narrator's strategic employment of his ambiguous racial identity enables him to escape the horror of lynching and to avoid the charge of transgressive interracial sex. It also allows him to access various communities that are configured differently from the black-white, North-South, and domestic-foreign binaries. As one of his acquaintances observes, his white skin allows him to venture any place in the Jim Crow South. With his unmarked racial difference, he engages in mixed-race encounters regularly, without detection—once again suggesting that miscegenation can produce new connections rather than foreclose them.

The Ex-Colored Man's racial hybridity also enables him to gain access to the Cuban community in Florida, where he learns to speak Spanish "better than many of the Cuban workmen at the [cigar] factory" (*The Autobiography*, 46). His performance as Latin American reinforces his belief that "cigar-making is one trade in which the color-line is not drawn" (43). Here, Johnson employs the trope of miscegenation as a potential transcendence of racial divides rather than as the overdetermined label that reinforces them. At the same time that *The Autobiography* celebrates a transnational Afro-Latino solidarity in the cigar-making culture in Florida, however, it omits other color lines that were being drawn and vigorously defended by white workers, like those in the cigar trade in California who excluded Chinese workers by creating local and national union labels and promoting hiring policies that maintained white exclusivity.[36] The romanticized role that the narrator plays enables him to foreground the Cuban workers' common class and national status while superficially glossing over the entrenchment of white racism in labor movements outside the small Cuban Florida town.

From his perspective, simultaneously ethnographic and uncritical, the narrator celebrates how the cultural and political ties shared by black and white Cubans (speaking Spanish, promoting Cuban independence) created an alliance around nationhood that challenged Jim Crow laws in the United States. Yet even this unifying (trans)nationalist association and apparent racial egalitarianism in the Cuban cigar factories required a deliberate resistance to the black-white binary that assigned Afro-Cubans to one category—the same as African Americans, despite cultural and language differences—and white Cubans to another after they arrived in the United States. Nevertheless, all Cuban immigrants were still considered outsiders by Anglo whites; transnational connections, ethnic solidarity, and liminal racial and national identities did not prevail over racialized bifurcation.[37]

The narrator's temporary membership in this community—his successful performance as a Cuban cigar maker and his revered role as a reader and translator for his fellow laborers—provides him with an even stronger sense of the deeply embedded color divisions in mainstream U.S. culture. However, his strategy for gaining entrance into the Cuban community—close study, imitation, and practice—suggests that his occupation of this role, based on a blend of racial, national, ethnic, and cultural performances, works only because of its social construction rather than because of any inherited genes. This vision of cultural identification echoes those of Cuban nationalists, like

José Martí, who encouraged Cubans to abandon the racist practices of the surrounding regions and states in the name of Cuban independence and solidarity.[38] It also recalls Johnson's conflicted role as consul in Central and South America: he benefited personally both from his elevated status as an agent of the U.S. government and from his liminal status as nonwhite and Spanish speaking.[39] His success was based on his distance from the racially marked category of black, similar to his narrator's self-proclaimed role as a racial performer. Johnson employs the performativity of race to emphasize contradictions between the narrator's ability to play Cuban temporarily and his inability to divorce himself completely from the elusive and "indefinable something" (*The Autobiography*, 120) that connects him to blackness.

Playing white is another role that the narrator acquires through the power of association. It could be argued that Johnson, as an agent promoting U.S. interests in Central and South America, elevated his own status by playing the role of white imperialist power broker or benefactor. The narrator's experiences traveling in Europe with his white millionaire patron reinforce his understanding of the limitations imposed by the strict racial classifications of the United States. His apparent mobility, because of his alignment with the unnamed millionaire, suggests that the powerful status of whiteness has as much to do with class and elite culture as it has to do with appearances. The millionaire's lack of a name reinforces the binary structure of race; he does not need a name because his powerful and racialized status as a member of the white imperialist elite is universally recognized and honored. This white supremacist dynamic echoed the contemporaneous imperialist politics that were unfolding in Europe, the United States, the Caribbean, and Latin America.

Once again invoking miscegenation, Johnson's staging of this homoerotic interracial liaison echoes the illicit heterosexual encounters between white male masters and black female slaves: the millionaire provides support and material comfort for the narrator as long as he abides by the millionaire's wishes. Their arrangement also invokes prostitution, since the narrator provides performances and favors in exchange for material compensation. Again, this uneven racialized power dynamic recalls Johnson's position as U.S. consul, as well as the history of white patronage for black artists. The narrative suggests that the protagonist willingly prostitutes himself for his own advantage. Alternatively, given the establishment of laws like the Mann Act (1910), used to police the mobility and agency of white women and to prohibit interracial relations, the idea of prostitution also associates the narrator's command performances for the millionaire with the sexual trafficking and exploitation of white women. The same rationale—that interracial intimacy was merely a ruse for the sexual exploitation by powerful men of white women—was used to arrest and prosecute the internationally famed black boxer Jack Johnson, who spurned mainstream white society's attempt to police his behavior and publicly defied convention by dating and marrying white women.[40] It also recalls the narrator's feminized image, described early in the text, aligning him more explicitly with his mother's role as the illicit nonwhite woman who is kept by and remains faithful to a powerful white man.

Even when the narrator decides to return to the United States to reconnect with his "black" heritage through the study of what he describes as primitive, indigenous southern music and culture, he maintains a distant and somewhat superior position. Unlike Reuel in *Of One Blood*, whose interaction with his ancestral roots provides him with a fuller understanding of his identity, the Ex-Colored Man considers this part of his journey more of a distancing project. His study of black culture functions like his participant-observer role in Cuban Florida. The fact that he chooses to associate himself with blackness emphasizes the uncertainty of his racial status. His benefactor reiterates this point when he asserts that the narrator is "by blood, by appearance, by education, and by tastes a white man" and that his plan "of making a Negro out of [himself] is nothing more than sentiment" (*The Autobiography*, 88). In the patron's estimation, the narrator's "whiteness" has not only been cultivated successfully, it has also been embodied through his blood, appearance, and behavior. From the millionaire's perspective, the narrator has earned his white credentials through his stellar performance.

For the book's protagonist, whiteness, like blackness, is something that he inhabits voluntarily and temporarily. His self-described role as a "privileged spectator" of black society reinforces his alignment with a white audience that consumes black culture. He moves through rather than into various southern black communities—educated and illiterate, rural and urban, middle class and poor—recording and absorbing but never discarding his distanced spectator's lens. This analytical perspective enables him to identify those aspects of racial identity that he considers performative, like what he calls a "mask" of laughter that black people use to negotiate anger and pain. He believes that improvisation and adaptation are the keys to black perseverance and survival in the face of racism, an observation that directly relates to his own ability to play diverse roles in distinct contexts.

Expanding his analysis of the specificities of blackness, the narrator also identifies the ways in which blacks successfully master the trappings of white, Western-identified cultural roles, regardless of geography. He has observed a black man in London who was the "perfect Englishman" and blacks in Paris who were more "Frenchy than a Frenchman" (*The Autobiography*, 93). For the Ex-Colored Man, this adaptability not only undermines the racial definitions that insist on the inferiority of blacks but also demonstrates the constructedness of racial (as well as national) categories. The precedence that nationality takes over race in these alternative spaces indicates that these identificatory categories carry different historical and cultural weight in non-U.S. landscapes, and thus they inform the different ways in which subjects are made intelligible. It also reinforces his belief that he could successfully stage the trappings of various racial and ethnic identities (black, white, Italian, Latino) in different contexts. The narrator's observations and experiences indicate that race is both assumed as a position and inscribed on particular bodies. Viewing it in this way, "all race identity is ... the product of passing,"[41] a type of racialized performance. However, the performance comes into full view only in and through the trope of miscegenation. This generative trope stands in for the context required to gain a fuller understanding of the complexities and hybridization of racial identity. The narrator is compelled by the intersecting performative strategies that he observes both in the United States and transnationally among the black diaspora. For him, these strategies expose the elasticity of seemingly static categories, as well as the power of performance to contest them.

The Ex-Colored Man's investigations of blackness eventually force him to confront the most insidious part of his identity: his own lies. In his house, he cannot maintain his stance as a removed observer and is consumed by doubts. The narrator's most poignant anxiety stems from his belief that his invisible black blood will jeopardize his relationship with his white fiancée. When he fears losing her, his masquerade as a white man—what he refers to as a "capital joke"—loses its humor. The stakes of staging miscegenation are too high. His anxieties about performing his role in a traditional, monoracial marriage point to one of the most threatening aspects of his racially unmarked position for white supremacists—interracial sex. Because the children produced by interracial unions, like the narrator, are considered contaminated bodies that can infiltrate "pure" white communities undetected, their existence literally and figuratively undermines the legitimacy of the color line that is used to prohibit miscegenation and promote racial segregation. As a child of what he calls "forbidden love," the narrator embodies the danger and corruption that white supremacists fear and loathe.

His paranoia about detection suggests that, despite his resistance, he has internalized many of the racist notions conflated with blackness. This self-imposed abjection emerges most explicitly after he tells his future wife that his mother is black. Recalling pseudoscientific and literary representations of atavism—exaggerated reversions back to racialized archetypes—the narrator fears that his disclosure will transform him into a repulsive image of blackness: "Under the strange light in her eyes I felt that I was growing black and thick-featured and crimp-haired" (*The Autobiography*, 123). Instead of experiencing relief because he has divulged his secret past to his fiancée, the narrator feels only regret and pain, and he fears the most explosive response that he has already witnessed—lynching. Unexpectedly, she eschews convention and chooses love over racial difference, but they pay the ultimate price for a few years of happiness, including two children: his wife dies. Although they did marry legitimately, their union was still haunted by the overdetermined pattern of devastation that accompanied most nineteenth- and early twentieth-century stagings of miscegenation.[42]

Individual Losses, Collective Cultural Gains

Neither Hopkins's nor Johnson's protagonists complete their transracial, transcultural, and transnational journeys unscathed. Both authors draw from the mythologies surrounding illicit interracial intimacies, reiterating the potential tragedy so often associated with miscegenation. In their reliance on deeply embedded cultural tropes, these two novels reveal how difficult it is—despite their many innovations—to break free from the status quo.

Hopkins's recuperative objective is not achieved without losses. As in other depictions of interracial encounters, those who engage in prohibited acts face punitive consequences for transgressing long-established societal and juridical rules. In *Of One Blood*, the costs are obvious: both Dianthe and Aubrey lose their lives. Aubrey forces Dianthe to drink the poison that she intended for him, and soon after Aubrey takes his own life. His self-inflicted death can be read as a sort of retribution for the past exploitative relationship between his white (slave-owning) father and his black (enslaved) mother. Meanwhile, Reuel experiences the shame of hiding his identity, which leads to the painful discovery not only that he has married his own sister (Dianthe) but that he is unable to prevent her death. For him, whiteness is temporary, but the damaging results of his role in the context of the racially polarized United States are permanent.

Like Reuel, Dianthe, and Aubrey, the narrator of *The Autobiography of an Ex-Colored Man* also sacrifices a great deal as a result of his unmarked mixed-race encounters, which are enabled through his racial performances. As a result of his decision to live as a white man and to inhabit blackness as a spectator, the narrator remains in a liminal and dissatisfying state of failed performance. His body and his life remain suspended in that in-between, multivalent, unresolved space. His attempt to create a white family fails: his wife dies, he does not reunite with his father, and he never meets his half sister. By the end of his narrative, it is clear that material success, children, and elevated status do not satisfy him; he remains incapable of coming to terms with his carefully constructed and performed identity. His career, masquerading abroad and in the South, and his ability to fool whites never completely fulfill him. As he brings his ruminations to a close, he claims that, at times, he is "possessed by a strange longing for [his] mother's people" and wonders if he has sold his "birthright for a mess of pottage" (*The Autobiography*, 126).

As I have shown, both Hopkins's and Johnson's spectacular representations reveal the potential repercussions of racial transgression. Yet neither narrative ends with only regret, pain, and sacrifice. Instead, both books offer recuperative, if not necessarily revolutionary, conclusions.[43] In *Of One Blood*, Reuel's fate can be read as a revision of the more conventional destiny assigned to those who cross racial borders and who, more often than not, are the children of interracial unions. Even though Reuel is the product of illicit interracial sex, he does not die. Instead, he serves as a link between the present and a long ancestral past, between black and white, between domestic and diasporic, and between sanctioned and illicit familial lines.

Reuel also represents a strategy for recuperating lost history. Hopkins maps his will to recover familial and cultural ties onto his sexual desire for Dianthe, which emerges because of their hidden connection. By returning to Telassar after confronting Aubrey and saying goodbye to Dianthe, Reuel discards his veiled and troubled identity for a new one. His new position as a mythological Ethiopian king can also be read as a performance, similar to his efforts to enact whiteness. His new identity, however, enables him to uncover and confront the past instead of burying it. Rather than offering a clear resolution, Hopkins's narrative points in an alternative direction. The conclusion resists endorsement or complete condemnation of racial transgression. Instead, the narrator claims that only "omnipotence can solve the problem" of "caste prejudice" and "race pride."[44] By relegating the resolution to an outside supernatural source, the text remains open ended. The gesture toward something beyond this world can be read as optimistic, because it looks to the future beyond the limitations of present-day society, or pessimistic, because it finds no attainable solution in the here and now.

Although Johnson's narrator retreats from any bold recovery of his black ancestry, his concluding remarks suggest that this sacrificed part of his identity is of great value and significance, even if he has left it untapped. For the Ex-Colored Man, the staging of race creates space for reevaluating racial subjectivity and his experiences in both black and white communities, but it does not radicalize him. Instead, Johnson uses his narrator's ambiguous identity to examine the public's response to an overt violation of the black-white binary. Attesting to the underlying knowledge that interracial mixture is a part of U.S. and global history, readers in 1912 did not doubt the book's veracity and were curious about the author. Later, Johnson even recalled one man who "tacitly admitted" to being the author of the narrative.[45] However, intrigue and excitement did not necessarily transform into immediate change in the early part of the twentieth century. In fact, the narrator's story was all the more fascinating to readers because of his risky transgression of the rigid racial codes that were still in place in the United States. Miscegenation was still a criminalized taboo, and his daring public confession did not change mainstream discourse, laws, or culture, even though his racialized mobility exposed the permeability of the segregated boundaries and the uncontainability of the bodies they were designed to circumscribe.

Both Hopkins's and Johnson's texts compel readers to rethink race, national origin, and diasporic identity by staging the complexities of whiteness and blackness: both are variegated, and neither is, or ever was, pure. Race, as these authors depict it, is performed, and miscegenation is the process through which it becomes legible. Hopkins pairs her reformulation of history, race, and diasporic identities with her anti-imperialist nonfiction. Johnson, equally observant of the intersections of domestic and international policies, frames his racial performance in global terms. His experiences of race, power, and culture, as well as U.S. imperialism, from his work and travel abroad lent to him "second sight" (Du Bois, 214).[46] Similarly, Hopkins's attention to the performance of racialized identity, normative unions, and white supremacy produces a provocative account of the miscegenated roots/routes of the U.S. and diasporic family tree. Both authors staged miscegenation differently from their predecessors (at times, even radically differently) as a symbolic platform to rehearse new conceptions of race, civilization, and culture based on the interactivity of distinct but interrelated diasporic communities.

Hopkins explores the possibilities of challenging mainstream beliefs about race and culture, while still appealing to the wide range of readers of her work.[47] Her writing functions as a springboard for identifying revolutionary possibilities, even if they are not explicitly articulated. At the same time, her text calls for a more immediate strategy of rethinking the relationships among different races, nations, and cultures as an intersecting network rather than as an inegalitarian hierarchy. For example, despite the era's centering of the hierarchical familial structure, with the white father as the symbolic head of the family and nation, Hopkins transforms the structure into one in which mothers and grandmothers have the power to reunify families and cultures. Similarly, spirituality and "superstitious" practices dismissed by mainstream science are recuperated through the mesmeric rituals that enable Dianthe and Reuel to uncover their intersecting ancestry and shared familial bonds.

Hopkins and Johnson demonstrate the many ways in which reductive definitions of blackness and whiteness are carefully constructed performances, while simultaneously articulating the complexities of these same racial identities, using their narratives to reevaluate the structures of U.S. and global race relations. Their innovative and performative texts pushed against the more limited discursive and literary forms that dominated turn-of-the-century discussions of race in order to offer thicker accounts of the interracial and intercultural influences that help constitute blackness, whiteness, and the range of identities in between. These representations mark and then transgress the boundaries of race while revealing how blackness and whiteness are made intelligible and distinct. At the same time, they reveal the fundamental arbitrariness of such classifications and show how these formulations are made meaningful not by any clear standard, but only through their relationship to each other. Moreover, they illuminate that even after definitions are established, they are enacted only when individuals occupy or refuse to inhabit them.

Although the endings of these two texts are neither romantic nor revolutionary, both Hopkins and Johnson reconfigure the typical finale of a miscegenation story into ironic and unsettling conclusions. They each repeat in various ways the historically embedded, conventional ending—both tragic and melodramatic—frequently used in prior narratives of miscegenation. Yet by transforming the stereotypical conclusion into something not so tragic, they reduce the hysteria surrounding miscegenation and expose the reiterative discursive process that reproduces and amplifies its destructive status. Thus their texts invite readings of the protagonists' fates that reevaluate their identities by connecting them to a broader canvas of interracial relations. Rather than remaining trapped by the inwardly focused and self-destructive narratives of a bifurcated and isolated nation, both novels encourage engagement with the domestic, diasporic, and transnational implications of miscegenation. In the early years of the twentieth century, these two works offered a range of possibilities rarely seen before in American culture; their creative visions seem less burdened by the fault lines of the Civil War and the half century that followed. Despite their ambiguous resolutions, these narratives offer a perspective that is aware of this past but not defined by it. Both texts stage miscegenation as a journey toward the future, a meaningful reckoning with the past that matters. By re-presenting miscegenation and putting these stories and characters into motion, these authors expose and critique the past but also remind us that it does not have to predetermine the future.

My discussion of Johnson's *The Autobiography* with Hopkins's *Of One Blood* lays a foundation, I hope, for continued exploration of these issues. As James Weldon Johnson writes in his autobiographical musings about the "American race problem" in which "the sex factor" is rooted, is indeed "the core of [its] heart," Americans' cultural obsession with sex—talking about it, prohibiting it, circumventing it—drives the passionate cultural preoccupation with miscegenation.[48] The sex factor is the root and also the route that must be explored in order to uncover the complex functions of polarized racial boundaries and conflict. The meanings and implications of interracial sex and intimacies shift over time, as the texts reveal. Their stagings of miscegenation demonstrate the ways that it has been used, what it represents, and how its meanings change; these revisions, however slight or radical, also indicate the degree to which U.S. culture changes and how Americans' attitudes about the concept of race itself change.

In various ways, Hopkins's and Johnson's works reveal the complexity and hybridity of identity, as well as the tangled histories of people of color within and outside the United States. Though the ideologies of these books may seem antiquated or their characterizations absurd, their concerns are not unlike those of today. These explorations are chapters in a vexing pursuit that is far from complete; more than one and a half centuries after the term "miscegenation" was coined, people still fight over how to talk about the various colors of skin and about what skin color says, or does not say, about the person underneath.

NOTES

This essay is modified from chapter 5, "The Futurity of Miscegenation," in Diana Rebekkah Paulin's *Imperfect Unions: Staging Miscegenation in U.S. Drama and Fiction* (Minneapolis: University of Minnesota Press, 2012), 187–227, and is reproduced courtesy of the Regents of the University of Minnesota.

1. James Weldon Johnson, *The Autobiography of an Ex-Colored Man* (1912) in Johnson, *Writings*, ed. William L. Andrews (New York: Library of America, 2004). Future references to this edition are provided parenthetically in the text. Pauline Hopkins, *Of One Blood; or, The Hidden Self*, in *The Magazine Novels of Pauline Hopkins*, ed. Hazel V. Carby (New York: Oxford University Press, 1988), 504. See Valerie Smith, *Self-Discovery and Authority in Afro-American Narrative* (Cambridge, Mass.: Harvard University Press, 1987); Robert B. Stepto, *From behind the Veil: A Study of Afro-American Narrative*, 2nd ed. (Urbana: University of Illinois Press, 1991); Samira Kawash, *Dislocating the Color Line: Identity, Hybridity, and Singularity in African-American Literature* (Stanford, Calif.: Stanford University Press, 1997); John Cullen Gruesser, ed., *The Unruly Voice: Rediscovering Pauline Elizabeth Hopkins* (Chicago: University of Illinois Press, 1996).

2. Susan Gillman, *Blood Talk: American Race Melodrama and the Culture of the Occult* (Chicago: University of Chicago Press, 2003); Sandra Gunning, *Race, Rape, and Lynching: The Red Record of American Literature, 1890–1912* (New York: Oxford University Press, 1996); Daphne Brooks, *Bodies in Dissent: Spectacular Performances of Race and Freedom, 1850–1910* (Durham, N.C.: Duke University Press, 2006); Lois Brown, *Pauline Elizabeth Hopkins: Black Daughter of the American Revolution* (Chapel Hill: University of North Carolina Press, 2008); Laura Doyle, *Freedom's Empire: Race and the Rise of the Novel in Atlantic Modernity, 1640–1940* (Durham, N.C.: Duke University Press, 2008); Siobhan Somerville, *Queering the Color Line: Race and the Invention of Homosexuality in American Culture* (Durham, N.C.: Duke University Press, 2000).

3. Brown, *Pauline Elizabeth Hopkins*, 407–41, 526–40. Brown provides detailed accounts of Hopkins's challenges in a male-dominated profession and of the calculated restructuring of the *Colored American Magazine* that pushed her out. The twelve-year age difference and time lapse between the peak of Hopkins's and Johnson's careers, as well as her disappearance from public life after 1916, generated different perspectives. Johnson was able to take full advantage of expanding opportunities for black men in areas from which Hopkins was excluded, such as entering the foreign service in 1906,

which enriched his transnational and intercultural background and experiences. As opportunities for black people expanded, so did Johnson's representation of miscegenation's possibilities.

4. James Weldon Johnson, *Along This Way: The Autobiography of James Weldon Johnson* (1933; rpt., New York: Penguin, 1990), 238.

5. Brooks, *Bodies in Dissent*. My discussion of the intersection of Hopkins and Johnson builds on Brooks's insights about how Hopkins "inherited and translated the field of historical and cultural performance into popular fiction paradigms" and thus empowered "performance as the insurgent site for dismantling imperialist and patriarchal discourses" and emphasizing "the resilience of black women's bodies" (301–2). Her reading of *Of One Blood* interrogates how Hopkins reformulated black nationalism, agency, self-representation, spectatorship, and pan-Africanism through an intertextual representation of black women's performance.

6. Brooks, *Bodies in Dissent* (301–2), argues that Hopkins undoes the erasure of black subjectivity by representing the cross-cultural and racial exchange of performance culture. She also talks about the interracial dynamic between the audience and the performers.

7. More rigid formulations of race at the time included the emergent black separatism envisioned by the likes of Marcus Garvey and increasingly entrenched forms of white terror and imperialism, represented by the Ku Klux Klan's resurgence at the turn of the twentieth century.

8. Brooks, *Bodies in Dissent*, 301–2. I build on Brooks's contention that Hopkins "sustain[s] a textual dynamism throughout the narrative" by capturing the shifting tensions between performers and spectators in her representation of the theatrical "contact zone[s]" as "terrain[s] of exchange and struggle."

9. Brooks, *Bodies in Dissent* (301–2), talks about the interracial dynamic of the audience and the performers, which gestures toward the productive possibility of staging miscegenation.

10. Despite Hopkins's great accomplishments, her activism and art did not receive the recognition it merited when she was still alive. Nellie Y. McKay, introduction to Gruesser, *Unruly Voice*, 2–5.

11. Hazel Carby, *Reconstructing Womanhood* (New York: Oxford University Press, 1989), 145. Hopkins authored her own text linking black Americans with classical culture and Africa: *A Primer of Facts Pertaining to the Early Greatness of the African Race and the Possibility of Restoration by Its Descendants* (Cambridge, Mass.: P. E. Hopkins, 1905). See also Gillman, *Blood Talk*; Gruesser, *Unruly Voice*; Thomas J. Otten, "Pauline Hopkins and the Hidden Self of Race," *English Literary History* 59 (1992): 248–49.

12. In order to disrupt notions of classical culture, the narrative emphasizes the authenticity of Ethiopian heritage. Although this attempt to present a cohesive and positive image of Africa can be read as essentializing African identities, it can also be read as a move to legitimize Africa in relation to the dominant history of white Western (classical) civilization.

13. Pauline E. Hopkins, preface to her *Contending Forces: A Romance Illustrative of Negro Life North and South* (1900; rpt., New York: Oxford University Press, 1988), 13–14. I am indebted to Kate McCullough, "Slavery, Sexuality, and Genre: Pauline Hopkins and

the Representation of Female Desire," in Gruesser, *Unruly Voice*, 27, for pointing to the significance of this preface.

14. See C. K. Doreski, "Inherited Rhetoric and Authentic History: Pauline Hopkins at the *Colored American Magazine*," in Gruesser, *Unruly Voice*, 72–91.

15. Editorial and publisher's announcements, *Colored American Magazine*, March 1903, 398, and Hopkins, "Venus and the Apollo, Modeled on Ethiopians," *Colored American Magazine*, May–June 1903, 465.

16. Claudia Tate, "Pauline Hopkins: Our Literary Foremother," in *Conjuring: Black Women, Fiction, and Literary Tradition*, ed. Marjorie Pryse and Hortense Spillers (Bloomington: Indiana University Press, 1985), asserts that in *Of One Blood* Hopkins's "effort to escape becomes total and comprehensive, as the story moves beyond the American social scene to a mysterious Atlantis-like region of an underground city in Africa" and that "instead of finding urgent social problems dramatized in a somewhat realistic fictional setting, we find remote landscape[s] of science fiction" (62). In contrast, others argue that Hopkins used forms such as melodrama to challenge and interrupt the unquestioned legitimacy of forms like biography, history, and science; see Sean McCann, "'Bonds of Brotherhood': Pauline Hopkins and the Work of Melodrama," *English Literary History* 64 (1997): 789–822; Doreski, "Inherited Rhetoric."

17. Carby, *Reconstructing Womanhood* (157–58), points out that Kirkland Soga's documentary article "Ethiopians of the Twentieth Century" ran concurrently with Hopkins's fiction, reinforcing Hopkins's assertion that contemporary black Americans were related to Ethiopians.

18. Carby, *Reconstructing Womanhood* (145), asserts that Hopkins incorporated formulas from various genres, like sensational fiction and dime and detective novels. Some of the characteristics Carby lists are suspense, action, adventure, complex plotting, multiple or false identities, and the use of disguise.

19. The parallels that white supremacists in the early twentieth century drew between incest and miscegenation reveal the contradictions of their antimiscegenation rhetoric, because the two acts are dissimilar. Their claim represents the legal and cultural reification of the taboo status of one (incest) in the service of pathologizing the other (miscegenation). Eva Saks, "Representing Miscegenation Law," *Raritan* 8 (Fall 1988): 53.

20. Hopkins, *Of One Blood*, 607.

21. Carby, introduction to Hopkins, *Magazine Novels of Pauline Hopkins*, xxxi–xlix.

22. Carby, *Magazine Novels of Pauline Hopkins*, 61–63; Paula Seniors, *Beyond "Lift Every Voice and Sing": The Culture of Uplift, Identity, and Politics in Black Musical Theater* (Columbus: Ohio State University Press, 2009), 22.

23. Johnson wrote a substantial portion of *The Autobiography of an Ex-Colored Man* while he was posted in Venezuela (1906–9) and completed it while serving as consul to Nicaragua (1909–12). Noelle Morrissette, introduction to James Weldon Johnson, *The Autobiography of an Ex-Colored Man and Other Writings* (New York: Fine Creative Media, Barnes and Noble Classics, 2007), xi–xii.

24. Johnson, *Along This Way*, 3–8.

25. See, for example, Harilaos Stecopoulos, "Up from Empire: James Weldon Johnson, Latin America, and the Jim Crow South," in *Our Americas: Political and Cultural*

Imaginings of the Americas, ed. Sandhya Shukla and Heidi Tinsman (Durham, N.C.: Duke University Press, 2007), 34–62.

26. Johnson, *Along This Way*, 64.

27. Stepto, *From behind the Veil* (97–105), asserts that Johnson's novel is a synthesis of Afro-American narrative history that fuses aspects of authenticating rhetoric to aspects of the generic narrative forms, like slave narratives and antislavery literature. Smith, *Self-Discovery and Authority* (50), argues that Johnson "simulated autobiography" in order to "explore a path he did not choose in life, but one that fascinated him." Donald C. Goellnicht, "Passing as Autobiography: James Weldon Johnson's *The Autobiography of an Ex-Colored Man*," *African American Review* 30, no. 1 (1996): 18–21, asserts that Johnson's text is a "parody" of "black autobiography" and that it plays with the promise of revealing a "total revision" of the "exotic."

28. Kawash, *Dislocating the Color Line* (147–55), argues that critiques of the passing in *The Autobiography of an Ex-Colored Man* still adhere to a presumption that underlying racial identities exist, but this narrative successfully demonstrates the fallacy of that logic by depicting the narrator's inability to name or perform any fixed racial identity.

29. Johnson, *The Autobiography of an Ex-Colored Man*, in his *Writings*, ed. William L. Andrews (New York: Library of America, 2004), 120. . *Writings* contains the 1912 edition of *The Autobiography*. Future references to this work are provided parenthetically in the text.

30. See Jeff Karem's essay in this collection for an alternative reading of audience, privilege, and promise.

31. This assertion is informed by Judith Butler, *Bodies That Matter: On the Discursive Limits of Sex* (New York: Routledge, 1993); and Gillman, *Blood Talk*, 24.

32. Johnson, *Along This Way* (168–69), provides a terrifying account of almost being lynched because the woman with whom he was meeting privately appeared to be white but was actually legally black. He narrowly averted mob violence and was cleared by a local authority who knew him and the woman.

33. See Robert Stepto's essay in this collection for an extended reading of this type of racialization.

34. Kawash, *Dislocating the Color Line*, 153–54.

35. Eugenia Collier, "The Endless Journey of an Ex-Colored Man," *Phylon* 3 (Winter 1971): 372.

36. Patricia A. Cooper, *Once a Cigar Maker: Men, Women, and Work Culture in American Cigar Factories, 1900–1919* (Urbana: University of Illinois Press, 1987). The labels certified white workmanship over that of the "alien" Chinese.

37. Nancy Raquel Mirabal, "The Afro-Cuban Community in Ybor City and Tampa, 1886–1910," *OAH Magazine of History* 7, no. 4 (Summer 1993): 19–22, http://www.jstor.org/stable/25162907.

38. Ibid.

39. See Johnson's discussion of his experiences as U.S. consul in *Along This Way*.

40. Kevin Mumford, *Interzones: Black/White Sex Districts in Chicago and New York in the Early Twentieth Century* (New York: Columbia University Press, 1997), 135–37.

41. Samira Kawash, "*The Autobiography of an Ex-Colored Man*: (Passing for) Black Passing for White," in *Passing and the Fictions of Identity*, ed. Elaine K. Ginsberg (Durham, N.C.: Duke University Press, 1996), 70.

42. This marriage and its outcome repeats a plot in Charles Chesnutt's *House behind the Cedars* (1900), in which the protagonist marries a white woman who dies in childbirth; their son survives.

43. Jennie A. Kassanoff, "The Politics of Representation," in Gruesser, *Unruly Voice* (174–75), argues that Mira's role is in fact revolutionary because as "the renegade mother" who appears as an apparition to her children, she cannot be contained by the text, and her utterances work to "destabilize the social order." Kassanoff goes on to assert that by "revealing her identity to her children, Mira reappropriates her own maternal body and thereby deconstructs all of the previously accepted genealogical structures in the novel."

44. Hopkins, *Of One Blood*, 621.

45. Johnson, *Along This Way*, 238.

46. Du Bois, *Souls of Black Folk* (1903), in *Three Negro Classics*, ed. John Hope Franklin (New York: Avon, 1965), 214. Du Bois refers to the double-consciousness or the bifurcated view that blacks in the United States develop because of segregation as a "second sight," an insight unique because of the history of enslavement and discrimination. In *The Autobiography*, 15–16, the narrator gives an extended description of how he learned to look at the world through "colored" eyes.

47. Hopkins engages in what C. K. Doreski describes as a "double-voiced pattern" so that she can both please the "accommodationist—black or white—and inform the militant race-and-culture leader" ("Inherited Rhetoric," 90).

48. Johnson, *Along This Way*, 170.

Blackness Written, Erased, Rewritten
James Weldon Johnson, Teju Cole, and the Palimpsest of Modernity

DAPHNE LAMOTHE

One hundred years separate the publications of James Weldon Johnson's *Autobiography of an Ex-Colored Man* (1912) and Teju Cole's *Open City* (2012), compelling me to ask if these novels can speak to each other across the span of time and, if so, what meanings they reveal to readers about the similarities and differences between the modernist New Negro era and the postmodern era of post-blackness.[1] I and other critics have argued that African American modernism is characterized by the efforts of progressive artists, activists, and intellectuals to construct a pluralist cultural nationalism.[2] This thesis necessarily assumes that early twentieth-century culture workers retained a geographically rooted and specifically (black) American notion of identity. For example, in an earlier reading of *The Autobiography*, I argued that Johnson "makes a case, through the protagonist's involvement with African American ragtime, for understanding America to be a multiracial and pluralistic nation in which African American cultural contributions have played an important role."[3] The protagonist's peripatetic travels (from North to South to Europe and back to the United States) function as a sign of his anxiety and ambivalence about his identity; yet always throughout the novel his actions are driven by the desire to identify and claim spaces of communal and national belonging.

Certainly, the transnational movement between the United States and Europe of the Ex-Colored Man functions as one of several migratory circuits that signal the contingency of his racial identity and alliances. In this essay, I extend that argument by considering how Johnson's transnationalism functions trans-historically as well. In other words, I make an argument for the value of reading Johnson intertextually, as part of a dialogic network that extends across the African diaspora and connects black literature's past with its present, by juxtaposing it to the fiction of Cole, a Nigerian-born, New York–based author. In *The Signifying Monkey*, Henry Louis Gates Jr. defines "intertextuality" as a narrative practice of "repetition and revision."[4] Reading Johnson—or, more specifically, his configurations of migration, race, racialization, and the problem of belonging—intertextually demands the presence of shared tropes and patterns of signification that pull various texts into dialogue with each other.[5] Such a connection rescripts Johnson's canonical African American narrative into a diasporic and transnational text. In this essay, I show that Johnson's and Cole's novels are tied together not only through the mirroring of their themes of migration, ambivalence, and belonging, but also through the authors' conceptualizations of race and belonging. Reading these novels intertextually also makes legible their narrators' capacity to function as a moral compass for the reader.

Johnson's and Cole's protagonists each grapple with the problem of alienation from self and other. The former is produced by the violence of the American color line and the latter by an existential crisis brought on by globalization. Both main characters work through the logic of the territorialization of identity, which resonates with Robert Reid-Pharr's critique of the notion of a "universal, transhistorical 'blackness.'"[6] Reid-Pharr musters legal, historical, and literary sources to support his contention that blackness is not only a social construct, but also a chosen identity. One example he uses is the 1896 *Plessy v. Ferguson* decision, reminding readers that the fair-skinned Homer Plessy would not have been identified, nor identified himself, as a person "of African descent" and that the U.S. Census retained the racial category "mulatto" until 1920.[7] These historical facts undergird Reid-Pharr's contention that the earliest black literature was the product of urbanization because southern black people's migration to northern cities was a process of "(Black) American community deformation and reformation."[8] In other words, readers of black literature must attend to the historical and social specificities of space and place in order to comprehend the emergence of definitions and redefinitions of blackness.

African American modernism is characterized by the longing for meaning and cohesion rooted in a reimagined and more inclusive cultural nationalism that is implicitly geographically bounded. In contrast, postmodernism and post-blackness are routinely described as deterritorialized and heterogeneous, resisting monolithic and unified constructions of identity. Yet I contend that even as *The Autobiography of an Ex-Colored Man* explores the anxieties and aspirations of twentieth-century black Americans, it also—with a thematic focus on cultural and racial hybridity through its representation of the protagonist's transformation as a musician and his grappling with his mixed racial heritage—anticipates the postmodern turn of this moment. Or, to return to Reid-Pharr's analysis: the Ex-Colored Man's racial indeterminacy forces him into a position of having to choose or reject blackness, and thus he must grapple with his moral responsibility to a community besieged by racial hostility. And just as the twentieth-century urbanization of black subjects forms the backdrop for the character's personal drama, the twenty-first century's urbanization of transnational black subjects leads to revisiting the themes of blackness, community, longing, and belonging in contemporary black literature. The physical and psychological similarities, as well as the similar philosophical conundrums of the protagonists of these two novels underscore how critical and foundational a text *The Autobiography* is to understanding twentieth- and twenty-first-century African diasporic racial formations. I move between the two novels in my analysis in order to expose their thematic similarities and to underscore the ways in which reading Johnson makes visible the still relevant and pressing questions of ethics and affiliation, which some contemporary social and political critics attempt to bury and suppress.

During the New Negro era, African Americans were reterritorialized: a predominantly southern, rural people reimagined themselves as northern and urban.[9] They were largely unified in the causes of racial uplift, social equality, and basic survival, though the leaders of the Harlem Renaissance parted ways over how to go about achieving these goals.[10] Certainly, class, gender, sexual orientation, and ethnic diversity existed within the category of blackness, but political exigencies demanded collectivist thought and action. The Ex-Colored Man acknowledges as much at the end of the novel when, even as he reflects on and rationalizes his decision to pass as white and abandon any outward signs of racial kinship with other African Americans, he looks admiringly at race men and activists such as Booker T. Washington: "that small but gallant band of colored men who are publicly fighting the cause of their race" with earnestness and faith.[11]

The relevance of these concerns to a non-American, racially mixed member of the African diaspora is far from self-evident. By foregrounding the story of an African immigrant to New York, Cole's *Open City* introduces a new framework for understanding blackness in the twenty-first century. The story of rural black Americans' migration (the subtext for the Ex-Colored Man's personal journey of self-exploration) is replaced with a narrative of transnational black migration, a foreseeable subject of interest in the contemporary publishing industry, given the rise of globalization and global economies. Like Johnson, Cole limns a narrative of dislocation, this time set on a global scale. Both the Ex-Colored Man and Julius, *Open City*'s protagonist, spend time in various European capitals, but Europe represents an idealized site of linguistic, musical, and artistic production for the former, who is momentarily captivated by the idea of living a life free of racism and full of art and culture if he were to remain there. Upon arriving in Paris, the Ex-Colored Man thinks to himself: "Paris became for me a charmed spot, and whenever I have returned there, I have fallen under the spell, a spell which compels admiration for all of its manners and customs and justification of even its follies and sins"

(*The Autobiography*, 94). The promised freedom of a cosmopolitan life tempts him keenly, though he ultimately decides to throw in his lot with the more unfortunate members of his race on American soil. The benefactor who has funded his travels until this fateful decision to return home makes explicit the bargain that the protagonist is forced to consider: "My boy, you are by blood, by appearance, by education, and by tastes a white man. Now, why do you want to throw your life away amidst the poverty and ignorance, in the hopeless struggle of the black people in the United States?" (105). The Ex-Colored Man's answer to this question, at least until he is brought face to face with the destroyed body of a lynched man, who embodies the tremendous costs of being black in a deeply racist society, is to embrace both the responsibility and the potential of working toward the collective building of the race's future, and he returns to attempt to reclaim his place in the national conversation on blackness through the creation of "Negro music."

For Julius, no such decision is ever forthcoming because he suffers from the malaise of postmodernity and refuses the responsibility of community and place. Julius's world is one in which the anchors of human experience—time, place, the body—have been destabilized and rendered nearly invisible and inconsequential.[12] Unlike the Ex-Colored Man, who struggles with both his feelings of alienation from his racial community and his feelings of guilt when he ultimately chooses to disassociate from that community, there is no unified (black) self from which Julius might feel estranged. As a consequence, his racial hybridity poses less of a crisis than does the Ex-Colored Man's because Julius, unlike his predecessor, faces no physical risks from crossing the color line. Instead, his identity—just as firmly rooted in a cosmopolitan indulgence in travel, taste, and aestheticism as the Ex-Colored Man's—is constituted solely through his accumulation of books, paintings, music, and languages. Julius is completely unmoored and alienated from family, community, and nation; he differs from the Ex-Colored Man in that the narrative never explicitly entertains the idea that he can, or even needs to, choose blackness, as his literary ancestor once considered doing, whether from a sense of political engagement or communal responsibility.

Johnson anticipated this in his novel by considering how notions of black cosmopolitanism carry with them the possibility of racial unmooring. Indeed, when the publisher Alfred Knopf reprinted *The Autobiography* in 1927 at the height of the Harlem Renaissance and two years after Alain Locke's publication of *The New Negro* (1925), there was an implicit invitation to readers to compare Johnson's portrayal of black cosmopolitanism to Locke's theorization of the same. Where Locke celebrates New Negro cosmopolitanism as proof of black people's urbanity, sophistication, and progressivism, Johnson's novel foregrounds more sharply the question of the relations between cosmopolites and the masses. The novel's political acuity persists today, since it also foretells the future of twenty-first-century black subjects, who might seem more free from racial caste structures—and indeed are freer than they have been in the past—and many of whom are also less motivated by clear and common goals determined by a unified community.[13] Then, and now, the decision to turn away from a collectivist identity or agenda carries with it, both authors suggest, a moral dilemma.

The Autobiography possesses an explicit moral compass that *Open City* lacks. It invites the reader's judgment of the Ex-Colored Man's eventual decision to renounce his racial kinship with black folks, even as it offers insight into the psychological and social factors that move him to do what he himself thinks is unethical: to choose, after all of his experiences, to pass as white. On the other hand, *Open City* operates on a more cerebral level, compelling the reader to follow Julius through his quotidian movements, narrating events from his perspective and without the clarity of distinguishing right from wrong, or victims from victimizers. Cole skims past the occasional moments of moral ambiguity, with his narrative obliging readers to draw their own conclusions about how a range of factors—race, gender, ethnicity, class—intersect and collude to produce Julius's central conflict, his alienation from self and others. Both novels are about ambivalence and are ambivalent about the integrity of their protagonists. Both grapple with the politics of race, explored from the perspective of the privileged professionals who at the turn of the twentieth century were known as the "talented tenth." And both explore the idea of blackness and the possibilities for black affiliation through unreliable narrators whose morally compromised natures implicate the reader. The reader's ability to navigate the novels' complicated geographical, political, and emotional terrains is enhanced when Cole's novel is anchored, through *The Autobiography of an Ex-Colored Man*, to the very particular history of African American passing, racial uplift, and the talented tenth.

Open City begins in media res, in the middle of an internal dialogue and with no clear introduction of either character or setting. The effect is to underscore Julius's lack of a starting place in his own life. The facts of his birth and upbringing in Nigeria and his eventual migration to New York for medical school and residency fail to capture the profound dislocation of his experiences, which are defined by his biracial and bicultural heritage (Nigerian father and German mother); the early death of his father and eventual estrangement for unknown reasons from his mother; the fleeting nature of his friendships and acquaintanceships; and the ambiguous reasons for the dissolution of the one relationship, with a woman named Nadège, that seemed to be the only constant in his life. Julius is defined more by lack and loss than by anything else, and he attempts to fill the gaps with long, leisurely walks around the city. The novel begins, "And so when I began to go on evening walks last fall, I found Morningside Heights an easy place from which to set out into the city."[14] Julius's external travel is an analogy for his interior quest for self-knowledge. The streets of upper New York and Morningside Heights that he travels are central because they define the protagonist. He declares, "New York City worked itself into my life at walking pace" (*Open City*, 3). In this novel, the city is a character, and the city builds the protagonist's character.

In contrast to the collective movement exemplified by the Great Migration, Julius's transplantation to New York is a singular and individual journey. His aloneness seems not to trouble him at first. He describes the bustle of the city as disturbing his tranquility and calm (*Open City*, 6). And when at home, he fills his silent apartment with private pleasures facilitated by modern technologies. Radio and the Internet transport his beloved classical music from Canada, Germany, and the Netherlands. He can tune out unwanted sounds like commercials (4) and allow in what he desires, specifically the compositions of Shchedrin and Ysaÿe. The music and the migrating geese that fascinate Julius are reassuring sounds and sights joined in the narrator's mind because they transport him from his present circumstances, which are more troubled than readers are immediately led to believe. "I turned the computer's speakers low and looked outside, nestled in the comfort provided by those voices.... Those disembodied voices remain connected in my mind, even now, with the apparition of migrating geese" (4–5). Here Julius apparently embraces the same logic of deracinated universalism espoused by the Ex-Colored Man's benefactor, who attempts to persuade him to take up permanent status as a "citizen of the world." The benefactor's appeal to the Ex-Colored Man includes the following observation: "Music is a universal art; anybody's music belongs to everybody; you can't limit it to race or country. Now, if you want to become a composer, why not stay right here in Europe" (*The Autobiography*, 105). Yet, like the Ex-Colored Man, Julius will eventually discover that social inequities (segregation in the early twentieth century and the policing of national borders in the post-9/11 era) make geographic mobility for black people far more elusive and dangerous than either protagonist's idealization of the traveling culture of music would have us believe.

Cole signals Julius's cosmopolitanism early in the novel, not only by noting his musical preferences (European, classical, and avant-garde) but also by presenting his friendship with Professor Saito, a Japanese American octogenarian and scholar of literature; the men bond over their shared appreciation of *Beowulf* and other classics. As Julius recalls, "He must have seen something in me that made him think I was someone on whom his rarefied subject (early English literature) would not be wasted" (*Open City*, 9). Over cups of coffee, Saito shares with Julius scholarly interpretations and tales of life in academia, as well as stories of his internment at the hands of the U.S. government during World War II. Even as Julius professes that "this last subject was so total in its distance from my experience," he nonetheless feels a close affinity to the man (9). This meditation on sameness and difference is not inconsequential in a novel in which the protagonist struggles to identify, control, and redefine the boundaries between himself and others.

Cole's description of the relationship between Julius and Saito is apparently concerned with the limits and potentials of affinity and affiliation across differences of age and ethnicity, whereas the dynamic between the Ex-Colored Man and his patron is defined by the proprietary, almost predatory attitudes of the benefactor toward his charge. Theirs is a relationship based solely on unspoken laws of cultural production and on consumption as a type of economic exchange. "Occasionally he [the patron] 'loaned' me to some of his friends. And, too, I often played for him alone at his apartments.... He would sometimes sit for three or four hours hearing me play, his eyes almost closed, making scarcely a motion except to light a fresh cigarette, and never commenting one way or another on the music" (*The Autobiography*, 88). Their bond is defined not only by a mutual appreciation of music, the universal language, but also by the Ex-Colored Man's willingness to produce music on demand in return for generous compensation. The benefactor's ravenous and selfish desire to consume (rather than share) the Ex-Colored Man's music ultimately taints their relationship, and the protagonist describes him as being like a tyrant, relentless in his demands.

In contrast, when surrounded by European literature and music, or communing with Saito over their shared appreciation of culture, Julius is at peace. One possible explanation for the lack of tension is the absence of the racial and ethnic hierarchy and power imbalance that marks the Ex-Colored Man's relationship to his benefactor and would-be mentor. Julius is freer to love all types of music because he is, compared to the Ex-Colored Man, more free. His appreciation of cultural artifacts invites greater scrutiny, however, when one considers how superficial this friendship, like most of his relationships, actually is. In other words, Julius's attachment to things implicitly calls into question his freedom (from people). For example, when Julius discovers that his neighbor passed away months earlier, he is shocked by the realization that her absence made no discernible impression on him. As he struggles to recall the woman's name and her husband's, he thinks, "A woman had died in the room next to mine, she had died on the other side of the wall I was leaning against, and I had known nothing of it.... I hadn't known him well enough to routinely ask how Carla was, and I had not noticed not seeing her around. That was the worst of it. I had noticed neither her absence nor the change—there must have been a change—in his spirit" (*Open City*, 21). Readers' understanding of the anonymity that defines city life absolves Julius of his ignorance of the small, personal tragedy unfolding beyond the wall that divides the two apartments. And yet this encounter plants a seed for the possibility that Julius's absorption in and love of books and music, which looks like aesthetic sensitivity from one vantage point, may be more akin to self-absorption and semipathological self-isolation from others.

One might be tempted to view Julius as a more extreme version of the Ex-Colored Man: Julius chooses isolation, as opposed to his predecessor, who is trapped by it. The Ex-Colored Man's difficulties in placing himself within a community have everything to do with factors beyond his control, namely his liminal racial and cultural status in a deeply segregated society. Yet the narrative pushes the reader to consider the implications of his allegiances, which are called into question whenever he enters a new community or, in the case of his childhood, when his identity is redefined within the context of that community. For example, in recounting his earliest memories as a schoolboy, the Ex-Colored Man recalls the white children—of which he believes himself to be a member—tormenting their black schoolmates, chasing after them and pelting them with stones. When his mother chastises him for this behavior and for using a racial slur, he says, "I did hang my head in shame, not because she had convinced me that I had done wrong, but because I was hurt by the first sharp word she had ever given me" (*The Autobiography*, 10). As the Ex-Colored Man grows and matures, the feeling of shame over misplaced allegiances will return, only tinted by his understanding of the nature and gravity of his betrayal. For much of the novel, however, he displaces the question of his racial identification, choosing instead to offer "detached" and sociological assessments of each community that he visits.

When living in Jacksonville, Florida, the Ex-Colored Man notes three classes of "colored" people: the desperate, who hate all whites; the servants, who are "simple, kind-hearted, and faithful"; and the independent tradesmen and the educated and well-to-do, who live in enclaves that are profoundly cut off from any contact with whites (*The Autobiography*, 55–58). Even New York, an apparently integrated city, offers very complicated models of interracialism, according to the protagonist. He describes the whites who frequent his favorite club, where he first learns to play ragtime, as either "sight-seeing, or slumming"; as minstrels who "came to get their imitations first hand from the Negro entertainers"; and as a small, mysterious group of white women, whose fascination with and eagerness to consort with black men belied their obvious wealth and educational status (78–79). American society's deeply stratified structure offers no easy or obvious resting place for Johnson's protagonist, who was raised by his mother in ignorance of his racial heritage, who acquires an understanding of his blackness as an adolescent and in early adulthood, and who must constantly negotiate his racial indeterminacy in a society that abhors racial mixing.

One hundred years later, Cole depicts an American social landscape that is many-hued, multiethnic, and apparently comfortable in its diversity. In the first chapter alone, he visits his Japanese American professor; takes note of the professor's Saint Lucian nurse; recounts a passing meeting with a Central or South American runner walking home after completing the New York City marathon (itself a celebration of internationalism); describes his neighborhood as inhabited by Senegalese immigrants and African Americans; and brings home a takeout meal of Jamaican curried goat and rice and peas. Yet the narrative suggests that these communities are little more than ephemera, much like the businesses that crop up and eventually fail in those same neighborhoods. Like the Ex-Colored Man, Julius takes note of the people he encounters. Whereas the former is driven by a sociological impulse to order and organize because he enters every community as an outsider, the latter is responding to a world that is defined by heterogeneity and multiplicity. One day, after a particularly long walk from his Harlem neighborhood to downtown and back, Julius reflects on the evening and on the city's refusal to mold itself to his intentions:

> That night I took the subway home, and instead of falling asleep immediately, I lay in bed, too tired to release myself from wakefulness, and I rehearsed in the dark the numerous incidents and sights I had encountered while roaming, sorting each encounter like a child playing with wooden blocks, trying to figure out which belonged where, which responded to which. Each neighborhood of the city appeared to be made of a different substance, each seemed to have a different air pressure, a different psychic weight: the bright lights and shuttered shops, the housing projects and luxury hotels, the fire escapes and city parks. My futile task of sorting went on until the forms began to morph into each other and assume abstract shapes unrelated to the real city, and only then did my hectic mind finally show some pity and still itself, only then did dreamless sleep arrive. (*Open City*, 6–7)

While the Ex-Colored Man never has to contend with the artifice of his social ordering, Julius recognizes almost instantly that he is attempting a fool's errand because the city and its inhabitants resist his easy categorization. This "failure" is a sign that his exceptional status as a highly educated, biracial doctor and world traveler does little to grant him any sort of special insight or analytical acuity—a notable counterpoint to the promise in the preface of *The Autobiography* that the Ex-Colored Man will give his readers "a glimpse behind the scenes" and "a bird's-eye view" of black Americans' racial drama.

All around Julius are reminders, like his widower neighbor, that freedom from attachments can be its own sort of prison. He is part of a community of strangers, and his accounting of what he sees while walking through Morningside Heights is simply a reflection of that fact. The city, Julius notes, is truly a place where one can be, as in a movie theater, "in the company of a hundred others but all strangers to me" (*Open City*, 29). Noting that his local Blockbuster video store is shuttering its doors, Julius thinks, "[National corporations] had made their profits and their names by destroying smaller, earlier local businesses. But I was touched not only at the passage of these fixtures in my mental landscape but also at the swiftness and dispassion with which the market swallowed even the most resilient enterprises" (19). Death haunts the city, and the only thing that thrives is the relentless pull toward profit and change. Madhu Dubey writes that the postmodern black city is marked by rupture in the assurance of a unified collective identity or, more accurately, in the idea of a "coherent community." One hundred years after the Ex-Colored Man lamented his refusal to choose blackness, readers of *Open City*, a novel about the postmodern black city, witness its protagonist's negotiation of a space in which "the idea of community [is] increasingly abstract and experientially unknowable."[15] Unlike the Ex-Colored Man, Julius appears to never be in a position to choose lines of affiliation and allegiance.

For the Ex-Colored Man, the sociological impulse to sort and order the black community of Jacksonville resonates on two levels: first, it betrays his emotional detachment from that community even as he lives within it; and second, he means to make blackness legible to a white readership. Like Johnson's protagonist, Cole's wants to believe in his ability to sort and order the world, but for entirely different reasons and in an entirely different context. In 2012 the novel need not assume a sociological imperative and can instead remain comfortably under the label of fiction. Moreover, contemporary society is organized differently and cannot be defined in the binary logic of white and black. And still, the problem of belonging lingers, as Julius is haunted by the history and the logic of blackness as an idea and ideology.

Chapters 3 and 4 of *Open City* begin to isolate and underscore the histories of violence enacted in the name of enforcing the racial and other boundaries that lie at the heart of Julius's conflict. I say this while noting that Julius never describes himself as in a state of emotional turmoil, nor does he interact long enough with any individual for a clear conflict to emerge. A vague sense of melancholy looms over the text, primarily centered around the fact that his girlfriend, Nadège, has broken up with him for reasons not entirely clear to the reader. The narrative hints at the kind of reading practice that would enable an understanding of his dilemma when Julius notes on his visit to Professor Saito, "I learned the art of listening from him, and the ability to trace out a story from what was omitted" (*Open City*, 9). Hence, readers are encouraged to understand Julius's dilemma from his juxtaposition of memories and experiences, though they appear at first glance to unfold in a haphazard manner, and he as narrator makes no effort to bring order. Readers move through Julius's narration of the personal to the political and historical, grasping to make meaning of it all.

Julius's past and present are defined by fragmentation and disconnection; indeed these are the conditions of the postmodern subject, from which there is no escape except through the veil of selective memory. He recalls his estrangement from his mother at the age of seventeen, which he connects to her estrangement from her own mother; the causes for this legacy of maternal alienation are "inchoate" (*Open City*, 34). Julius fondly recalls the single visit by his German grandmother, Oma, to the family home in Nigeria: "I was eleven when she came to visit, and I could see that both my parents were barely tolerating this strange old lady (my father sided with my mother). I also knew that part of what I was had come from her, and on this basis a sort of solidarity was established" (34). Julius's memories take on a nostalgic film when he remembers a trip taken to a sacred historical site noted for its warm springs. There, he and his grandmother sat in harmonious silence: "my parents were gone an hour, and in that hour we two communed almost wordlessly, simply waiting, sensitive to the wind in the trees nearby, watching lizards scuttle over the smaller rock formations that pushed through the earth like prehistoric eggs, listening to the thrums of motorcycles on the narrow road some two hundred yards away" (35). This memory stands as a powerful antidote to Julius's urban malaise and alienation. It echoes in many ways the Ex-Colored Man's memories of happiness and feelings of wholeness before the full awareness of his mixed-racial identity sets off a lifetime of searching and confusion. For the Ex-Colored Man, the memory of his mother holding him close, "softly crooning some old melody without words, all the while gently stroking her face against my head" is a counterweight to his emotional turmoil (*The Autobiography*, 5). He states, "The memory of that picture has more than once kept me from straying too far from the place of purity and safety in which her arms held me" (5). Yet neither character can escape the familial estrangement that is also their inheritance. Julius's parents never encourage Oma to visit again, and indeed he never sees her after that single visit. His refusal or inability to reconcile with his mother makes any desire to recover or recreate this harmonious moment impossible. After he shares the memory of his grandmother Julius visits the American Folk Art Museum and wanders through the galleries admiring the art. He finds the portraits calming, but also sealed off and hermetic, much like his memory of Oma. "Each of the portraits was a sealed-away world, visible from without, but impossible to enter" (*Open City*, 37). Julius will remain cut off from the possibility of interpersonal connection signified by that single and singular memory of his grandmother, and I would suggest that he simultaneously wills himself to remain detached from other, more painful memories that also recall the violence of estrangement.

In place of harmonious communion, Julius is left with urban alienation and conflict, illustrated by an anecdote in which he refuses to cede a taxi to a woman during a rainstorm. Julius surprises himself by raising his voice in anger at the woman's appeal to chivalry, an attempt to implicitly appeal to his sense of communal, albeit gendered, obligation. He refuses such pressure in this instance, and then ignores his communal obligation in the very next: he enters the cab and self-centeredly focuses on his immediate thoughts and needs. The state of his umbrella, recalling an address, remembering the museum visit—all of this filters through his mind before he finally looks up and speaks to the cabbie, an African like himself. "'So, how are you doing my brother?' The driver stiffened and looked at me in the mirror. 'Not good, not good at all, you know, the way you came into my car without saying hello, that was bad. Hey, I'm African just like you, why you do this?'" (*Open City*, 40). The driver's anger at Julius's refusal to obey the rituals of racial and cultural solidarity is matched by Julius's resentment. He thinks, "I was in no mood for people who tried to lay claims on me" (40). But, of course, the reader wonders if the thing he resents is also the very thing for which he longs.

A subway ride to lower Manhattan brings together all of these themes. Julius emerges from underground and walks to the site of the former World Trade Center. As he overlooks the ruins and the new construction overlaying it, Julius thinks, "This was not the first erasure on the site" (*Open City*, 58). Before the towers' construction, the streets had crossed residential neighborhoods, which were razed in the 1960s to make way for the World Trade Center; before that, those neighborhoods had replaced a late nineteenth-century enclave of Christian Syrians and Lebanese, who in turn had overtaken the Lenape whose "paths lay buried beneath the rubble. The site was a palimpsest as was all the city, written, erased, rewritten" (59). Here the reader can start to make connections and tie the strands of this narrative together, for the events of 9/11 provide the most obvious rationale for a twenty-first century dominated by policies that work toward the retrenchment of national borders, coupled with a widespread paranoia about the presence of black and brown migrants.

In *Color Me English*, Caryl Phillips ruminates on the themes of identity, belonging, and migration in the Black Atlantic. Phillips notes how both U.S. and British ideologies and practices of belonging and unbelonging have been intensified and transformed by the global "war on terror." Examining the anti-black and brown ideologies masquerading under the guise of national security, Phillips concludes, "Of course, most of the discourse is just plain, simple, old-fashioned malevolence towards the outsider, the person who not only looks different, but who dresses differently, or who worships in a place other than a church. It is an old European game and we have all seen and heard it before."[16] The interpersonal connection that Julius seeks may be always already elusive, but his peripatetic ruminations suggest that a true understanding of the world and his place in it will start with the ability to recognize and reckon with the past. The narrator implies as much when Julius looks out across the river and catches sight of the Statue of Liberty and Ellis Island: "the focus of so many myths; but it had been built too late for those early Africans—who weren't immigrants in any case—and it had been closed too soon to mean anything to the later Africans like Kenneth, or the cabdriver, or me" (*Open City*, 54–55). The dashes in this sentence signal a present absence in the text between the early and later Africans: the African American descendants of "those early Africans," who flocked to northern cities, and New York in particular, in a famed attempt to force the nation to live up to its democratic ideals. Perhaps these migrants' journeys and unrealized dreams need not be mentioned because they are a haunting presence, shadowing the next group of migrants' attempts to do the same.

These ruminations trouble the novel's initial depiction of black life in the present day as free from racial, class, or cultural boundaries. Just as the optimism felt by the southern migrants of the early twentieth century was tempered by the continuing facts of racial segregation and violence, so is Julius's middle-class existence revealed to be a distraction from the reality of most twenty-first-century black immigrants, who are not welcomed with open arms. For example, Julius remembers an excursion with an organization affiliated with Nadège's church, ironically named "the Welcomers," to a detention center in Queens that houses undocumented immigrants. There, he and the Welcomers joined a line of documented immigrants—Africans, Latinos, Eastern Europeans, and Asians—all there to visit people hidden away in a nondescript, one-story building, which Julius describes as "a long, gray metal box" (*Open City*, 62). Once admitted, he spends time talking to a Liberian man named Saidu Caspar Mohammed, who tells a harrowing story of his travel to America. Saidu recounts a tale of persecution during war, the brutal killing of his family, and his exhausting journey through Nigeria, Guinea, Tangier, Spain, and Portugal. After fighting to overcome national borders, linguistic barriers, and grinding poverty, he finally saves enough money to pay for a forged Cape Verdean passport and a flight to JFK, where he is promptly detained at Customs. Rather than receiving asylum or having the opportunity to breathe free air and step foot on American soil, Saidu is transported to the "gray metal box," where he waits indefinitely for the time when he will be returned to Lisbon, his port of entry.

Though he appears moved by this story of exile, Julius has really only joined the Welcomers and listened to this man because he wants to impress Nadège with his "compassion" (*Open City*, 70), and the episode ends with yet another account of unexplained separation: he and Nadège "drifted apart." One suspects that their breakup has something to do with Julius's lack of a moral center, which the anecdote about Saidu reveals to the reader. Julius cares more about how he appears to Nadège, whom he hopes to impress, than about what kind of human being he really proves to be. Other encounters reveal him to be emotionally cold, in love with his own cultural "sophistication" and worldliness and incapable of empathizing with those who are different from him. Even when he claims to identify with other Africans in their shared status as the unwanted or unseen, as in his observations of Ellis Island, one gets the sense that these are abstract musings rather than a concrete, lived reality.

Reading Julius's halfhearted attempts at empathy and affiliation in comparison with the Ex-Colored Man's efforts to relate to African Americans in *The Autobiography* sets into relief not only the flawed character of both protagonists, but also the context for understanding their unreliability. When first returning from Europe on a ship traveling back to the States, the Ex-Colored Man strikes up a friendship with an African American physician, one of the only other black men aboard the ship. During these long, far-ranging conversations on racism and racial progress, the narrator makes an attempt at racial affiliation: "We walked the deck for an hour or more, discussing different phases of the Negro question. In referring to the race I used the personal pronoun 'we'; my companion made no comment about it, nor evinced any surprise, except to raise his eyebrows slightly the first time he caught the significance of the word" (*The Autobiography*, 110). In this passage, "we" is clearly the most significant word because it represents the protagonist's efforts to live up to and act on his politically progressive intentions. Yet this friendship, again brief and temporary, precedes the Ex-Colored Man's final sojourn, which anticipates Julius's personal failures set against the backdrop of the failed promise of American opportunity and democracy. Johnson explores the idea of blackness as a choice in his depiction of a black man who has the option of choosing to pass. Though the Ex-Colored Man's ability to choose is connected to his unique racial makeup, his predicament foreshadows a historical moment when some black people—albeit a very select few, like Julius—have the financial, social, and cultural capital to entertain the notion of choosing to turn away from the violence directed against blackness and its legacy.

Back in the States, the Ex-Colored Man travels the country gathering materials and inspiration for his music, while finding refuge in the homes of local black people. This happy existence ends when in one town he witnesses a lynching. Surrounded by the sight and smells of burned human flesh, he thinks, "A great wave of humiliation and shame swept over me. Shame that I belonged to a race that could be so dealt with; and shame for my country, that it, the great example of democracy to the world, should be the only civilized, if not the only state on earth, where a human being would be burned alive" (*The

Autobiography, 137). Similarly, after the episode with the detainee and a surrealist conversation with a Haitian bootblack in Penn Station (surreal because the man's life story, recounted as he shines Julius's shoes, spans an improbable length of time and includes references to the Haitian Revolution and vague allusions to slavery and emancipation), Julius emerges from underground and imagines that he sees on the crowded streets the body of a lynched man hanging from a tree. Though only a figment of his imagination, it is an omen, a portent of death.

What does death mean in these contexts? For Johnson, the lynching he witnesses is a reminder of the hard inescapability of the color line. His musical aspirations pale in comparison to the threat of racism and racialist thinking, so in choosing to pass as white, the Ex-Colored Man chooses to run from death. *Open City* is not a passing novel in the traditional sense of the genre; Cole never suggests that his biracial protagonist's complexion is light enough to allow him to pass. But perhaps the point is that in the twenty-first century, education, financial security, and status as a professional give enough leverage to allow him to pass in spirit if not in fact. Julius's class affiliation is only one of the factors that contribute to his experience of crisis in communal cohesion. It certainly frames readers' understanding of his encounters with the Liberian and Haitian men, for they, unlike he, are submerged and hidden from the sight of the dominant society, one housed in a metal box, the other toiling away in the bowels of the New York subway system. Like the Ex-Colored Man, Julius runs from death or, stated differently, from the idea of abject blackness. Like Johnson, Cole acknowledges that the social and material obstacles faced by black migrants are unequal.

Cole's novel proves itself to be a literary descendant of *The Autobiography*, for they both use the black migrant in the (post)modern city to reflect on the challenges of race, identity, and belonging. And just as the Ex-Colored Man is pulled to look outside of himself and to grapple with his failure to live up to his own and others' expectations that he would act on his feelings of communal responsibility, so too does Julius. A hundred years after its initial publication, *The Autobiography of an Ex-Colored Man* continues to resonate for contemporary readers, who recognize its prescience in its depiction of blackness not only as a condition that one is born into, but also as a choice to enter into community spurred on by feelings of love, longing, responsibility, and loss.

NOTES

1. "Post-blackness" is a concept that articulates the heterogeneity and contingency of racialized blackness. When I use this term, I do not mean to invoke the more neutered idea of the "postracial," a notion that assumes that it is possible in twenty-first-century America to "transcend" race and lead a color-blind existence.

2. Daphne Lamothe, *Inventing the New Negro: Narrative, Culture, and Ethnography* (Philadelphia: University of Pennsylvania Press, 2008); George Hutchinson, *The Harlem Renaissance in Black and White* (Cambridge, Mass.: Belknap, 1997).

3. Lamothe, *Inventing the New Negro*, 69.

4. Henry Louis Gates Jr., *The Signifying Monkey: A Theory of African-American Literary Criticism* (New York: Oxford University Press, 1988), 60.

5. Proving Cole's familiarity with, or intention to signify on, *The Autobiography of an Ex-Colored Man* in *Open City* is unnecessary to claiming their intertextuality: a careful reading of each book reveals their working with and through a set of shared tropes that have signaled outsiderness and belonging in multiple black diasporic literary works.

6. Robert Reid-Pharr, *Once You Go Black: Desire, Choice and Black Masculinity in Post-War America* (New York: New York University Press, 2007), argues that naturalized conceptions of racial identity were neither inevitable nor compelled, but instead were deliberately chosen by black intellectuals acting on their perceptions of civic and communal obligation.

7. Ibid., 15, 16.

8. Ibid., 13–14.

9. Alain Locke, "The New Negro" (1925), in *The New Negro: Voices of the Harlem Renaissance*, ed. Arnold Rampersad (1925; rpt., New York: Touchstone, 1997), 3–18; Farah Jasmine Griffin, *Who Set You Flowin'? The African-American Migration Narrative* (New York: Oxford University Press, 1996).

10. Nathan Irvin Huggins, *Harlem Renaissance* (New York: Oxford University Press, 1971); David Levering Lewis, *When Harlem Was in Vogue* (1979; rpt., New York: Penguin, 1997).

11. James Weldon Johnson, *The Autobiography of an Ex-Colored Man* (1912; rpt., New York: Penguin, 1990), 154. Future references to this edition are given parenthetically in the text. Johnson's impetus to consider the meaning of blackness was the turn of the new century, well before the Harlem Renaissance, the movement that reinvigorated the reading public's interest in the novel and gave it yet another layer of complexity.

12. Jean-François Lyotard, *The Postmodern Condition: A Report on Knowledge* (Minneapolis: University of Minnesota Press, 1984).

13. The irony of this statement is that the promise of racial progress lies in close proximity to the persistence of antiblack violence and institutionalized racism, which renders this perspective more myth than reality. I return to this point later in the essay.

14. Teju Cole, *Open City* (New York: Random House, 2012), 3. Future citations to this work are given parenthetically in the text.

15. Madhu Dubey, *Signs and Cities: Black Literary Postmodernism* (Chicago: University of Chicago Press, 2003), 2.

16. Caryl Phillips, *Color Me English: Reflections on Migration and Belonging* (New York: New Press, 2013), 8.

Dead Ambitions and Repeated Interruptions
Economies of Race and Temporality in *The Autobiography of an Ex-Coloured Man*

BRUCE BARNHART

At a particularly important moment in his life, the narrator of James Weldon Johnson's *The Autobiography of an Ex-Coloured Man* finds himself on the receiving end of some rather bleak advice. In an attempt to discourage the narrator from returning to the United States, his wealthy patron tells him: "to attempt to right the wrongs and ease the sufferings of the world in general is a waste of effort. You had just as well try to bale [sic] the Atlantic by pouring the water into the Pacific." The narrator has just told the patron of his ambition to compose a classical composition "on Negro themes," a musical project that would voice "the hopes and ambitions of the American Negro."[1] The narrator sees his composition as a work that will play a part in bettering the conditions of African Americans. Like Johnson himself, he sees music and other forms of art as weapons in the struggle for African American equality.[2]

The narrator's plan is hopeful and ambitious. It aims at a changed future, a future qualitatively different from the present. When the patron argues against this plan, he is essentially arguing against hope, ambition, and meaningful change. He tells the narrator to give up his idea of "making a Negro out of yourself" (*The Autobiography*, 145) and to give up on the idea of a future that is anything but a repetition of the present. The patron's advice is an attempt to deny the future to the narrator and to negate his racial ambitions. Nobody else in the novel speaks to the narrator in this way, but there are a number of other forces that work to deny the future to him. The most powerful of these is a fiery lynching that delivers the final blow to the narrator's musical and racial ambitions. Both the lynching and the patron's advice are part of a system that works to deny futurity to the Ex-Coloured Man. This system is a racialized one, which works to forbid futurity to African Americans and to reserve its privileges for white subjects. Johnson's novel makes this quite clear: as a "coloured" man, the narrator's ambitions are repeatedly thwarted, but as an "ex-coloured man," he quickly achieves a stable and secure future by way of real estate speculation.

This racialized denial of futurity has a long and persistent history in the United States. Perhaps the clearest statement of it comes from Frederick Douglass's 1845 *Narrative*, in the form of a slave owner's reply to Douglass's request to hire out his own time. Douglass's description of his owner's reply reads as follows: "He told me if I would be happy, I must lay out no plans for the future.... he advised me to complete thoughtlessness of the future."[3] For Douglass's owner, as for the wielders of racialized power in Johnson's period and in the present, the future is a zone reserved for the reflective and speculative operations of white subjects. The kind of temporal segregation embodied in the advice of Douglass's owner continued to operate in Johnson's time period and throughout the twentieth century. The latest version of this kind of advice shapes the racialized working of the twenty-first-century trade in subprime mortgages.[4] Johnson's novel provides an insightful reading of this denial of futurity. It gives a rich sketch of the different forms it can take, and it compellingly dramatizes the effects they have on the narrator's life. These effects are psychic and interior as well as practical; one of the most compelling aspects of *The Autobiography* is its account of the narrator's psychic life and of the way this psychic life is shaped by external economic and social forces as well as internal conflicts and desires. What I am suggesting here is that a crucial part of the lasting importance of *The Autobiography of an Ex-Coloured Man* is what the novel tells us about the relationships between race, subjectivity, and temporality.

Johnson's narrator is divided between the lure of the white world and the pull of racial responsibility, but he is also divided between different temporal trajectories and different rhythms of attunement to the world. What Johnson's novel exposes are the discrepant trajectories at work within the subject, trajectories that are both inherent in any human existence and that take on their particular shape and rhythm through the specific ways in which the subject suffers the weight of the social. These trajectories push and pull the subject in different temporal directions; the novel asks readers to pay special attention to the relationship between race and the different temporal trajectories that structure the subject.

Subjectivity is a temporal structure, because no matter how it is conceived, it must have some form of continuity across time. To be a subject is to have some way of connecting the present to both the past and the future.[5] Without a temporal rhythm linking different moments in time, and without a temporal form binding its different psychic rhythms together, the subject cannot exist. The subject is given a particular set of temporal coordinates by a whole host of social institutions, including aesthetic forms like music and literature. The novel is a literary form of particular importance in understanding the relationship between time and subjectivity. As both Mikhail Bakhtin and Georg Lukacs have argued, the novel is a genre that works to both codify and critique each society's treatment of time.⁶ Novels work to give the passage of time a meaningful narrative form; the ways in which they do so reveal much about the rhythms and temporal patterns each social formation and the subjects that inhabit it use to give themselves a coherent, workable form.⁷ Johnson makes full use of the resources of the novel to explore the ways the social forces of the U.S. landscape work to inculcate a particular temporal orientation in its subjects. *The Autobiography* gives a rich and compelling portrait of the psychic rhythms at work within its narrator and of the way conceptions and practices of racialization affect the shape and valence of these rhythms.

One of the primary ways in which race works to structure the narrator's psyche is by dint of the forces that work to prohibit to him and to other African Americans a productive trade with the future. The forces of racialization that Johnson's narrator encounters work to confine his imaginative energies to the present. In doing so, they operate on one of the major axes of all subjective orientations. Every form of subjectivity is divided between two different temporal orientations: the repetitive and the speculative or futural. On the one hand, every subject is immersed in a regime of social habits: momentary, diurnal, weekly, and seasonal rhythms of repetitive actions and reactions that the subject accommodates itself to and incorporates into its own-most structure.⁸ On the other hand, every subject has a speculative, futural dimension: a component that reaches out of the given and the habitual by way of desire, ambition, hope, and other forms of social and subjective investment in a future that is in at least some small way different from the present.⁹

Johnson's treatment of his narrator shows the way that racial prescriptions and prohibitions work to cut off full access to these two dimensions of subjectivity, cutting up the subject and standing in the way of its attempt to productively coordinate both temporal orientations. When the narrator encounters his patron's argument against hope, it is one instance of a welter of forces that work to curtail the speculative dimensions of his subjectivity and heighten the importance of its repetitive dimension. In psychic economies as well as social ones, the primary result of excising the future is to make the present more repetitive. This tradeoff is evident in Johnson's novel: as his narrator continues to have his hopes and ambitions thwarted, he becomes more aligned with the vicissitudes of repetition. In the narrator's movement between "coloured" and "ex-coloured" positions, the working of racial division on subjective structures is made apparent. The racial system that the narrator encounters is a kind of temporal apartheid; it takes the division between the repetitive and the speculative that is internal to the subject and uses racial distinctions to hypostatize it and project it onto the divide between black and white subjects.¹⁰

The contrast between the economic positions that the narrator inhabits as a "coloured" man and as the Ex-Coloured Man is an exemplification of how this racialized logic functions.¹¹ In his life as a "coloured" man, the narrator consistently inhabits positions dominated by repetition and by precarity, the possibility that he might need to start all over again at any moment. Both as a worker in a cigar factory and as a gambler in New York, the narrator lives with repetition and makes part of its dictates into a component of his psychic structure. In his life as an ex-colored man, he occupies a position in which repetition is muted and in which he gains success as an economic agent. With the narrator's success as a speculative buyer and seller of real estate, his economic future expands and his psychic structure adapts to this new prominence of futural and speculative energies.[12]

Most of Johnson's novel is concerned with the impact that the racialized denial of futurity and the resultant emphasis on repetition have on the narrator's consciousness. The next part of this essay attempts to account for the insights that *The Autobiography* delivers about this relationship between race, repetition, and the structure of subjectivity. My aim is to show the way Johnson's novel lays bare the significance of repetition, both exposing its utilization in unjust racial regimes and tracing the outlines of its productive role in creating subjective and social structures that work to transform these regimes.

Repetition as Imposition

The narrator spends most of the novel as a subject intimately acquainted with repetition. The dictates of a racialized economy give him his first job as a roller of cigars, a repetitive task in which remuneration is directly tied to the number of times one can repeat the actions necessary for the assembly of a complete cigar. This job can lead to a relatively high salary and a lucrative career, but it does not lead to any upward progress through the ranks of the tobacco industry. In the cigar factory and in most of his "coloured" life that follows, the narrator's race and circumstances shape him in accordance with the dictates of repeating and restarting. To repeat is often to restart, to go back to a beginning point that has been gone through before. Both repetition and restarting play a crucial part in psychic life and are an unavoidable part of any social life. In addition, as I discuss below, Hortense Spillers and James Snead argue that repetition and African American strategies for harnessing it can be crucial components of productive psychic structures and vital cultural formations.

However, despite the necessity of repetition to existence, and despite the positive role that it can play in psychic and social life, there is something maliciously unjust in a system that makes racial difference an excuse for forcing African Americans into a position in which they must start all over again, giving up their previous ambitions and hard-won social and economic positions. The fate of Johnson's narrator dramatizes this injustice. In *The Autobiography*, the shape of his life is determined by a number of events that forcefully knock him off his established path and force him to restart, rethink, and repeat his forward movement. The Ex-Coloured Man is forced to rethink his plans and restart his adult life when his tuition money is stolen. He is forced to start all over again when the tobacco plant in Jacksonville is closed down. He is forced to repetitively restart his career as a ragtime pianist when he is involved in a shooting at "the Club." The terrifying force of a brutal lynching ends his plan of becoming a classical composer and forces the narrator to restart his life in New York City, where he becomes a white real estate speculator. Again and again, the narrator is forced to go back to a beginning that seemed settled and repetitively restart his life.

In his portrayal of these forced repetitions, Johnson shows the way that the racial system of the United States differentially apportions the need for repetition. The narrator's fate as a "coloured" man functions as a critique of an unequal and racially determined requirement to repeat and restart what had already seemed settled. This imposition of repetition is one half of a system of racial injustice that works to reserve the easiest paths and the most rewarding futures for white subjects.[13] Johnson's novel dramatizes the narrator's forced intimacy with repetition as determined by a series of events that violently shake the narrator and violently dispossess him of his economic means and volitional power. The novel focuses most overtly on the pragmatic effects of these events, but Johnson's detailed sketch of the narrator's interiority also shows the way this racialized insistence on repetition affects the subject on the deepest level, shaping his relationship to language and to himself.

Repetition and Utterance

The relationship between repetition, racism, and subjectivity is one that Hortense Spillers foregrounds in "All the Things You Could Be by Now, if Sigmund Freud's Wife Was Your Mother." Working with a Lacanian model that emphasizes the entanglement of psychic and linguistic structures, Spillers reworks the psychoanalytic model to account for the way that racial prohibitions penetrate to the very core of the subject. This penetration has everything to do with repetition, as Spillers makes clear: "To speak is to occupy a place in [a] social economy, and, in the case of the racialized subject, his history has dictated that this linguistic right to use is never easily granted but must be earned, over and over again, on the level of a personal and collective struggle that requires in some way a confrontation with the principle of language as prohibition, as the withheld."[14] Here Spillers shares with Johnson an emphasis on the way in which repetition is a necessity imposed by racism. She shows subjectivity to be a function of one's place in a social economy and one's right to linguistically articulate one's satisfaction or dissatisfaction with this place.

Unlike a white subject that is easily granted the right to linguistic articulation, the racialized subject has to linguistically repeat "over and over again" both its own identity and the mechanics by which it claims a right to speak or be heard.[15] In its encounters with society's different discursive fields, the racialized subject encounters hostility, prohibition, and/or indifference. The result is a heightened anxiety about the reception of the subject's speech and a heightened reflexivity about the effects of repetition.

The racist structure of American society forces the African American subject to confront prohibition again and again, both linguistically and socially. Johnson's narrator is banned from eating in certain places (*The Autobiography*, 57), from participating in certain occupations, and from pursuing his artistic ambitions without the terrifying threat of racial violence. Like Johnson, Spillers critiques these racial prohibitions and shows how they create a crippling environment that is psychic as well as social. However, and also like Johnson, Spillers suggests that this repetitive confrontation with forms of prohibition can give the racialized subject an acute insight into the workings of both the American social system and subjectivity itself.[16] Spillers asserts that this repetitive need to establish one's right to speak makes the racialized subject more aware of language as prohibition—as a force that cuts the subject off from her or his desire. The racialized subject is compelled to articulate its identity and its desires again and again because no articulation is fully successful. Part of this lack of success is the fact that no articulation can entirely remove the need for repetition; the most successful linguistic act(s) can force some recognition from the (white) world and can effectively articulate some desire, but it cannot, given the weight of history and the stubborn persistence of racism, succeed in securing a place for the racialized subject's next utterance. In other words, what the racialized subject can never successfully establish is duration, a reorientation of the racialized social and discursive field lasting long enough to obviate the need for racialized subjects to repetitively fight for the right to articulate themselves and their desires. In this sense, language is prohibition because it blocks its unchallenged appropriation by the racialized subject.

On a deeper level, language is prohibition because of its incommensurability with the nonlinguistic world of desire. From a Lacanian perspective, language can never fully articulate desire because language and desire are two qualitatively different realms. The two realms come in contact with each other, but they only overlap in that small instant in which the subject is speaking. As a result, language can never capture desire; it can only get at it elliptically, by way of its entanglement in subjective, intersubjective, and social economies. Language does not function primarily as a description of this entanglement; it functions as a provocation used to elicit a response from the subject's social surroundings and to push both the subject and its surroundings closer to the subject's desires. Language marks the subject's situatedness in what Spillers calls "the crossroads of conflicting motivations" and is its primary access to the "constant commerce in real and symbolic capital among struggling intersubjectivities" that make up U.S. social relations.[17] There is an irreducible incompatibility between language, which belongs first and foremost to the social field, and desire, which comes to the social from the outside. Language and desire constitute overlapping gravitational fields, and the subject exists at the point of their overlap.

The result of this overlap is a doubleness that has a strong affinity with Du Bois's "double-consciousness," a form of which shows up in *The Autobiography*. When Johnson's narrator feels his thoughts and words "dictated" by race, he feels himself acquiring "a sort of dual personality" (*The Autobiography*, 21). Like Johnson, Spillers describes the doubleness of the racialized subject in ways that make the dictates of linguistic experience central and that also suggest the possible upside of this subject's forced familiarity with the need to repeat and start over. Her description couples a sense of language as a marker of social position with the linguistic and psychoanalytic distinction between the speaking I (the "subject of the *énonciation*") and the spoken I (the "subject of *énoncé*"). When one uses the pronoun I to articulate identity, one is divided between the spoken I, which leaves the subject's lips or pen and travels in the world of discourse, and the implied but unspoken I, which utters the linguistic I but stands detached from it in a realm asymptotic to language. The spoken I is meant to stand for the subject (or the speaking I), but once it is uttered it is determined by its reception, by its relationship to other signifiers, and by the whole social realm of discourse and positionality that gives language meaning. In other words, once it leaves the subject's lips, it is determined by forces largely out of the subject's control. This aspect of the divided subject, the spoken I, is socially determined, discursively shaped, and in some sense removed from the other aspect of the divided subject, the speaking I. Social forces wrest the spoken I away from the speaking I, bending it to fit already existing linguistic patterns and social expectations.

Here is how Spillers describes this distinction: "The 'one' . . . is both a position in discourse—the spoken subject of *énoncé* that figures a grammatical instance, and a consciousness of positionality—the speaking subject of *énonciation*, the one in the act of speaking as [a] consciousness of position. As the former is mapped onto his/her world by discursive social practices, the latter comes into the realization that he/she is the 'one' who 'counts.'"[18] The language that Spillers uses to describe the division between the part of the subject determined by one's positionality in the social field and the part of the subject conscious of but undetermined by this positionality suggests that this model does not only apply to the racialized subject. The division she describes is drawn from Lacanian psychoanalysis, a discourse that has little to say about race.[19] So, on the one hand, Spillers's distinction does not necessarily appear to be raced. On the other hand, both Lacan and Spillers suggest that this division is something that the dominant fictions of any culture work to cover up or evade. As Johnson's novel forcefully shows, race is the dominant fiction of U.S. culture. In the United States the fictions of white subjectivity work to evade the division of the subject and the truth that a significant part of its being is determined by forces outside of its control. What Spillers shows in her account of the racialized subject's need to repetitively claim the right to speak is that the realities of race work in the opposite way for subjects racialized as black, brown, or yellow: these subjects are painfully familiar with the divide between their desires and the resistances of the social field. In other words, the consciousness of speaking subjects that their utterances are carried away from them by the resistances and prohibitions of the social world is a consciousness that comes easier to the racialized subject. The narrator of Johnson's 1912 novel and the African American subjects that preceded and followed him are shaped and constrained by a welter of prohibitions; the primary medium of these prohibitions is language. The African American subject lives in a social world where language and prohibition often go together; this fact places this subject in a place where a consciousness of language's resistance to desire and volition comes relatively easily.

This consciousness of language as prohibition and the resultant reflexivity about repetition, division, and the social structure of language are key elements of the way Spillers and Johnson limn the structure of racialized subjectivity. This is evident in Johnson's account of the narrator's entry into his life as a "coloured" man. When the narrator first becomes aware of his race, it alters his perception, his consciousness, and his relationship to language. When he learns that he is black, he "pass[es] into another world" and finds his "thoughts ... coloured," his "words dictated," and his "actions limited by one dominating all-pervading idea which constantly increased in force and weight until I finally realized in it a great, tangible fact" (*The Autobiography*, 11). At this moment, the narrator feels the heavy hand of the social world upon him. It does not just limit him from the outside; "the great, tangible fact" of race prescribes and proscribes the shapes and patterns of his interior mental life and "dictates" the ways in which he will articulate his identity and desire. His words are not his own; he feels the power of language as an alien force that moves through him and divides him from his innermost sense of who he should be and what his social position should be. After this moment, the narrator will again and again approach language with a new wariness, a consciousness that each time he speaks he is doing battle with this interior alien. He gains a canny, reflexive awareness of the fact that if he does not carefully craft his utterances to take account of the social powers that work to make his language alien to his desires, he will constantly be consigned to an undesirable social position.

This moment in the novel establishes the template for everything that will follow. It is the first instance of an arbitrary or unmotivated event that forces on the narrator the need to repeat or rethink a beginning that he has already been through. It also gives the outlines of the alien but intimately interior force that he will have to repetitively confront again and again: "the great, tangible fact" of race. At the moment that the narrator is racialized, he is exposed to the insistent force of repetition and the power of language as a social force that is indifferent or hostile to his desires. At the same time, when the interrelated forces of race, language, and repetition strike the narrator, he becomes less of an individual. He does not become less human, but he is less structured by the fictions of self-possession, control, and self-containment that constitute individuality. To say this is to say, along with Spillers, that individuality is historically constituted by the interactions of social and economic forces. As she puts it, the "individual" is a "particle in constant bombardment ... between and within races, and according to a modern cultural synthesis, brought on by industrialized capital in its precise historic formation and its aftermath that divide and specify 'persons' from 'land,' 'family,' and 'other.'"[20]

"Individuality" is a name for a position within an overlapping web of economic and social relations that emerged in the eighteenth century. The black subject is not outside this web, but he or she does have a different relationship to almost every element of its different social and economic strands. The white subject becomes an individual by virtue of her or his specific position in this web. Left outside of some its strands, more heavily enmeshed in others, the black subject becomes something else, something both more and less. This something else is what Spillers refers to as the "one." In her attempt to bend the protocols of psychoanalysis in ways that make it accountable to the distinctive shape and movement of the racialized subject, Spillers undoes the assumed structural necessity of any particular form of subjectivity. Individuality is one form of subjectivity, but there are others, and each one is heavily entangled in its constitutive social and economic milieu.

This last fact is made compellingly clear in *The Autobiography*. Johnson moves his narrator into and out of a number of clearly drawn socioeconomic milieus, and in each the narrator takes on a markedly different shape. The Ex-Coloured Man is a bit of a sponge; his high sensitivity to his surroundings allows Johnson to deliver a series of case studies about the way in which social and economic relations move in and through the narrator. The narrator's life as a "coloured" man includes stints as a gambler, as a reader in a cigar factory, as a ragtime performer, as a composer, and as a student. In each situation the narrator stages himself differently, and in each situation his cathexis by the social and economic forces that surround him gives his subjectivity a different form. In his depiction of each of the narrator's incarnations, Johnson depicts race as the mode through which social forces cathect the subject, and subjectivity is presented as a coagulation of social forces that can take many shapes.[21] Each episode is an argument against individuality as the exclusive form that subjectivity can take, and each is an argument against individuality conceived as a "subjectivity hermetically sealed off from other informing discourses and practices."[22]

Repetition and the One

When Johnson and Spillers foreground the historically determined nature of subjectivity, they work to denaturalize individuality, but they do something more as well. In Johnson's literary account of the narrator's racialized schooling in repetition and in Spillers's theoretical account of the subject formed by repetition and division, one can see the outline of a different form of subjectivity, one that is not just a fractured or lacerated version of individuality but that also has its own set of possibilities, limitations, and productivities. Spillers refers to this other, racialized form of subjectivity as the "one"; she distinguishes it from individuality on the basis of repetition, reflexivity, and collectivity. The one is not totally distinct from the individual, but it is a configuration that posits a different relationship to the repetitive nature of the present and to the speculative energies that tie the present to the future.

Spillers describes the "one" in ways that extend her insights about the repetitive nature of the racialized subject's relationship to linguistic utterance and social positionality: the one is "a structure in this instance: the small integrity of the now that accumulates the tense of the present as proofs of the past that would warrant, might earn, the future."[23] Here, the racialized subject's relationship to repetition takes on a more positive valence. The "now" that defines the one necessarily occurs over and over again, and it is through its repetition that the one can accumulate the energies that gain it access to a beneficial future. Unlike the individual, the one does not permanently link itself to a stable, discursive identity. It repetitively stages itself in recognition of the antiphonal relationship between itself and its surroundings. Its familiarity with language as prohibition makes the one aware of the divide between the speaking I and the spoken I and capable of manipulating this divide. Standing apart from the fictional integrity of the individual, the one knows that its utterances are not linked to it by the bonds of ownership and possession but that they are performative gambits working to create a space for the subject in the shifting and contradictory terrain of the social world.[24] The individual assumes a stable platform for identity and a broad integrity of the now that link the past, present, and future in a structure of necessity and continuity. The one insists in and on the "small integrity of the now" as the momentary point of enunciation in which the speaking I repetitively launches an articulation of itself (the spoken I) into the world.

The one stages itself in the "small integrity of the now" every time it speaks itself against the sounding board of the social world; it accumulates the "tense of the present" when its utterances echo off this sounding board and earn for it a reflexive knowledge. The repetitions of these echoes are cumulative and help the one earn knowledge of how its utterances are received in a complexly reflexive social world. Just as skilled ragtime or stride piano players' repetition of the same piece can help them anticipate how their specific musical utterances will be responded to by dancers and listeners, so can the one earn a reflexive knowledge of how its uttered articulations of its own needs, desires, and claims for recognition will be received by interlocutors in the realm of social discourse.

For Spillers, the way the one accommodates itself to a world of repetition is one of its most productive strengths, the source of its reflexive knowledge of language and of its own structure as well as a strategy closely aligned with the one's collective properties. Repetition is a defining attribute of the one, and in her allusions to the music of Charles Mingus, Spillers suggests an affinity between African American music's treatment of repetition and the shape of racialized subjectivity. This is a connection more overtly made by the critic James Snead. His article "Repetition as a Figure of Black Culture" describes a forthright confrontation with the vicissitudes of repetition as the defining element of black culture, of black music, and—implicitly—of the subject aligned with both. Snead posits the centrality of repetition as an inescapable fact of the social and natural world. For him, culture is a technology that social collectivities use to either confront or evade the facts of repetition. The distinction he makes between cultures that engage repetition and cultures that evade it lines up with Spillers's distinction between the one and the individual and with Johnson's distinction between his narrator's temporal shape as a "coloured" man and as an "ex-coloured" man. Like Johnson and Spillers, Snead shows the way a sophisticated treatment of repetition gives the African American subject productive possibilities unavailable to any subjective or social formation that evades the centrality of repetition.[25]

Snead's insights about repetition are important not only because they help to elaborate the significance Johnson and Spillers assign to repetition but because his approach gives a clear indication of the importance of musical treatments of repetition in Johnson's text and of the way these treatments are linked to structures of subjectivity that have a powerfully collective component. Snead uses musical and literary examples to theorize the way repetition works in black culture. He shows how the performance strategies of John Coltrane, Elvin Jones, and James Brown exemplify a set of philosophical insights into the relationship between repetition and social life. He also shows that the complex dialogic interactions enabled by these performers' treatment of repetition exemplify the kind of subjective and social interactions possible in cultures and social structures that foreground repetition. The participatory, improvisational, and egalitarian impulse in jazz and other forms of African American music depends on the necessary relationship between repetition and any robustly collective social formation.

Snead demonstrates the collective implications of African American music, and this is something that Johnson shows as well in his depiction of the social spaces of ragtime performance and, even more clearly, in his account of the powerful community feeling generated by the repetitive and antiphonal performance practices of a religious revival meeting that the narrator attends in the South. This last is the "Camp Meeting," a space in which the musical mastery of Singing Johnson creates an intense experience of social affiliation and collective identity. Johnson's account emphasizes the role of repetition at the camp meeting in creating a set of collective affiliations that bind its participants together. Even though it is made up of "people from different communities," the congregation at this meeting responds to both the singing and the preaching "with the precision of a company of well-drilled soldiers" (*The Autobiography*, 176). The interactions of the congregation with the preacher, John Brown, and the singing leader, Singing Johnson, are a model of well-coordinated, participatory social form. These interactions and the collectivity they generate depend on repetition: when Singing Johnson sings the leading lines of "Swing Low, Sweet Chariot," the author of *The Autobiography* provides the repetitive response of the congregation.[26] The congregation marks the moving point of collective enunciation with a line that is repeated four times—"Coming for to carry me home," the last repetition of which is marked by an ellipsis indicating the open-ended and ongoing iterative performance of social coordination. The congregation repetitively articulates the "small integrity of the now" as the site of their collective attempt to open up this "now" to the future.

At this moment in the text, James Weldon Johnson gives a sketch of community and collectivity that is in sharp contrast with the isolating individualism of the narrator at the end of the novel. The camp meeting is the strongest of several moments that show the narrator immersed in a situation that exemplifies an important aspect of Spillers's "one": its collectivity. Spillers refers to this collective aspect as the one's "iconic thickness," its imbrication with other subjects: "the individual-in-the-mass and the mass-in-the-individual."[27] For Spillers, the individual is formed in "opposition to the mass,"[28] but the one takes on an iconic thickness by way of its awareness of the social energies, rhythms, and trajectories that it shares with others. The subject as the one is thick because it is an aggregation of the social field's thickness and density. The thick subject does not imagine itself separated from the rhythms and trajectories that pass through it and shape its milieu; at the camp meeting, part of the enthusiasm and collective effervescence is generated by a celebration of shared rhythms and by the subject's capabilities of shaping and being shaped by these rhythms and repetitions.

At the camp meeting, the narrator is in close contact with a form of subjectivity that is collectively engaged in performing and celebrating repetitions. This subject is collective because it is repetitive. Snead stresses that "beat is an entity of relation,"[29] and whether the beat is musical, linguistic, or social, the subject's attunement to the beating repetitions of its lifeworld makes it aware of its dependence on repetitive rhythms generated by others. Snead points to the way that "one rhythm always defines another in black music" as an example of how an attentiveness to repetition militates for collectivity and interdependence.[30]

Repetition also facilitates collective participation by the way it constantly makes available a starting or entry point that is either happening right now or that is about to be repeated again. Snead refers to this as the performance of a "beat that is there to pick up," a pattern of repetition that is "amenable to restarting, interruption, or entry" by other members of a musical or social ensemble.[31] When music or cultures are repetitive, they are more open to participation by all members. Because repetition creates a certain kind of regularity that is easy to anticipate, and because repetition is aligned with starting over and returning to beginnings, it creates a movement that any participant can join. Cultures that foreground repetition make no effort to hide the fact that culture is constantly and repetitively performing itself in a movement that depends on the contributions of its members.

The connection between music and social form foregrounded by Snead and alluded to by Johnson leads to an understanding of social form itself as a performance dependent on repetition. Social form has to maintain itself; it depends on "a certain continuance in the nurture of those concepts and experiences that have helped or are helping to lend self-consciousness and awareness to a given group."[32] Snead sums up this point: "'Culture' . . . also means the culture of culture."[33] Culture always has to be cultured or cultivated, which means that the practices, forms, mental habits, and relations that are its constitutive elements need to be repeated. Culture performs its ongoing form by way of repetition, and any attempt to break the rhythm that racialized cultural forms use to perpetuate themselves needs to take this fact into account. This means that the strategies for managing and harnessing repetition that show up in Johnson's novel are not just technologies for shaping and reshaping the self but contain important strategies for transforming and reforming the social world. This is how Johnson presents repetition in his novel: not as something one can choose to use or not use, but as an ineluctable force of social life that can be used to either constrain or unfetter the subject.

Repetition as Ending

Repetition is an inescapable component of every form of subjectivity, and Johnson attests to this fact by the way his novel ends. On the last page, the narrator affirms his commitment to his current life as a white subject secure from the need to repeat or restart. He claims a freedom from any "desir[e] to be otherwise," but this complacent freedom is disturbed by an "and yet" that announces the disruptive presence of repetition: "and yet, when I sometimes open . . ." At those repeated moments in which he opens up the box containing the remnants of his classical composition on "Negro themes," he confronts his "dead ambition" and realizes that in taking up his life as a white man he has acquiesced to the racial regime working to thwart African American futurity.

When the Ex-Coloured Man "sometimes" opens the lid of his repressed past, he is repetitively called back to a series of alternative futures that do not eschew repetition. He feels the repetitive calls of his "dead ambition" and "vanished dream," the calls of access to a future that do not depend on any social or psychic investment in whiteness. These repetitive interruptions of his stable, white present call him back to an experience of repetition that might earn or warrant access to a different future, one in which race is not a force that cuts the subject off from valuable psychic resources but functions as the positive condition of a more capacious treatment of social and psychic energies. In the ending's conjugation of repetition with traces of an alternative mode of futurity, *The Autobiography* suggests the possibility of social and subjective formations that couple the productivities of repetition with access to a speculative future that is something more and something other than a hopeless repetition of the past and the present.

NOTES

1. James Weldon Johnson, *The Autobiography of an Ex-Coloured Man* (1927; rpt., New York: Hill and Wang, 1960), 146, 148. This essay uses the 1960 Hill and Wang edition of *The Autobiography*, in which Arna Bontemps's introduction asserts that the book feels "as if [it] had been written this year." In addition to Bontemps's introduction, this version also includes the 1927 edition's British spelling and authorial attribution and the novel's original 1912 preface. Bearing the marks of the 1912, 1927, and 1960 iterations, this edition highlights the complexity of the novel's ongoing engagement with different historical contexts and foregrounds the novel's rich treatment of repetition, the subject of my essay. Future references to this work are given parenthetically in the text.

2. Johnson is clear about this in his preface to *The Book of American Negro Poetry*: "The status of the Negro in the United States is more a question of national mental

attitude toward the race than of actual conditions. And nothing will do more to change that mental attitude and raise his status than a demonstration of intellectual parity by the Negro through the production of literature and art" (Johnson, ed., *The Book of American Negro Poetry* [New York: Harcourt, Brace, 1931], 9).

3. Frederick Douglass, *Narrative of the Life of Frederick Douglass, an American Slave* (1845; rpt., New York: Penguin, 1986), 139.

4. See Tayyab Mahmud, "Debt and Discipline," *American Quarterly* 64, no. 3 (2012), esp. 477–79.

5. Frantz Fanon writes: "Every human problem must be considered from the standpoint of time" (*Black Skin, White Masks*, trans. Charles Lam Markmann [New York: Grove, 1967], 14–15). See also Martin Heidegger, *The Concept of Time*, trans. William McNeill (Hoboken, N.J.: Wiley-Blackwell, 1992).

6. Georg Lukacs, *The Theory of the Novel*, trans. Anna Bostock (Cambridge, Mass.: MIT Press, 1971); and Mikhail Bakhtin, *The Dialogic Imagination*, trans. Caryl Emerson and Michael Holquist, ed. Michael Holquist (Austin: University of Texas Press, 1981).

7. Paul Ricoeur calls the novel "a prodigious workshop for experiments in the ... expression of time" in *Time and Narrative*, trans. Kathleen McLaughlin and David Pellauer (Chicago: University of Chicago Press, 1985), 2:8.

8. For a thoroughgoing account of the role of repetition in psychic structures, see Gilles Deleuze, *Difference and Repetition*, trans. Paul Patton (New York: Columbia University Press, 1994), esp. ch. 2.

9. The literature on the speculative or futural dimension of subjectivity is vast, but three important texts are Heidegger's *Being and Time*, trans. Joan Stambaugh (Albany: State University of New York Press, 2010); Freud's *Beyond the Pleasure Principle*, trans. James Strachey (New York: Norton, 1989); and Ernst Bloch's *The Principle of Hope*, vol. 1, trans. Neville Plaice, Stephen Plaice, and Paul Knight (Cambridge, Mass.: MIT Press, 1995). The particular way in which Johnson's narrator renders himself speculative by "forsaking" the past (*The Autobiography*, 190) and "den[ying]" the present (195) makes *Beyond the Pleasure Principle* and Frankfurt school appropriations of it particularly relevant. See Herbert Marcuse, *Eros and Civilization* (New York: Vintage, 1961); and Theodor W. Adorno and Max Horkheimer, *Dialectic of Enlightenment*, trans. Edmund Jephcott, ed. Gunzelin Schmid Noerr (Stanford, Calif.: Stanford University Press, 2002), esp. ch. 2.

10. I am not making an argument about any kind of natural connection between repetition and African American existence. What I am arguing is that all cultures and all forms of subjectivity depend on repetition. Johnson's novel exposes some of the historical coordinates contributing to the distinctive weight that repetition has come to have in economies of African American existence. For a critique of formations that posit a "natural" link between race and repetition, see Ronald Radano's "Hot Fantasies: American Modernism and the Idea of Black Rhythm," in *Music and the Racial Imagination*, ed. Radano and Philip Bohlman (Chicago: University of Chicago Press, 2000). See also Saidiya Hartman's account of the relationship between repetition and African American experience in the nineteenth century: *Scenes of Subjection* (New York: Oxford University Press, 1997), 49–78 (esp. 76).

11. Elsewhere, I have argued that the narrator's successive engagements with improvised ragtime and classical music are indexes of his engagement with different forms of temporality. Part of the richness of Johnson's novel is its examination of the ways in which all the different layers—aesthetic, economic, ideological—of U.S. social formations participate in shaping race and time. See Barnhart, "Chronopolitics and Race: Rag-time and Symphonic Time in *The Autobiography of an Ex-Colored Man*," *African American Review* 40, no. 3 (2006): 551–69.

12. For a compelling historical and theoretical reading of the links between racial distinction and the assignment of economic positions, see Lindon Barrett, "Mercantilism, U.S. Federalism, and the Market within Reason," in *Accelerating Possession*, ed. Bill Maurer and Gabriele Schwab (New York: Columbia University Press, 2006), esp. 106.

13. For an account of the ways in which the legal system enforces whiteness as a privileged relationship to the future (in the form of "reasonable expectation"), see Cheryl Harris, "Whiteness as Property," in *Critical Race Theory*, ed. Kimberle Crenshaw et al. (New York: New Press, 1995), 276–91.

14. Hortense Spillers, "'All the Things You Could Be by Now, if Sigmund Freud's Wife Was Your Mother': Psychoanalysis and Race," *Boundary 2* 23, no. 3 (1996): 108.

15. I follow Spillers in referring to the subject position of people of color as "racialized." This does tend to suggest that the white subject is not racialized; however, implicit in my argument is the belief that the white subject *is* racialized, only in ways that are not as overt and that tend to present whiteness as racelessness.

16. "I believe it to be a fact that the coloured people of this country know and understand the white people better than the white people know and understand them" (*The Autobiography*, 22).

17. Spillers, "All the Things," 95.

18. Ibid., 101.

19. Although Lacan did not discuss issues of race, there is a growing body of work that uses a Lacanian framework to address these issues. See Arlene Keizer, "African American Literature and Psychoanalysis," in *A Companion to African American Literature*, ed. Gene Andrew Jarrett (West Sussex, England: Wiley-Blackwell, 2010); Ranjana Khanna, *Dark Continents: Psychoanalysis and Colonialism* (Durham, N.C.: Duke University Press, 2003); Mikko Tukhanen, *The American Optic: Psychoanalysis, Critical Race Theory, and Richard Wright* (Albany: SUNY Press, 2009); and Kalpana Seshadri-Crooks, *Desiring Whiteness: A Lacanian Analysis of Race* (London: Routledge, 2000).

20. Spillers, "All the Things," 92.

21. Stuart Hall writes, "Race is the modality in which class is lived," in "Race, Articulation and Societies Structured in Dominance," in *Policing the Crisis: Mugging, the State, and Law and Order*, ed. Stuart Hall et al. (London: Macmillan, 1978), 394.

22. Spillers, "All the Things," 103.

23. Ibid., 102.

24. I use the word "performative" in an attempt to do justice to the rich connections Johnson's novel suggests between his narrator's struggles with identity and the performance strategies of African American music. I do not use it to suggest that any individual or subject can easily "choose" to perform or not perform race. This last is a

view critiqued by Johnson: he puts a similar view in the mouth of the narrator's patron, and the narrator's lament over his "sacrificed" past belies any facile notions of race as "mere" performance. For a theorization of race that takes full account of both its unremitting fixity and its performative dimension, see Fred Moten, *In the Break: The Aesthetics of the Black Radical Tradition* (Minneapolis: University of Minnesota Press, 2003).

25. James Snead, "Repetition as a Figure of Black Culture," in *The Jazz Cadence of American Culture*, ed. Robert O'Meally (New York: Columbia University Press, 1998). For Snead, the chief virtue of black culture's stance toward repetition lies in the way it utilizes the powers of social imbrication, relationality, and improvisation.

26. Jeffrey Nealon writes, "In the blues tradition, of course, repetition with a difference is linked to the structure of call and response" (*Alterity Politics: Ethics and Performative Subjectivity* [Durham, N.C.: Duke University Press, 1998], 125). See also Bernard Bell, *The Afro-American Novel and Its Tradition* (1970; rpt., Amherst: University of Massachusetts Press, 1989), 27.

27. Spillers, "All the Things," 101.

28. Ibid., 100.

29. Snead, "Repetition," 75.

30. Ibid., 68.

31. Ibid., 71.

32. Ibid., 63.

33. Ibid.

PART THREE

Poetics
Sound, Affect, and the Archive

The Autobiography as *Ars Poetica*
Satire and Rhythmic Exegesis in "Saint Peter Relates an Incident"

BEN GLASER

In a survey of 1935's black literature for *Opportunity* magazine, Alain Locke develops a criterion for black poetry that may seem surprising: not James Weldon Johnson's famous call for "symbols from within" comparable to the achievement of Synge and Yeats, not a call for native rhythms and folk forms, and not Langston Hughes's turn to the "eternal tom-tom beating in the Negro soul—the tom-tom of revolt against weariness in a white world."[1] Rather, Locke sought "the full flavor of tragic or comic irony as applied to Negro experience" that he had found in the "sturdy, incisive verse" of Sterling Brown:

> For years we have waited for the sealed vials of irony and satire to open and for their purging and illuminating fire to come down in poetic flashes and chastising thunderbolts.... The puny thrust that passes for irony, the burlesque smirk that masquerades as satire try one's critical soul, until one remembers that outside antiquity, only the Irish and the French have the gift of it. But it might have been in the gift-box of the Negro, seeing he had such need of it.[2]

One difficulty with satire—the reason it remains a mere "smirk"—is that it tends to destabilize its origins as much as its target.[3] Melvin Tolson stages this truth in *Harlem Gallery* (1965), as do earlier authors like George Reginald Margetson in "The Fledgling Bard and the Poetry Society" (1916) or Countee Cullen in "Heritage" (1925)—both of whom thematize self-denial and avoid racial essentialism.[4] Satire is doubly unstable for black poets because it might not even register with either the white or the black half of what Johnson, in 1928, termed the "double audience."[5] The best example of this may be the cakewalk, whose historical origin as a parody of white dances was lost not only on whites, who parodied it in turn, but on the black narrator of *The Autobiography of an Ex-Colored Man*. Despite the present sense that a poem like Cullen's "Heritage" satirizes atavistic yearnings for Africa, even Sterling Brown criticizes the poem for rendering Africa "literary," "romanticized," and "too close to Vachel Lindsay's 'Congo, creeping through the black.'"[6] Brown may seem to misread Cullen's sophisticated irony, but his reading constitutes a necessary protective gesture against the projection and consumption of racial fantasies.

In James Weldon Johnson's poetry, as in Cullen's and Brown's, poetics and prosody guard against such romanticized "creeping through the black." In this essay I suggest that Johnson's satire in "Saint Peter Relates an Incident of the Resurrection Day" occurs not only at the level of theme and character, but also in its engagement with the reader's prosodic expectations and specifically the expectation for black rhythm. *The Autobiography* and its many scenes of performative crisis anticipate this focus on the intersection of racial identity and rhythm. Studying this intersection in the novel helps one to understand the decisively rhythmic mode of exegesis in Johnson's exploration of black identity and collectivity as framed by a heterogeneous modern audience.

In December 1929, enraged at the second-class treatment of the Negro Gold Star Mothers, James Weldon Johnson wrote and then privately published the satirical "Saint Peter Relates an Incident of the Resurrection Day."[7] Five years later, while preparing the collection *Saint Peter Relates an Incident: Selected Poems* (1935), he penciled into the foreword: "driven by a spirit of angry irony he wrote rapidly, the time consumed being a matter only of hours."[8] He did not publish this remark, however, perhaps because it might have solidified the poem's status as propaganda.[9] The more important achievement of the poem, I argue, is the transformation of anger and irony into its metrical and rhythmic body. Johnson's prosodic development of this poem *is* its complex mode of satire; it is a satire that does not merely adopt and then deform traditional white forms, but deforms the very process of writing and receiving these forms. In ways best seen by looking at Johnson's drafting process, the poem toys with the limits of the reader's ear and expectations for black performance. Although there is limited space here to explore how poets of the New Negro Renaissance negotiated the history of meter and rhythm, I contextualize Johnson's intense focus on the mediation of sound, on scansion and ear training, by looking at his pedagogical methods in courses he taught at Fisk University in 1932–33.

In a retrograde movement from *God's Trombones* (1927), whose rhetorical power remains united with musical efficacy, the sound in "Saint Peter" remains irrecoverably rhetorical (rather than natural, lyrical, or even racial in any simple sense). I read *The Autobiography* as an extended ars poetica for poetic sound's rhetoricity: a study of how rhythm emerges, is disfigured by rhetorical pressures, and potentially reemerges as a powerful mode of black rhetorical—signifying—sound. Stripping away the established Anglo-American poetic tradition without promising collective musical and racial expressivity, "Saint Peter" returns to and renegotiates the soundscape laid out in *The Autobiography*'s failure to foreclose the violence of passing through mere glimpses of the rhythmic and exegetical community provided by the speeches of Shiny and the oratory of John Brown. "Saint Peter," whose black unknown soldier is a similarly potent figure for rhythmic power at once black and universal, performs the instability of antiphonal community in its destabilized prosody.

Johnson's *The Autobiography* begins with an unusual symbol of organic form: bottles that grow like flowers until the young narrator is spanked for digging them up. Friedrich Hölderlin imagined poetic expression that might be this organic: "the word originates like the flowers."[10] The organic structure of the romantic image is swiftly dispelled for Johnson's narrator: not, as in Hölderlin or Wordsworth, by the immanent failure of tropes to sustain the ideal of poet-as-maker/namer—although the need for rhetorical effectiveness is at issue in the book—but because of the tragic birth of double-consciousness. The narrator's love of music in particular—artifice become innate "feeling"—dissolves steadily in *The Autobiography* under double-consciousness's "warping, distorting influence."[11] Restoration cannot flow from ragtime but only through the rhythmic mode of rhetorical existence thrillingly embodied in the preacher John Brown.

One reading of *The Autobiography*, aware perhaps of Johnson's praise of ragtime in his prefaces to *The Book of American Negro Poetry* (1922) and elsewhere, might consider that black music transcends double-consciousness by providing an alternate genealogy of expression, a route back from white artifice to something innate or embodied. The spirit of the flower bottles does indeed return in the narrator's memory of his mother's playing "largo . . . freer, because she played by ear" and of her "old melod[ies] without words" (*The Autobiography*, 7–8). Yet at the novel's conclusion the reader must recognize the untruth of the narrator's claim that maternal memories "kept me from straying too far from the place of purity" (8). The narrative shows double-consciousness predetermining music's capacity for open racial expression. The narrative pushes against Johnson's own hope for an "interracial model of culture" in which "performance is emphasized through the black [here, maternal] body without its reduction to deforming stereotype."[12]

Johnson's extension of double-consciousness to what he calls "the problem of the double audience"[13] emphasizes the circulation and mediation of all expressive forms and performances. Tsitsi Jaji, discussing the black British composer Samuel Coleridge-Taylor's setting of Paul Laurence Dunbar's "Corn Song," shows how a musical arrangement that seems to lift the poem (and its dialect) from the text and into our ears must be read as a further mediation: it "makes the poetry audible without suppressing the estrangement entailed in voicing what is always already an anomaly on the page."[14] Estrangement remains in the sound; the narrator's youthful "strange harmonies" and preference for the "black keys" (*The Autobiography*, 7), though preceding his racial awareness, foreshadow a dissonant career with no racial uplift. *The Autobiography* suggests that what Jaji calls "the page" is the ineluctable product of double-consciousness. In a way, the page might represent a supposedly white poetic tradition and its rhythms: a prosody deeply meaningful to black poets (including Dunbar) and yet bottled up *avant la lettre* as alien. Yet the narrator's fate—selling his racial heritage for the pottage of passing—precludes the conclusion that orality, folk heritage, or natural musicianship are aesthetic guides available to replace the white tradition or "page."

The Autobiography seeks out passionate and communal acts of rhythmic exegesis outside of the presumed organicism of oral folk rhythms. The motivating ars poetical question of *The Autobiography* is how the rhythmic exegesis and rhetorical skill of speakers like Shiny and John Brown, alongside the song leading of Singing Johnson, could model a black poetics without merely forcing tropes of raced voice, bodily movement, or musical swing. Moreover, how could poetry's audience (white as well as black) participate in shared affective acts without presupposing that such tropes functioned (as African American poets of this period did not and could not)[15] to sustain both collective and individual identity?

The first roots of rhythmic, exegetical poetics lie in the narrator's musical style, but they remain a limited basis for identity because they fail to circulate. The narrator plays well, avoiding the flaws that might have come with too much focus on technique: "I never played the piano like a child, that is, in the 'one-two-three' style with accelerated motion. Neither did I depend on mere brilliance of technique ... but always tried to interpret a piece of music; I always played with feeling" (*The Autobiography*, 17). In music, at least, he has not "strayed" from his mother's "largo" style. The terms of the description here directly link interpretation and feeling. This link depends on rhythm, especially manifest in the narrator's footwork on the pedal, which renders the piano a "sympathetic, singing instrument" (17). Here again he has learned from his mother: his ability is "due not entirely to natural artistic temperament, but largely to the fact that I did not begin to learn the piano by counting out exercises, but by trying to reproduce the quaint songs which my mother used to sing, with all their pathetic turns and cadences" (17). Yet the path remains rough from the maternal tradition to the flexible voicing Johnson would later lay out in *God's Trombones*. Problems emerge when one turns from the narrator's piano style, his interpretive playing in relative isolation, to his relationship with an audience. Rather than becoming a ground for community, as is the case with John Brown's rhythmic exegesis of the Bible, interpretation gets in the way the moment another "soloist" enters: "I have never been a really good accompanist because my ideas of interpretation were always too strongly individual. I constantly forced my accelerandos and rubatos upon the soloist, often throwing the duet entirely out of gear" (18).

More severe are the patterns of thought forced upon the narrator when he performs for his white father. The narrator plays well, but the circuit of performance is convoluted. When his father is introduced, the Ex-Colored Man involuntarily stutters, "'Father, Father,' that was the word which had been to me a source of doubt and perplexity" (*The Autobiography*, 22). As with the duet, the pairing of word and feeling is skewed. The narrator fails to embrace his father, not because of anger or confusion, but because he believes the gesture would be "melodramatic." Thus, in his literally musical drama, "melos" ironically names an outdated aesthetic mode, a mode, moreover, implicitly associated with Victorian women's poetry of the sort his mother could well have appreciated. The "old melodies without words" she played are now heard within that atavistic category.

As for his music, the narrator plays well only because his father "displayed that sincere appreciation which always aroused an artist to his best effort, and, too, in an unexplainable manner, makes him feel like shedding tears" (*The Autobiography*, 21). Melos returns then to fill the void opened when sentimentality passes from maternal bulwark to rejected artifice, but song returns framed by a hyperawareness of spectatorship, impersonality, and notably rigid prose. That the early drafts of the novel were edited to increase the hypotaxis suggests an effort on Johnson's part to complicate the syntax.[16]

This split moment, with his mother in actual tears but the artist twice removed from tears (by his father's spectatorship role and by his only "feeling like" crying), recalls the narrator's description of the "dual personality" (*The Autobiography*, 14) constructed and endured by African Americans (and performers in particular). Maternal sentiment, off the stage, is a "freemasonry" (14, 40) that does not mimic sentiment; yet the narrator, despite having learned music from his mother, masks his relation to emotions as "feeling like." While this is not so extreme a case as the "antics" of the minstrel stage (14), it is precisely the point that even in such an intimate circumstance as being reunited with his father, the painful mediation of self-spectatorship takes over.

Thus *The Autobiography* unexpectedly frames music not as a maternally guided tradition and form of self-expression but as an institution corrupted by its performance and reception. In its place Johnson elevates rhetorical skill, which is described, like rhythm, in a figurative language of electricity and waves.[17] Two characters stand out for their rhetorical and prosodic prowess: the narrator's grammar school classmate Shiny and the preacher John Brown.

Early in the novel Shiny is responsible for delivering Wendell Phillips's speech "Toussaint L'Ouverture" at graduation. The narrator had been applauded for a piano solo, but "the real enthusiasm was aroused by 'Shiny'":

> He made a striking picture, that thin little black boy standing on the platform ... his eyes burning with excitement, his shrill, musical voice vibrating in tones of appealing defiance, and his black face alight with such great intelligence and earnestness as to be positively handsome. What were his thoughts when he stepped forward and looked into that crowd of faces, all white with the exception of a score or so that were lost to view? I do not know, but I fancy he felt his loneliness.... I think that solitary little black figure standing there felt that for the particular time and place he bore the weight and responsibility of his race.... as the words fell from 'Shiny's' lips their effect was magical.... When in the famous peroration, his voice trembling with suppressed emotion rose higher and higher and then rested on the name Toussaint L'Ouverture, it was like touching an electric button which loosed the pent-up feelings of his listeners. They actually rose to him. (*The Autobiography*, 25–26)

Perhaps even more compelling than the "vibrating," "trembling," and "electric" oratorical skills of Shiny is the description of his effect on the audience and narrator. The audience is "swept by a wave of sympathy and admiration," and the narrator in particular feels the old wound of "dual personality" stitched up: "the effect of 'Shiny's' speech was double; I not only shared the enthusiasm of the audience, but he imparted to me some of his own enthusiasm" (26). The coordinated syntax here ("not only ... but") differs sharply from the hypotaxis and convoluted logic of spectatorship in the narrator's earlier scene with his father. It seems critical that whereas readers cannot hear the narrator's music, they could look up Phillips's speech and enact it themselves. Indeed, the Ex-Colored Man's imaginative response not only to Shiny's performance but to the conditions of that performance marks an ongoing and productive mediation of racial conflict from the Haitian Revolution (another suppressed Romantic origin) to Phillips's abolitionist evocation of L'Ouverture as evidence of racial equality and through to the novel's present.

Shiny's performance is the skillful execution of a set piece. While it is more elocution exercise than aesthetic development, it insists on the central role of audience reception and participation in such development. Later in the novel, with the description of Brown's sermon, there are multiple levels of productive mediation and a more thoroughgoing, polyphonic, and rhythmic weave of audience, performer, and narrator:

> He seized the Bible and began to pace up and down the pulpit platform. The congregation immediately began with their feet a tramp, tramp, tramp in time with the preacher's march in the pulpit, all the while singing in an undertone

a hymn about marching to Zion. Suddenly he cried, "Halt!" Every foot stopped with the precision of a company of well drilled soldiers, and the singing ceased. The morning star had been reached. Here the preacher described the beauties of that celestial body. Then the march, the tramp, tramp, tramp, and the singing was again taken up. Another "Halt!" They had reached the evening star. And so on.... He took his hearers through the pearly gates, along the golden streets, pointing out the glories of the City, pausing occasionally to greet some patriarchal members of the church, well known to most of his listeners in life, who had had "tears wiped from their eyes, were clad in robes of spotless white, with crowns of gold upon their heads and harps within their hands," and ended his march before the great white throne.... I was a more or less sophisticated and non-religious man of the world, but the torrent of the preacher's words, moving with the rhythms and glowing with the eloquence of primitive poetry swept me along. (*The Autobiography*, 92)

These feet may be well drilled, but they are not overdetermined or disciplined like Gerard Manley Hopkins's generations that have "trod, and trod, and trod,"[18] or the work rhythms of a chain gang. As in Sterling Brown's wry version of a chain-gang song in "Southern Road," John Brown's sermon develops a mode of counterpoint that intentionalizes otherwise rote repetition.[19] For instance, the rhetorical journey taken by the parishioners is on its face absurd: the "morning star" and "evening star" both refer to Venus. This travel is circular or static, however, only from the perspective of location, not time. By "tramping" from the morning star to the evening star the preacher renders place dynamic by injecting return with difference: the journey is metaphysical as much as rhetorical, oriented around the subjectivity of those who see a morning star in the East and an evening star in the West as symbolic, perhaps even of the Middle Passage continued westward until it arrives in Zion and the "new Jerusalem."

The heightened rhythm of John Brown's prose parallels this vision of space transformed by rhythmic repetition. His words form a well-regulated but fluid iambic hymnal stanza, which can be lineated through a stress count as either 3-4-4-3 or 7-7 ("fourteeners"):

> [had] *tears wiped* from their *eyes*,
> were *clad* in *robes* of *spotless white*,
> with *crowns* of *gold* up*on* their *heads*
> and *harps* with*in* their *hands*

Though lacking full rhyme, substantial consonance and assonance further structures these lines: wiped/eyes/white, heads/harps/hands, and clad/crowns. These help create what the narrator calls "tone pictures." The sermon's prosodic structure potentially translates the effect on the narrator to *The*

Autobiography's reader, something Shiny's unheard speech cannot achieve. Brent Hayes Edwards notes of the sermon-poems of *God's Trombones*, "There is no music in the sermon itself.... Johnson is looking for a musical figure of vocalization."[20] This formulation should be amended for Brown's sermon, in which there is deliberate rhythm (if not music) though it remains mediated by its strange, hybrid presence in prose and outside the narrator's explicit recognition.

The Autobiography considered as ars poetica is less about the shape of communal or specifically black rhythm than the conditions of production and reception encountered by the performer. With Shiny's and Brown's rhetoric the reader sees the productive mediation of both the recent past and biblical narrative through dynamic repetition. Shiny's and Brown's ability to embrace and control their performance context contrasts with other cultural forms that appear less successful in exposing and combating the alien reframing of genres—especially black genres. The narrator's classical piano playing is one such example: it is unable to transcend his father's control or even sustain a duet with less poignant racial conditions. (The duet foreshadows the pyrrhic victory of the Chopin piece, which reunites the narrator and his white wife as a white couple; she plays a few bars before he takes over and "silence[s]" the room [*The Autobiography*, 126].) The narrator is starkly aware that whites viewed black middle-class strivings as "putting on airs" and "monkey-like imitation" rather than as people "obeying an impulse common to human nature" (50).

The novel also considers two more conventional (and conventionally raced) performance genres, the cakewalk and ragtime. The narrator sees in the cakewalk, a rhythmic movement contest, proof of the "power in creating that which can influence and appeal universally" (*The Autobiography*, 54). That it was much imitated by whites in both America and Europe seems to be evidence of this power to the narrator. But this "power in creating" is less than half of the story of the cakewalk, and the narrator is mistaken in defining it with help from "Parisian critics," who "pronounce it the acme of poetic motion" (54). In the minstrel show's debased adoption of the cakewalk, and the subsequent shame associated with it, one can see the limits of rhythm as a self-sustaining social ground. The rhetorical aim of the narrator at this moment is to convince blacks to be proud of the dance, but his advocacy comes off flat. Perhaps this is because Johnson's narrator (but not Johnson) has forgotten the real history of the cakewalk and replaced it with a deracinated contemporary "acme"—part of what Wallace Thurman calls the "present epidemic of negrophilia."[21] Shiny's speech, like Frederick Douglass's famous "What to the Slave Is the Fourth of July?"[22] derives its power from suggesting a past that is alive because it is unsatisfied by the present. The narrator does not know the cakewalk's past, that it began not as the acme of "motion" but as the acme of black *satire*. The cakewalk is proof that a rhythm or prosody taken to be uniquely racial in character—for instance, the syncopated cadences referenced in works as different as T. S. Eliot's *The Waste Land* (1922) and Langston Hughes's "The Weary Blues" (1925)—are best understood as citations of rhythm that in many cases, including Hughes's poem, foreground the racialized history of rhythm's circulation.

The cakewalk's shuffle step, as Brooke Baldwin has shown, began as a takeoff of white plantation dances. The white dancers immediately read its ludic character as a failure of imitation and subsequently represented it as such in the minstrel show, but the pre–minstrel show black performers were entirely aware of its satirical intent.[23] Johnson, like later commentators, knew this deep imbrication of performance and history. Why then is Johnson's narrator either unconscious of or unwilling to include this important history? There is a similar kind of dramatic irony in the Ex-Colored Man's effort to trace his skill at ragtime back to his mother's influence without considering ragtime's (and black music's in general) "double audience." In contrast, black poets from Paul Laurence Dunbar and Claude McKay to Sterling Brown and Hughes, as well as singers like Paul Robeson and Roland Hayes, were highly aware of ragtime's advance framing by alien demands on both its form and content. As Baldwin notes, ragtime was just as burdened as the cakewalk by "images inherited from the minstrel stage"; eventually the commercialization of ragtime debased its form, turning its African polyrhythmic elements into "chaotic parades of arpeggios and trick fingering."[24] In his treatments of both music and the cakewalk the narrator reveals himself to be an ahistorical lyric striver in pursuit of pure forms and universality, a would-be flowering bottle. His eventual failure as either musician or spokesman can be chalked up to his blindness about historical mediation and his resulting inability to recognize and pass ironic judgment on the racial rhetorics of his surrounding culture. In "Saint Peter" Johnson sets out to correct this specific failing by paying heightened attention to the framing and figuration of black rhythm.

The novel's ragtime players, including the narrator, appear as rhythmic virtuosos who seem to equal Shiny in that they "demanded physical response," yet they remain limited in situations that call for more complex rhetorical and ironic poise. "Guided by natural musical instinct," one ragtime player's "lavish natural endowment" seems almost too "natural," too "barbaric" to benefit from formal training: "Perhaps [with training] he wouldn't have done anything at all; he might have become, at best, a mediocre imitator of the great masters in what they have already done to a finish" (*The Autobiography*, 63). Again "imitation" threatens "nature," revealing the ideals of native musicality to be deeply unstable if not themselves constructed. The German pianist who renders ragtime "classic" also reinforces the novel's "troubling, ambiguous framing of blackness."[25] The narrator does not recognize that his plan to render the spirituals "classic" is no less precarious.

Ragtime and other musical modes that demand an ideology of authenticity are not, then, safer than the cakewalk or the "black Shakespearian" whose tragic ambitions earn only laughter "at the size of his mouth," rendering his performance unintentionally tragic (*The Autobiography*, 65). It is only the narrator's wealthy white patron (who demands the narrator play at all hours) who can safely (if ironically) espouse unattainable humanist and aestheticist ideals: "Music is a universal art; anybody's music belongs to everybody; you can't limit it to race or country. Now, if you want to become a composer, why not stay right here in Europe? I will put you under the best teachers" (87). The seemingly contrasting ideas that ragtime is both natively black and universal both work to obscure its mediation, circulation, and audience. Thus even before the pivotal lynching that pushes the narrator to pass, the novel ambivalently frames his desire to go to the American South to recover "the hopes and ambitions of the American Negro, in classical music form" (102). Music, in its abstract and universal guise, lacks the power to make these transatlantic and transcultural voyages. The real challenge is to "free black expressive culture from the binary trap of racial determinism or universalism."[26] This means freeing black culture from the perception of immediacy. In this way *The Autobiography* crucially anticipates Johnson's poetic oeuvre, which as Edwards succinctly puts it, "discards the mediating figure of music" and "transfer[s] the swing from the vernacular, performing black body or bodies into the very formal body of the poem; in the manipulations of line, measure, and punctuation, the poem itself begins to be sketched out as a 'breathing,' 'syncopating' body."[27]

To understand Johnson's complex construction of that "formal body" in "Saint Peter" it helps to explore how he reframes black sound in his editorial and pedagogical practices. Edwards notes that Johnson's prefaces to *The Book of American Negro Poetry* and *The Book of American Negro Spirituals* (1925) explore the "interface" of music and writing rather than claiming to be audible transcriptions of musical forms on the page.[28] Johnson's anthologies of spirituals and sermon-poems differ from other "folk" collections (including the Ex-Colored Man's attempt to be an archivist of black folk forms)[29] in his deep skepticism about the movement from text to sound: "I doubt that it is possible with our present system of notation to make a fixed transcription of these peculiarities that would be absolutely true; for in their very nature they are not susceptible to fixation."[30] In a draft of the preface to *God's Trombones* he is similarly skeptical about cueing stress contours for the reader: "I would be tempted to indicate by italicizing the words [where] the voice stresses fall except for the fear that it would [be] a clumsy if not confusing chore."[31] The draft asks readers not to prioritize scansion via syllable count: "the number of syllables makes no difference—Just as in music—any number of syllables may be syncopated into the rhythm."[32] But in its final form the preface to *God's Trombones* drops commentary on italicization and syllable counting to recommend only "a decided syncopation of speech—the crowding in of many syllables or the lengthening out of which must be left to the reader's ear."[33] That so much must be left to the ear, however, concerned Johnson and other writers who knew how the double audience tainted dialect spelling or apparent musicality.[34] The question for Johnson became how a destabilized, precarious poetic prosody might initiate new modes of collective hearing.

The drafting of *God's Trombones* reveals an extensive and intentional destabilization of the audience's prosodic and genre expectations. Johnson originally included an introductory framing poem, "The Gospel According to Jasper Jones," written in heroic couplets reminiscent of Chaucer and focused on Jones's vocal style: "the pause for effect, the rapid, sudden rise, / Through sharp staccato to the grand surprise / Of an electric climax."[35] The poem was withdrawn, leaving readers with a different preface and a "preliminary prayer" whose crucial "antiphonal" element Johnson does not even "attempt to set down."[36] All told, the final version of *God's Trombones* removed three elements that might have made it more translatable into dramatic sound and sense: the figure or imagined presence of music, dramatic framing through a given character, and diacritical marks of any sort. The question then was how to make the preacher Jasper Jones, a figure the public would have recognized too well, into James Weldon Johnson's hybrid literary sounding. Just as *The Autobiography* "offer[s] not the thrill of access to a 'veiled' world, but the threat of incomprehension,"[37] so too *God's Trombones* deconstructs and reframes a supposedly unique black sound and black identity. Even God experiences this existential crisis during "The Creation," as he tries to "make me a man."[38]

In *The Autobiography*, the rhythmic and deeply context-driven oratory of Shiny and John Brown reverberates through their audiences and the narrator, forming a new and positive figure of transmission that replaces lyrical music. Brown's oratory, crucially, is aided by Singing Johnson: an indispensable figure who knows all the hymns and when to sing them and thus pulls together diverse congregations. Because such direct antiphonal support is unavailable in James Weldon Johnson's poems, he turns, I argue, to the mercurial prop of poetic prosody. The question then is what the "formal body of the poem" can look like when, as *The Autobiography* and Johnson's other writings insist, the poem must "discard" pure music in favor of new modes of rhythmic, rhetorical power. How can Johnson's satirical reinterpretation in "Saint Peter" create a medium as "sharp," "surprising," and "electric" as Jasper Jones and his forerunners John Brown and Shiny? In my reading the rise of vernacularity reverberates not in the unknown soldier's black body but in the patient undermining of Anglo-American prosody and its transformation—literally visible in the drafting process—into a new rhythm.

Renovating or overcoming past prosodic contracts was a modernist concern at the forefront of Johnson's teaching as well as his poetics. Johnson's treatment of prosody and scansion in his 1932 course in creative literature at Fisk University shows a sustained effort to provide students with a flexible frame for mobilizing the rules of versification. During the poetry lessons he insists first that "too strict scansion must be avoided" in the writing of poetry, and then more trenchantly that one must not perform scansion "by drumming the meter out with your fingers to see if all the feet are of the proper size and length" as determined by "rules ... for the most part, borrowed from Greek + Latin."[39] Conscious that his students may have heard prosody's siren song of cultural capital and aesthetic order, he asks: "How many of you have studied English prosody? Then you know all about iambic, trochaic, anapestic, dactylic feet. Well, for the purposes of this course, forget them! NO practicing poet knows very much about them."[40]

Yet Johnson is anything but dismissive of scansion as a means of encountering and reframing poetic traditions. Johnson's foremost example of poetic rhythm is Hopkins's "Spring and Fall," chosen in part because of its importance to I. A. Richards's *Practical Criticism* (1929). Johnson seems almost delighted (unlike Richards) to observe that his students will have "some trouble in making the metrical scheme" of its sprung rhythm.[41] The poem's "ever changing modulations," Johnson lectures, permit "no monotony. Hardly any two consecutive lines in the same rhythms, and yet what perfect music." Hopkins embodies Johnson's ideal use of rhythm: "much like a musician establishe[s] a theme and then varies it—But the theme must be *established* and in the variations *never lost*" (emphasis in original).[42] With this "perfect music" Johnson returns to a figure that did not serve in *The Autobiography* or even in *God's Trombones*. This figure works, however, not through a musicality proper to Hopkins or obvious to his readers, but rather through Johnson's diligent and interpretive scansion. This essay is not the place for a reading of the poem, or for Johnson's reading of the poem. It is helpful, however, to observe Johnson's transformation of one of the most intransigent lines of "Spring and Fall"—"And yet you will weep and know why," a line that I. A. Richards observed all but the choicest students failing to perform or understand—into a double scansion, double voicing, and double interpretation:[43]

$$\left\{\begin{array}{l} \smile - \smile - - \smile - - \\ \smile - \smile\smile - \smile\smile - \end{array}\right. \begin{array}{l} = \text{You persist in weeping and knowing why} \\ = \text{Some day you will weep and know why} \end{array}$$

Johnson's students were subsequently asked which of the "two totally different meanings" of the line they preferred. His practice in teaching was shot through with exercises in scanning both poetry and prose less for precision than to "stimulate [students'] powers" through attention to the prosodic features of language. Unlike Richards, who remained dedicated to a singular voicing of the poem, Johnson deliberately framed the challenge of interpretation as one of scansion. His bracketed double scansion, written out for students, visibly incarnates an ambiguity that need not be resolved into a unitary voicing. Using Hopkins's poem allows Johnson to transform his students' practice of exegesis into a rhythmic exegesis, rather than simply pushing them toward new musical or rhythmic expression.

In the course's final "practical work" Johnson asked his students to explore the racial component of how sound is framed and interpreted. The predetermined theme of the creative option looks strikingly like a rewriting of *The Autobiography*: "Mozart Brown a little colored boy, so named by his mother because of her ambitions he become a great musician. Mozart is shortened into Moze by his playmates and friends. A. Moze has real talent and does through a series of experiences develop into something beyond his proud mother's expectation, perhaps even her comprehension. B. Moze has no exceptional talent and fails in spite of the hopes and efforts of his fond mother."[44] The vernacular shortening of the name is the key detail. Whereas the narrator of *The Autobiography* can be either Mozart (or Chopin) or Moze, but in effect neither, Johnson seeks a path back from the Moze-aic exodus to the promise of Mozart. This is the ineluctable path through the racing of form to its musical ideal, through the bad dichotomy of the white, Anglo-American tradition and its black rhythmic other to the rhythmic exegesis modeled in the scansion of Hopkins. "Saint Peter" charts that path in its prosody.

Johnson's lesson of a transformed Anglo-American tradition resonates in Sterling Brown's response to the poem's "notes of irony":

> I think the ironic approach is excellent. It isn't at all one of those "damn you, take that" sort of things.... There is quite a swing to the lines; they catch you up before you know it.... The whole poem keeps to its tone of high wit, and tempered irony. And it's not "wise-cracking"—it's the spirit best seen in Dryden and Pope, at their best. I think the use of the couplet form was well chosen; they [the couplets] are fluid, and pointed—and to me at times "drawling"—which accents the wit—and the other stanzaic variations lend variety—and each form suits the function it performs in the narrative.—the raillery may be gentle—but it is trenchant:—there's so much real social criticism compassed in such a small space—
>
> ... The note of irony which is so frequently struck by our people is missing in our poetry.[45]

Brown's genealogy of satire focuses on English origins because these are the high-water marks for the couplet, the crucial medium for the Augustan wit of Alexander Pope, John Dryden, and Jonathan Swift. The "drawling" here is not some native syncopation belonging to Johnson's voice, or Brown's ears, but is the same fluid relation to the couplet tradition for which Brown would later praise Cullen.[46] Johnson's drawl nonetheless suggests that his lines might become a literary embodiment of the unknown soldier's own "loose, long stride." The goal then might seem to be a positive form of rhythmic racing that does not depend on a presumed folk source or nativeness—already co-opted in the blunt cadences of Vachel Lindsay, the popularized form of the cakewalk, and the "chaotic parades of arpeggios" in "pseudo-rag."[47]

Johnson's path to a new prosodic as well as national identity comprehends that demand—separating a priori musical virtue from the black body of the soldier or poem—and turns instead to the couplet as both the medium and object of his satire. Ultimately "Saint Peter" cannot be read as transcending the white poetic tradition to achieve a black version of Hopkins's "musicality": there is no transfusion of the spirituals and Chopin, of Moze and Mozart. The spirit of irony drives instead "ever changing modulations" that poignantly disfigure the national and prosodic tradition he associates, in this poem, with the treatment of black soldiers and their families, the failure of the Dyer Anti-Lynching Bill, and the legacy of Reconstruction more generally.

The process of drafting the poem manifests modulation and variation that could scarcely be called musical. With the exception of a few shortened lines, the thirty quatrains of the first four sections are in heroic couplets. The drafts show that although the poem was written quickly, Johnson took the time to return almost obsessively to certain lines to manipulate their rhythms, usually within the constraints of meter. The drafts are littered with synonym lists meant for putting together metrical lines. Yet the metrical revisions are idiosyncratic. The drafts move from anger to wit not by smoothing out irregular lines or even by introducing conventional variations (caesuras, limited inversions or counterpoints, enjambments, shifts of stress) but by making lines jagged and even confrontational. (There is also a second type of revision, no less confrontational, oriented back toward musical measure.) These revisions are unlike the ideal of "establishing a theme" without losing it in variation; rather, they are a satire of false modulation leveled at the English tradition and its audience (loosely equated with white nationalist groups). The poem's rhythmic assault on these groups occurs both in couplets and in its "drawling" or "loose, long stride" as it is charged with the unknown soldier's presence. This prosodic drama leads directly to the poem's central question of whether the satire and its implied audience can be surpassed for the new vision of collectivity first found in *The Autobiography*'s rhythmic oratory.

Several of the revisions suggest that Johnson was trying to make "Saint Peter" a bouquet of blunt, arch-Augustan rhythmic and rhetorical effects. Before settling on the heavily alliterative and bouncily metrical second line, "Hung heavy on the hands of all in heaven," Johnson tried out five different ornate, bad, less metrically regular lines, including "Hung like a heavy opiate in heaven" (requiring a three-syllable "opiate"—and are there light opiates?) alongside a list of metrically distinct adjectives—"tedious, soporific, monotonous, somnolent"—so florid that Johnson could not have missed the irony of using them to help render his line metrically tedious. One quatrain, concerned with the gathering of peoples for revelation day, stands out for its prosodic, rhetorical, and descriptive absurdity:

> Swift-winged heralds of heaven flew back and forth
> Out of the east, to the south, the west, the north,
> Giving out quick commands, and yet benign,
> Marshaling the swarming milliards into line.

Johnson heavily worked and reworked these lines. The first line came about in part after Johnson played with several patterns of scansion, indicated by his own classical, quantitative symbols (the ones he urged his students away from). The mock-epic collocation "swift-winged heralds" was in Johnson's scansion a choriambic (‾ ˘ ˘ ‾) or dactylic (‾ ˘ ˘) opening leading into a triple rhythm.[48] The second line had several incarnations, each with a different ordering of the directions, suggesting that the final form exists primarily for its rhythmic contour. This, like the previous line, begins in triple rhythm before shifting back to iambs. The third line is more metrically regular, but was heavily modified to contain the flourish of a syntactically ornate hendiadys. Drafted as several variants of "directing and guiding every tongue and nation," Johnson in the final form chooses the syntactic transformation that pushes the adjective "benign" to the end of the line and in so doing regularizes the meter at the expense of syntax (or, rather, toward ironic syntax). The final line brings these lines "into line" with the more regular rhythm that guides most of the quatrains.

Why, if Johnson excluded scansion from the poet's toolbox, preferring (in typically modernist fashion) a more musical ideal, do his modulations here seem so canned or vestigial? He was in part parodying metrical culture—the angels "chanting the selfsame choral aeon after aeon"—and yet Johnson knew that poets like McKay, Cullen, and himself in poems like "O Black and Unknown Bards" (1908) used well-modulated meters to great effect and not to escape from questions of race. How then does Johnson's parody become one of whiteness and racism, rather than the typical modernist rejection of older forms? The direct answer comes at the end of the poem in the new black rhythm figured by the soldier's "loose, long stride." At that moment the reader sees the full fruits of Johnson's rhythmic exegesis, the way he lends his feet (no longer classical, but almost literal) to the unknown soldier's embodiment. But equally important is Johnson's willful failure to modulate the white meters that frame the angels, the KKK, and other nationalist groups. The drafts show that Johnson edited the poem not to produce bluntly metrical lines (he was capable of doing that without much revision), but to disfigure his own metrical facility. This prosodic disfiguring reveals a constructedness that reveals in turn the constructedness of white prosody. In this, the poem's meter performs a function similar to *The Autobiography*'s overall deep irony, noted by Aldon Nielsen, of presenting white audiences with "an exemplary life" that is not the advertised and expected "inner life of the Negro in America" but that of "an ordinarily successful white man who has made a little money." "Saint Peter" also fits Nielsen's description of *The Autobiography* as "at least in part a cognitive mapping of a world in which 'white' does not 'know' the truth of its own blackness."[49] In both novel and poem this means coming to terms with the nonimmediacy, rather than the given otherness, of blackness and with a nonessential whiteness.

I now offer several examples where Johnson distresses the line, shifting from iambic cadences to differing modes of rhythmic raggedness (often at moments where the content concerns rhythmic movement or linear organization). In each case the irregular moments—additional syllables between stresses or stresses in normally unstressed positions—are italicized. The accents help show the underlying pentameter:

1. their voices show the strain → their tone revealed *voice* strain
2. and then the line was thrown into the flurry → Then, through the long *line* ran a sudden flurry (the word "line" goes from a stressed to an unstressed position but clearly keeps its accented nature)
3. Gave rise *to a*nother puzzling question → Gave rı́se *to a* ráther mètaphýsi*cal* qüestion → Gave rı́se *to a* ráther nı́ce *meta*phýsi*cal* qüestion ("nice" forces the first syllable of "meta" out of its previously stressed position, as with "line" in example 2)
4. directing, guiding → guiding and shepher*ding* → direc*ting and* guiding every tongue and nation → Giving out quick commands, and yet benign[50]

These examples all overload, counterpoint, or stretch the iambic line found in their first iterations. Pairing these changes with the overdose of vestigial rhetoric and pseudoclassical inventions, Johnson created a deliberately frayed poetics that allowed his angriest and most mocking lines to pass through meter into memory. Angels "chanting the selfsame choral, aeon after aeon" and "The G.A.R., the D.A.R., the legion" line up plot and form as "compliantly" as the lined-up men: these are lines that Sterling Brown reported reciting and laughing over again and again with his wife. Thinking back to Johnson's lectures on meter, one sees a poignant contrast between free modulation, which allows meter to refresh itself, and a composition that either marks out and thematizes thumping meter or willfully disturbs the ground so the weeds of the "great white" tradition can reemerge. This occurs repeatedly in "Saint

Peter," with alternate lines diverging from the base pattern before snapping back to attention with brutal consequences. For instance, after the unknown soldier is revealed to be black:

Bedlam: They clamored, they railed, some roared, some bleated:	[extra syllables]
All of them felt that somehow they'd been cheated.	[strict]
The question rose: What to do with him, then?	[mismatches of stress]
The Klan was all for burying him again.	[strict]

Johnson is cakewalking here, parodying the Klan's movements through the very mechanicity he cautioned his students against. Johnson is playing with modulation itself, with a version of faux and foreclosed syncopation that (like the Klan's racism and the treatment of the Negro Gold Star Mothers) never truly skips a beat.

It is against this critique that the poem's other modulation takes form. The syncopation of section 5 is not merely "black," but a variant on variation. It is a modulation that goes to the heart of measure and wrenches the decasyllabic line into a heterogeneous form that is, like the sermons of *God's Trombones*, no longer trackable or scannable by ears trained for the syllabic play of Dryden and Pope. As the poem shifts into antiphony, with the italic text of "Deep River" accompanying Saint Peter's oratory, the quatrains in regular typeface begin to "drawl" in a poetic sense: shifting from modulation at the level of the line toward a large-scale stanzaic and phenomenological disturbance.

> I rushed to the gate and flung it wide
> Singing, he entered with a loose, long stride;
> Signing and swinging up the golden street,
> The music married to the tramping of his feet.

The poem is still near enough to heroic couplets that the syncopation can be felt in the missed beats on "with" (line 2), "up" (line 3), and "to" (line 4). The following stanza, however, shifts without any warning to a completely different musical analogue:

> Tall, black soldier-angel marching alone,
> Swinging up the golden street, saluting at the great white throne.
> Singing, singing, singing, singing clear and strong.
> Singing, singing, singing, till heaven took up the song:
> *Deep river, my home is over Jordan,*
> *Deep river, I want to cross over into camp-ground.*

Returning to Johnson's drafts one can see in process a striking transformation. From the first line he removed the word "all" from "marching all alone," thereby avoiding a more regular alteration of stress at the line's end. Into the second line he inserted the words "great white"—a massive addition in terms of phonological weight, rendering the line completely excessive to the iambic pentameter base still present in the preceding stanza. The third line was initially "singing, singing, singing, so sweet and strong," which could still count as a highly counterpointed iambic line. The fourth "singing" makes that impossible, however, and brings the line into parallel with the fourth line, a full six-beat alexandrine split along the caesura into two measures of potential singing (three beats and an implied rest each). The fourth line was initially "The angels listened and heaven took up his song," which is even more regular. One draft suggests an almost manic desire to have the looping script g's of "singing" override whatever hint there was of iambics:

> Swinging up the golden street, saluting at the [great white] throne
> Singing, singing, singing[, singing] sweet and strong
> Singing, singing, singing, till heaven
> ~~The angels listened and heaven~~ took up his song[51]

"Singing" is at once a narrative intervention, a prosodic intervention at the level of scansion, and a material means of antagonism exercised by Johnson's own hand.

Though lacking the italic lines' direct allusion to musical support, Johnson's transformation of this section of the poem into longer, two-measure lines brings it toward a quasi-musical measure of the sort seen in John Brown's hidden hymnal fourteeners. Insofar as scholars can ever take the progression of drafts as a meaningful process—and given the improvisatory nature of preaching and biblical exegesis, this seems acceptable—one finds that "Saint Peter" contains a transformation within the final quatrain that mirrors (however concealed until now) the poem's hoped-for "crossing over" into a postrevelation, postdiasporic prosody. Indeed, the one variation visible in the transcribed spiritual is the insertion of "Lord" and an accompanying relineation echoing and reconfiguring Johnson's stretched "singing" quatrain:

> *Deep river, my home is over Jordan,*
> *Deep river,*
> *Lord,*
> *I want to cross over into camp-ground.*

Yet the rhythmic and musical convergence of Johnson's sermon-poem and the transcribed spiritual is more asymptotic than suggested by the phrase "heaven took up the song." Johnson's horizon of circulation, including the two hundred people to whom he sent the original printing and the wider audience of the 1935 edition, is hardly equivalent to the "angelic hosts" who take up the spiritual. Babylon is still hovering over prosody, as it does in "Lift Every Voice and Sing" (published in 1901 and also reprinted in 1935): "lest our feet stray from the places ... where we met Thee." All of the anxieties about audience and audition that Johnson expressed throughout his career, beginning with *The Autobiography*—the "long convention" that dictates the hearing of dialect, the continued dependence on the reader's uncertain ear, the figurality of "black music"—persist in the formal fissure between Saint Peter's speech and the italicized song of the unknown soldier. The reader cannot see his "loose, long stride" and cannot hear him "singing clear and strong," and so the new marriage of "singing and swinging" is at once beautiful and phenomenologically obscure.

Johnson's poem charts a trajectory for black poetics between brilliant prosodic satire and the spiritual with which its penultimate stanza closes. The final stanza, an isolated, unheralded sestet, leaves heaven resounding with a rhythm that is neither satire nor spiritual and in fact has no definition at all: a formal embodiment of its final lines, "Something that quivered / 'twixt tears and laughter." "Saint Peter" is a sustained rhythmic exegesis of this amorphous but overdetermined laughter-and-suffering: an analysis via prosody of how both black forms and subjects, whether ragtime, the Negro Gold Star Mothers, or the narrator of *The Autobiography*, circulate in contemporary America. Above all "Saint Peter" must forcibly depart from rhythmic and performative traditions before an alternate phenomenology is in place. This is the lesson taught by *The Autobiography* but in poetic form: its narrator struggling for a musical self-relation free of the veil. Johnson's satirical, rhythmic exegesis of Anglo-American poetics and its "great white" world deprives the poem of such immediacy, focusing but not resolving the struggle for black poetics in a world projecting and consuming alien versions of blackness.

NOTES

1. Johnson, "Preface to the Original Edition," *The Book of American Negro Poetry* (1922), in his *Writings*, ed. William L. Andrews (New York: Library of America, 2004), 713; Hughes, "The Negro Artist and the Racial Mountain," in *Poetry in Theory: An Anthology, 1900–2000*, ed. Jon Cook (Malden, Mass.: Blackwell, 2004), 142.

2. Alain Locke, "Deep River, Deeper Sea: Retrospective Review of the Literature for 1935," *Opportunity* 14 (1935): 10.

3. Friedrich Schlegel calls this a "permanent parabasis." Quoted in Paul de Man, *Aesthetic Ideology* (Minneapolis: University of Minnesota Press, 1996), 178–79.

4. Margetson's poem is excerpted at length in Johnson's *Book of American Negro Poetry*, 109. The speaker calls himself "A rustic ranting rhymer like by chance / Who thinks that he can make the muses dance," treating the poem's own form—based on Wordsworth's stanza from "Resolution and Independence"—as markedly vestigial. But

Margetson reveals that vestigiality to be the product of a poor fit between black vernacular expression and America's desire for a national poetics: "The Scotchman tunes his pipe and drum, / Old Ireland's Harp is never dumb, / We make our rag-time banjo hum / To Uncle Sam's swift pace."

5. "The Dilemma of the Negro Author" (1928), in Johnson, *Writings*, 745.

6. Brown, *Negro Poetry and Drama* (Washington, D.C.: Associates in Negro Folk Education, 1937), 73.

7. "Saint Peter Relates an Incident of the Resurrection Day" was published in 1930 for two hundred recipients.

8. JWJ MSS 49, box 64, folder 261, James Weldon Johnson and Grace Nail Johnson Papers, Beinecke Rare Book and Manuscript Library, Collection of American Literature, Yale University, hereafter JWJ BRBL.

9. It was read this way nonetheless. Newspaper mentions of "Saint Peter" tended to highlight its propagandist punch: "America's unknown soldier may be a Race Man, is the suggestion contained in a new poem" ("Poem by James Weldon John'n Very Revealing," *Chicago Defender*, October 12, 1935).

10. Quoted in Paul de Man, *Rhetoric of Romanticism* (New York: Columbia University Press, 1984), 3. De Man finds Hölderlin's trope to be rhetorically unsustainable, as is the case in *The Autobiography*.

11. James Weldon Johnson, *The Autobiography of an Ex-Colored Man* (1912; rpt., New York: Norton, 2015), 13. Future references are given parenthetically in the text.

12. Noelle Morrissette, *James Weldon Johnson's Modern Soundscapes* (Iowa City: University of Iowa Press, 2013), 61.

13. Specifically, Johnson is referring to the black writer's rhetorical dilemma of whom to address given a biracial audience with "opposite and often antagonistic points of view" ("The Dilemma of the Negro Author," 745).

14. Tsitsi Jaji, "Art Song Poetics: Performing Samuel Coleridge-Taylor's Setting of Paul L. Dunbar's 'A Corn Song,'" *J19: The Journal of Nineteenth-Century Americanists* 1, no. 1 (2013): 202.

15. Morrissette, *Modern Soundscapes*, puts it succinctly: "Sterling Brown, Johnson, and others were wary of the reception of their poetry as pure performance, the response to their use of vernacular as mere vaudeville, mere source, mere transcription, not poetry" (140).

16. JWJ MSS 49, box 50, folder 115, JWJ BRBL.

17. See Jason Rudy, *Electric Meters: Victorian Physiological Poetics* (Athens: Ohio University Press, 2009), on nineteenth-century associations between prosody and electricity. Langston Hughes's 1954 children's book, *The First Book of Rhythms*, invites children to draw a range of oscillating waves and to observe the same in nature.

18. "God's Grandeur," in Hopkins, *Poems and Prose of Gerard Manley Hopkins* (1953; rpt., New York: Penguin, 1985), 27.

19. As Max Cavitch notes in his brilliant essay "Slavery and Its Metrics," in *Cambridge Companion to Nineteenth-Century American Poetry*, ed. Kerry Larson (Cambridge: Cambridge University Press, 2014), the association of "experimental prosody and political liberty" by the mid-nineteenth-century prosodist Sidney Lanier and others made it a challenge to hear in plantation music something more than what

Francis Gummere called "instinctive perception" and "social consent" (103). Cavitch argues, however, that once the audience members' ears are trained away from a mere disdain for repetition, they may feel in it the extreme unnaturalness of forced labor. Audiences must listen, he suggests, not for "metrical iconoclasm" but for the "somatic experience of lasting estrangement" (110). In this passage from *The Autobiography* readers are given a test of tolerance for repetition; clearly the church scene involves literal and figurative repetitions, but it also points to a transcendence of rote repetition, which is difficult to hear because it lacks a new form to contain it.

20. Edwards, "The Seemingly Eclipsed Window of Form: James Weldon Johnson's Prefaces," in *The Jazz Cadence of American Culture*, ed. R. G. O'Meally (New York: Columbia University Press, 1998), 593.

21. Thurman, *The Collected Writings of Wallace Thurman: A Harlem Renaissance Reader*, ed. A. Singh and D. M. Scott (New Brunswick, N.J.: Rutgers University Press, 2003), 185.

22. The speech was first given on July 5, 1852, in Rochester, New York. It was printed as a pamphlet shortly afterward.

23. Ishmael Reed refers, in *Mumbo Jumbo* (1972), to "dazzling parodying punning mischievous pre-Joycean style-play of your Cakewalking." Amiri Baraka notes poignantly: "I find the idea of white minstrels in blackface satirizing a dance satirizing themselves a remarkable kind of irony." Both are quoted in Brooke Baldwin, "The Cakewalk: A Study in Stereotype and Reality," *Journal of Social History* 15, no. 2 (1981): 212.

24. Baldwin, "Cakewalk," 212.

25. Brent Hayes Edwards, *The Practice of Diaspora: Literature, Translation, and the Rise of Black Internationalism* (Cambridge, Mass.: Harvard University Press, 2003), 43.

26. Morrissette, *Modern Soundscapes*, 120.

27. Edwards, "Seemingly Eclipsed Window," 595.

28. Ibid., 580.

29. This is Jacqueline Goldsby's precise characterization of the narrator's effort to be a collector and reproducer of black folk music, an effort foreclosed by the violence of lynching, in her introduction to *The Autobiography of an Ex-Colored Man* (New York: Norton, 2015), xvii.

30. Johnson, preface, *The Book of American Negro Spirituals* (New York: Viking, 1925), 30.

31. JWJ MSS 49, box 59, folder 202, JWJ BRBL.

32. Ibid.

33. Johnson, *Writings*, 840.

34. In her memoir, *Negroland* (New York: Pantheon, 2015), Margo Jefferson gives a poignant example of how the culture of dialect performance has infected black vernacular poetry. She recalls that she and her sister travestied Langston Hughes's "Mother to Son" by hunting for the "I'se" and "dropped *g*s," adding "heavy downbeats" and reading with sustained "mezzo forte." Their mother corrected them by reperforming the poem, mother to daughters, "turning dialect into vernacular" (102–3).

35. An instance reminiscent of Chaucer: "But reader, I have made too long a speech; / hear for yourself the Reverend Jasper preach." JWJ MSS 49, box 59, folder 202, JWJ BRBL.

36. Johnson, *Writings*, 841.
37. Edwards, *Practice of Diaspora*, 41.
38. Johnson, *Writings*, 843.
39. JWJ MSS 49, box 78, folder 573, JWJ BRBL.
40. Ibid.
41. Ibid.
42. Ibid.
43. Material in curly brackets was inserted by Johnson in the manuscript.
44. JWJ MSS 49, box 78, folder 573, JWJ BRBL.
45. Letter from Sterling Brown to Johnson, n.d., JWJ MSS 49, box 4, folder 66, JWJ BRBL.
46. See Sterling Brown, *Outline for the Study of the Poetry of American Negroes* (New York: Harcourt, Brace, 1931), 32.
47. Quoted in Baldwin, "Cakewalk," 215.
48. ¯ = long, ˘ = short. Johnson is more or less converting this pattern into stress: / x x /, with "wingèd" suggested to be bisyllabic. He knew all the Greek quantitative feet, though he correctly considered them irrelevant to the rhythm of English poetry (making such moments all the more curious).
49. Aldon Nielsen, *Writing between the Lines: Race and Intertextuality* (Athens: University of Georgia Press, 1994), 178.
50. Beneath these lines Johnson wrote out a distinctly non-iambic five-stress pattern: ˘ ˘ ¯¯ ˘ ¯¯ ˘ ˘ ¯¯ ˘ ¯¯ ˘ ˘ ¯¯. This pattern of inserted double offstresses nearly matches the alternative that begins "directing and guiding."
51. The last line is crossed out by the loops of the *g* in singing.

The Composer versus the "Perfessor"
Writing Race and (Rag)Time

LORI BROOKS

In the sixth chapter of James Weldon Johnson's *The Autobiography of an Ex-Colored Man*, the protagonist arrives starry-eyed in New York City and offers an account of its black nightlife, including his first encounter with ragtime music: "the stout man at the piano began to run his fingers up and down the keyboard. This he did in a manner that indicated that he was a master of a good deal of technique. Then he began to play; and such playing! ... It was music of a kind I had never heard before. It was music that demanded physical response, patting of the feet, drumming of the fingers, or nodding of the head in time with the beat." Johnson's richly detailed description of the new music highlights all that was novel and even revolutionary about ragtime—its "barbaric harmonies" and "audacious resolutions" featuring "abrupt jump[s] from one key to another." The Ex-Colored Man thrills at the pianistic brilliance of the musician, whose technical facility is more closely associated with the concert hall than the nightclub. Johnson notes with relish that "the dexterity of [the pianist's] left hand in making rapid octave runs and jumps was little short of marvellous; and with his right hand he frequently swept half the keyboard with clean-cut chromatics which he fitted in so nicely as never to fail to arouse in his listeners a sort of pleasant surprise at the accomplishment of the feat." Through the Ex-Colored Man, Johnson puts forward both a definition of ragtime and a sense of the music's awe-inspiring power in the hands of a master. "This," he notes with satisfaction, "was rag-time music."[1]

Central to the Ex-Colored Man's appreciation for the genre's innovations was a notion of ragtime as the source of a distinctly American school of classical composition, a project of redefining ragtime and its potential for a national musical culture that both James Weldon and his brother, John Rosamond, made central to their work from the late 1890s to the second decade of the twentieth century. The "ex-colored" man was one of a number of prototypes of the "Negro composer" that the Johnsons constructed in essays, manifestos on national culture, speeches, and fictional sketches for the stage and page. By moving away from a dominant image of the ragtime "perfessor," an innately musical but unlearned entertainer, to the ragtime professor or "Negro composer," a conservatory-trained interpreter of a musical nationalism, the Johnsons sought to redefine ragtime at a time of heated national debate in the United States about cultural values and morals, the impact of popular culture on Americans, and the political future of African Americans. Johnson's *The Autobiography of an Ex-Colored Man* presented African American music as a historical narrative, documenting the origins and originality of ragtime through a protagonist who, in recognizing the genre's place in the historical evolution of black Americans' history, simultaneously seeks the elevation of ragtime and his own status as a music professional. At the same time, Johnson's narrative argues for the instrumentality of ragtime in facilitating modern America's interpretation of itself.

Johnson's attention to pianistic technique, directed through his narrator's observation of ragtime, marks his own roots as a student of the piano, an instrument that played a central role in his artistic development and even more for Rosamond. Like many Victorian homes, the Johnsons' parlor contained a piano, an instrument that they and most Americans in this period saw as representing the highest attainment of musical skill. Growing up in Jacksonville, Florida, the boys vied over which brother had the best piano skills, a contest that Rosamond won. He would go on to attend the New England Conservatory of Music in Boston and to demonstrate his skills as a pianist and arranger in the fields of classical and popular music. The brothers' rivalry also centered on which could beat the other in acquiring the latest popular march or clever tune. James recalled introducing his brother to a musical selection he had found in the newspaper and torturing Rosamond by refusing to reveal his source. As adults, they became collaborators rather than competitors, forming a unique team among American songwriters. As the Cole-Johnson Trio, the brothers and Bob Cole found unparalleled success among African American composers in Tin Pan Alley, New York City's collection of music publishing firms; however, they remain mostly unsung in the history of popular songwriting in the United States. By the end of the nineteenth century, Tin Pan Alley had transformed not only American tastes and appetites for popular songs but also the methods by which popular songs were promoted in national theaters and music halls and mass marketed to the American public. Although their collaboration lasted for little more than a decade, the trio penned numerous popular songs together, and by the first blush of the twentieth century they could boast of having a song in nearly every hit musical theater production in Manhattan. "The three of us worked as one man," James recalled, and "with an almost complete absence of pride of authorship," making them frequently unsure about what role each had played in the final product. Often, two of the composers worked as a pair while the third acted as "a sort of critic and adviser," a collaborating style that, to Johnson's knowledge, was unique among Tin Pan Alley songwriters.[2] By 1903, the Cole-Johnson combination had secured a status as one of the most successful songwriting partnerships, black or white, of Tin Pan Alley's first golden age. Between 1898 and 1905 the trio held the record for more "successful coon [sic] songs and march songs, as well as ballads, than any other men in the profession," surpassing even the prolific white songwriter Harry Von Tilzer with more than two hundred songs.[3]

James would soon turn his attention to literature and politics, but it was largely his role that gave the trio a reputation for writing what one journalist referred to as "literary ragtime," songs that retained a "racial" flavor without the crude stereotypes of blacks found in other ragtime songs. Sometimes referred to as "coon" songs, this wildly popular style of Tin Pan Alley song traded in stereotypes of black men as violent and oversexed idlers and black women as coldhearted and materialistic. In James's absence, Rosamond and Cole continued as a songwriting and performance duo, maintaining the trio's singular style of collaboration. Each man's special talents as a lyricist or composer enhanced the work of his partner; they continued to work so closely as to make it difficult, a contemporary noted, to tell where one talent ended and the other began.[4] At a time when African American men rarely performed on stage without blackface—a holdover from nineteenth-century minstrelsy—Cole and Rosamond formed a high-class vaudeville act in 1902, appearing onstage in full evening dress with a grand piano, both rarities in vaudeville. Cole and Johnson's "pianologue" combined dialogue and music, not only their own compositions but also classical pieces for piano, ballads, and other song selections. As James noted in his memoir, the duo's trademark tuxedoes and grand piano became much emulated in early twentieth-century vaudeville.[5]

With such credentials, the Johnson brothers had earned the right to advance arguments about ragtime's cultural value to the nation. But as ragtime's popularity waned, most young Americans were ignorant of the music's true racial origins. By the 1910s, ragtime had been identified with songs like Irving Berlin's "Alexander's Ragtime Band," a 1911 sensation of Tin Pan Alley's second generation and a tune with only muted references to African American themes and folk elements. Although some historians of ragtime have disavowed the genre's roots in African American folk music, the Johnsons in their day put forth the argument that ragtime's true roots lay in the folk rhythms of antebellum African American music and dance.[6]

Syncopation—a rhythmic swing in which accented beats fall outside the primary four-beat meter of the music—was ragtime's most characteristic feature. Ragtime syncopation, as Johnson's Ex-Colored Man describes it, featured "intricate rhythms in which the accents fell in the most unexpected places, but in which the beat was never lost" (*The Autobiography*, 99). Chroniclers of the music of enslaved people had attempted to describe black polyrhythms and syncopation, but most Americans had heard little of it in the days before the development of sound recording. In the last decades of the nineteenth century, syncopated rhythm was perceived as a novel musical element that distinguished ragtime from other styles of popular music. Although today it has become so customary as to be almost unnoticeable, in an essay on the genre's potential as a national music, Rosamond astutely elided ragtime's roots in both African American vice districts and Tin Pan Alley's "coon song" craze of the mid-1890s, even glossing over the midwestern school of "classic" piano rags epitomized by the African American pianist and composer Scott Joplin in the same period.[7] Ragtime's deeper roots, Rosamond argued, could be found in the cultural forms that emerged from antebellum slavery, from, as he described it, the foot patting of the "old darkey" while strumming on his banjo accompanied by the syncopated hand clapping of "pickaninnies."[8] In support of his argument, he included a musically notated example of how this rhythmic counterpoint sounded for readers unfamiliar with African American forms of syncopation. Ragtime, he argued, was a joyous expression of black people embracing their freedom, the affective counterpart to the spirituals. When sung in all-black contexts, the spirituals sounded "the note in music which is not heard with the ears" (*The Autobiography*, 178), as the Ex-Colored Man describes it, an elegiacal "testament to black suffering under slavery" that the African American intellectual W. E. B. Du Bois, a contemporary of the Johnson brothers, referred to as "sorrow songs."[9] This idea appears in both Rosamond's treatise on ragtime and James's writings about music, including through the character of the Ex-Colored Man.

The sense of newness that facilitated ragtime's rise to popularity jolted Americans out of their aural complacency, fomenting a radical shift in the way audiences heard music and how they responded to it. The impact of black syncopated music on turn-of-the-twentieth-century aurality has yet to be comprehended and appreciated. A century after its publication, Johnson's novel urges readers to reattune to ragtime as a revolution in sound in the waning years of the nineteenth century and the first two decades of the twentieth. The author's characterization of ragtime and his construction of the Ex-Colored Man as the archetype of the modern American cultural hero resonates with both James's and Rosamond's views on ragtime, race, and national culture, expressed in their antiracist intellectual and artistic projects preceding the Harlem/New Negro Renaissance of the 1920s. The project to elevate ragtime to the status of a national classical music was a shared mission, then, inaugurated not with Johnson's novel but with the work of the Cole-Johnson Trio dating back to the late 1890s. After Cole's untimely death in 1911, the project reached a crescendo in the brothers' mature careers and became the heart of a collective manifesto that was for them central to the race question. As they argued, the future of African American culture hinged on the status of blacks within the broader national cultural life and was inextricably linked to the larger question of the political status of blacks in the United States.

The War against Ragtime

By the end of the nineteenth century, ragtime emerged as central to larger cultural and political debates about the impact of industrialization and urbanization on modern life and especially the aesthetic value and impact of African American culture on Americans as a whole. Such debates were not only cultural but racial and thus political, centering on the question of the role that African American culture—and, more important, African American *people*—would play in the nation. The exponential growth of mass-marketed popular culture, the increased migration of African Americans to northern cities, and the impact of northern forms of discrimination and racial segregation were all deeply intertwined in these debates. But these debates also referenced the more abstract question about which forms of culture best represented the United States and the broader issue of the professionalization of American musicians and where to draw the line—if one needed to be drawn—between their identity as artists and as laborers. Such ideological position-taking often centered on the role of ragtime in the repertoires of American musicians and the meaning of its popularity among the American public.

From the late 1890s until well into the next century, newspapers regularly featured stories about the impact of ragtime on Americans' taste in music. Often such stories were tied to the actions of local and national musical societies that had "banned" the performance of ragtime by their members or decried the public's demand for ragtime from white bands and orchestras. Musicians unions and other music and dance associations weighed in on the impact of ragtime's popularity. In 1902, the *New York Sun* noted an "acute" split among the ranks of the Chicago Federation of Musicians over ragtime, a divide that had led the Denver branch of the American Federation of Musicians to pass a resolution the prior year condemning ragtime and recommending that its members cease playing it. The Dancing Teachers Association of America and the National Music Teachers Association joined in the outcry with the latter organization vowing "to discourage the use of ragtime in every manner possible."[10] The backlash against ragtime, which continued long after the genre's decline, had less to do with changing musical tastes among Americans than the fact that American musicians (many of them displaced by Europeans in American orchestras) were willing to meet that demand for the purposes of work as well as their own enjoyment. The ragtime "craze" served as an opportunity to bring to the fore questions of musical taste and aesthetics, but was inextricably linked to the perceived value of black culture in the United States. The professionalization of American musicians and the question of whether they were artists or laborers—central issues to musicians unions in this period—were bound up in ragtime as a discourse of race and aesthetics.

The American Federation of Musicians had declared a "state of emergency" in 1901 and, in a futile effort, banned the public playing of ragtime by its members. The union, founded in 1896, framed its dissent by blaming an uneducated musical public who compromised the talent and professionalization of classical musicians by demanding to hear ragtime. Significantly, attitudes toward ragtime racialized the discourse of professionalism among American musicians, as union officials counterposed the artistic enlightenment and education of American audiences to the "denigrating" influence of ragtime as a music rooted in African American vice districts. On the local and the national level, musicians unions and neighborhood and municipal music societies saw ragtime as a music that degraded the tastes of Americans. Their mission, as they saw it, was to "protect" and educate the tastes of American audiences. "The musicians know what is good," they desperately claimed, "and if the people don't, we will have to teach them." One reader protested, "Leave us our 'Coal Black Lady.'"[11] As the historian George Seltzer has noted, American musicians perceived themselves as being under attack in the musical marketplace. Many were loath to see themselves as laborers in the traditional trade unionist sense, even though they, like other American workers, suffered from inadequate pay and job shortages. In the 1870s and 1880s, many American musicians struggled to protect their jobs against the double threat of European musicians and amateurs. The latter, which included popular musicians, were referred to as "imposters and impecunious musical quacks."[12] The National League of Musicians, the most effective American musicians union at the end of the nineteenth century, had passed a resolution against ragtime in 1886, appealing to musicians' local solidarity and national allegiance by making both foreigners and itinerant musicians suspect. The resolution was an attempt to push out those musicians considered to be less skilled but who were, in actuality, viable threats in the music job market. Amid arguments claiming that musicians were artists, not laborers, the league split over the question of whether to join the larger labor movement. The defectors formed the American Federation of Musicians. In the attempt to extricate ragtime from the repertoires of unionized classical musicians, ragtime was made to signify a crisis in taste, education, and skill among the American musical public.

The culture war over ragtime—which claimed that it degraded the musical skills of otherwise well-trained musicians—was based on the racist assumption that because this music was "black," it was therefore neither serious nor valuable. But regardless of the views of the genre's musical value, ragtime was in demand, and much of the furor had to do with the fact that many musicians were willing to comply with that demand. Within a broader discourse of modern life, aesthetic taste, and social and moral degeneracy, ragtime shaped the professionalization of American musicians at the turn of the twentieth century even though musical standard-bearers saw the syncopated music of the African American tradition as reflecting the demeaned tastes of an emerging popular music industry and an inferior race. There were, however, exceptions. Although he believed that most musicians no more noticed ragtime than "if it were the beating of tom-toms outside a side-show," Hiram Moderwell, the music critic for the *New Republic*, credited the genre as being "the one original and indigenous type of music of the American people."[13]

Elevating Ragtime and Writing African American History

The trajectory of James Weldon Johnson's thinking on national culture can be traced back to his brief career as a Tin Pan Alley lyricist before his emergence as a national race activist, literary figure, and architect of the Harlem/New Negro Renaissance. Almost unchanged, many of the arguments central to Johnson's larger thesis resurfaced as shaping forces of 1920s black modernism, and Johnson, now an elder statesman of African American culture and politics, began to steer black artists of the Harlem/New Negro Renaissance toward using black folk forms as the basis of their art. In the preface to his *Book of American Negro Poetry* (1922), Johnson argued, "A people may become great through many means, but there is only one measure by which its greatness is recognized and acknowledged. The final measure of the greatness of all peoples is the amount and standard of the literature and art they have produced. The world does not know that a people is great until that people produces great literature and art. No people that has produced great literature and art has ever been looked upon by the world as distinctly inferior."[14]

Johnson saw what he referred to as the "art approach to the race question" as the path of "least friction."[15] In other words, in the rare moments when African Americans were credited with making *any* contribution to American culture, most often it was for their work in music, dance, and humor. The most effective way, then, for African Americans to combat accusations of intellectual inferiority was to persuade nonwhite Americans—and even other African Americans—that black people had the capacity to produce great art. White imitations of black cultural forms, Johnson argued, more often than not resulted in condescending depictions of black intellect, inauthentic and forced representations of what Johnson perceived to be an "innate" black gaiety, and denigrating forms of mimicry. Whites regularly criticized conservatory-educated African Americans for incorporating European classical techniques into their work (from spirituals to the cakewalk and ragtime), decrying what they perceived to be the imitative nature of blacks, who destroyed the authenticity of African American culture with poor versions of European and European American culture. Yet, Johnson noted, the history of white appropriations of black culture in minstrelsy, ragtime, and popular dance revealed that whites, not blacks, were the real imitators.[16] Johnson's Ex-Colored Man addresses this paradox. When he wonders whether education might enhance or destroy his beloved pianist's facility with ragtime, he determines that the musician would become either a mere imitator of Western greats or an atonal musical modernist who "avoid[s] melody." Neither outcome was satisfactory, and neither would be as "delightful" as the pianist's untutored version of ragtime (*The Autobiography*, 102). But after performing for a European audience, the Ex-Colored Man witnesses a European classical musician transform the ragtime he has just played into classical music. "It can be done," he determines. "Why can't I do it?" (142). From this point the Ex-Colored Man sets himself on a path to elevate ragtime to the status of an American classical music.

Johnson returned repeatedly to the argument that African Americans had taken the raw materials of European culture and transfused them with the distinctive and characteristic elements of their own culture, creating something that had become identified in an international context as "American." To prove that African American culture was the nation's true indigenous folk culture was to demonstrate how blacks in the United States had not simply assimilated the best of Western religious, political, and cultural values but had contributed a unique ability to distinctively imbue other forms of culture with their own. Like a black musician ragging the classics, this transmuting quality adapted the raw materials of other cultures into something completely distinct but identifiably African American.[17] Johnson offered an example of this when he explained in a 1936 speech how he developed the voice of the black preacher in his poem *God's Trombones*. He described the preacher's voice as evolving not from "exterior" perceptions of black comicality rooted in popular racist forms of American culture but from the imagined interiority of the black preacher, who sought "to give an art-governed expression to the dream he strove to utter."[18] By creating a "white-skinned" black character in *The Autobiography*, Johnson suggested that the artistic expression of this interiority was closely tied to the power of individuals to articulate their own racial alliances rather than allow society to dictate their views for them.

In his speeches and writings, Johnson returned repeatedly to three primary arguments supporting this idea: African Americans had made significant and racially distinctive contributions to the American culture; peoples were known and respected largely as a result of the quality of the art they produced; and if such contributions remained unrecognized within the nation, then the artistic impact of African American culture must be assessed from a transnational perspective. In Johnson's estimation, the most important of these racial contributions to the national culture were the spirituals that emerged from slavery, the Uncle Remus stories, ragtime music, and the comic cakewalk, an antebellum black dance that mocked the pretensions of whites. As "the popular medium for our national expression," ragtime had been "all-conquering," known throughout the world and associated with the United States more than any other genre of music. For these reasons, ragtime was quintessentially "American" to Johnson.[19]

Almost word for word, the Ex-Colored Man voices the same arguments as James Weldon Johnson and his brother, Rosamond. Both brothers published important early compilations of African American poetry and folk music in the 1920s: James put out *The Book of American Negro Poetry* in 1922 and wrote the prefaces for *The Book of American Negro Spirituals* and *The Second Book of American Negro Spirituals*, a two-volume compilation that he coedited with Rosamond in 1925 and 1926. Their treatises about black art in the United States became opportunities to reiterate the above-mentioned arguments about the centrality of African American folk culture to U.S. national culture. Using the comparatively highbrow contexts of poetry and classically arranged folk music, James and Rosamond sought to rectify the public's association of ragtime with lowbrow culture, namely, its brothel origins and its association with Tin Pan Alley. In another setting, James decried the idea that ragtime's "vulgar" origins justified its dismissal as a nationally representative music, calling such notions "a most absurd standard of criticism."[20] In this context, James responded directly to the public criticism of his thesis by the influential American music critic Henry Krehbiel who, though he authored one of the earliest studies of African American music, referred to ragtime as a "degraded form of music."[21] Krehbiel had chided Johnson for eliding the subject of ragtime's brothel roots, neglecting the importance of spirituals, and giving ragtime undue emphasis in his preface to his collection of African American poetry. In essence, Krehbiel sought to challenge Johnson's central argument that ragtime was a form of African American folk music.

James addressed Krehbiel's criticisms in the *New York Tribune* in 1922 but more fully in his preface to Rosamond's collection of spirituals. There, he took issue with the notion that spirituals were imitations of European music, noting that there was never a question of the spirituals' black origins until their "beauty and value" had been demonstrated. The same forces of racism, he insisted, were at work in those who doubted the role of African Americans as the "originator[s] of America's popular medium of expression."[22] By drawing a parallel between the spirituals and African American secular music, Johnson was able to make the claim that the different rhythms or swing between the two genres had much to do with the needs they filled for African Americans: the former largely psychological and the latter physical. As he noted,

"Religious ecstasy fittingly manifests itself in swaying heads and bodies; the emotions that call for hand and foot patting [in secular music] are pleasure, humor, hilarity, love, just the joy of being alive." In both genres, the prevailing practice was for the pianist to play with the fundamental beat, "pounding it out with his left hand" while juggling it with his right.[23] Echoing his protagonist, Johnson cites ragtime's "bizarre harmonies, its audacious resolutions often consisting of an abrupt jump from one key to another, its intricate rhythms in which the accents fall in the most unexpected places but in which the fundamental beat is never lost" (*The Autobiography*, 95).

The real question was whether Americans would accept ragtime as "American" and place its characteristic musical elements in classical settings.

The Evolution of Ragtime

Central to the Cole-Johnson Trio's approach to songwriting was an effort to rid "Negro dialect" songs from both buffoonish humor and cloying sentimentalism. Cole noted, "What we aim to do . . . is evolve a type of music that will have all that is distinct in the old Negro music and yet which shall be sophisticated enough to appeal to the cultured musician. We want the Negro spirit—its warmth and its originality—to color our music; we want to retain its marked rhythms; but we are trying to get away from the minor strain that used to dominate it."[24] Their music had too much artistic merit to be dismissed as just another "coon song," and they sought to rescue the genre from Tin Pan Alley hacks and the forces of mass production, entities that increasingly tried to push culturally irrelevant material down Americans' throats. Others agreed. "There is hope for the 'rag-time' ditty after all," said one critic, calling Cole and Johnson "the musical Moses to lead the 'coon song' into the Promised Land!"[25]

By adopting a more literary style and the techniques of European classical music, the trio sought to move beyond the limitations that James perceived in the work of Paul Laurence Dunbar, the recognized poet laureate of African Americans at the turn of the century. Dunbar's use of black dialect read inauthentically to Johnson, and he felt that his friend could not achieve sentiment without catering to the extreme poles of humor and pathos. African American artists must, he believed, imbue African American folk speech with a greater elasticity and emotional depth while retaining an authentic black voice.[26] As a duo, Cole and Rosamond Johnson hewed closely to the same belief. "We try to write in our songs the finer feelings of the colored race," Cole remarked to the press, because the black man has his sentimental side "just as the white man has." In contrast to the rough and coarse qualities of commercial "coon songs," "we try to retain the racial traits, not only in the syncopated time of the music, but in the lyrics as well, and want the verses to sound as well recited as when sung."[27] James's poetic skills had been crucial to the Cole-Johnson Trio's early success and their ability to raise the standard of Tin Pan Alley's black-themed songs. It was a role that he felt he could not commit sufficient time to but that he approached with great seriousness.[28]

In their quest to nudge the public's taste away from "coon songs" and eventually to a classical American music, the trio's artistic project fell in line with ideals established by Antonín Dvořák during his tenure at the National Conservatory of Music in New York between 1892 and 1895. Harry T. Burleigh and Will Marion Cook had studied there, as had other leading African American classical performers like the organist and pianist Melville Charlton and the soprano Deseria Plato. For a time Burleigh taught voice there, likely the first African American faculty member at a white conservatory in the United States. As a student, Burleigh was said to have sung the songs of southern slaves to the Bohemian composer in his studio and was credited with making Dvořák familiar with Negro spirituals. Burleigh became a well-regarded arranger of spirituals, placing them in art-song settings so that classical musicians could perform them alongside a European classical repertoire. Dvořák counseled young American composers of all races to draw on the folk material of African Americans. Dvořák believed that American composers could create a native classical music by imbuing their work with the folk spirit of the indigenous musical cultures, and African American folk culture should be one of these indigenous sources. Although he did not advocate direct quotations from folk music, he did quote the spiritual "Goin' Home" in his symphony *From the New World*. Dvořák set out to prove that composers could integrate the spirit of this music into their compositions without amateurishly relying on direct quotations of African American folk music.[29]

In an attempt to avoid the stereotypical trappings of the "coon song," Rosamond put forth an elitist definition of ragtime that served as the musical equivalent of social programs of racial uplift. In doing so, he not only disregarded the music's living folk roots but also ragtime's black working-class roots in urban brothels and saloons across the nation. In "Why They Call American Music Ragtime," published in the *New York Age* in 1908, Rosamond described ragtime as "a slang name for that peculiarly, distinctive, syncopated rhythm originated by the American Negro. And not until it reaches that higher development, only to be accomplished by scholarly musicians, will it be called 'ragtime.'"[30] Like the Spanish bolero, Rosamond argued, ragtime was a genre without respect in its own country, even though both types of syncopated music served as the direct and indirect expression of the national folk music. Here, Dvořák's ideas greatly influenced Johnson's approach to music composition. Based on a belief that a national culture could only be built on the culture of a people rooted in the soil of a country (an argument advanced by the German philosopher Johann Gottfried Herder), Rosamond described syncopated music as "the direct expressions of the American peasant, the Negro."

In alignment with the racial uplift ideology, the two poles of this folk culture were the "light-hearted" expressions found in ragtime and the more serious, plaintive plantation and jubilee songs of the African Americans of the slavery and Reconstruction eras.[31]

To dismiss the brothers' mission as simple elitism would be erroneous. They consciously positioned themselves within the field of professional musicians and literary artists not to distance themselves from their roots in popular musical theater and Tin Pan Alley but rather to angle for particular levels of national recognition. They sought, first, the recognition that African American folk music is the legitimate indigenous folk music of the United States; second, the (re)insertion of African Americans into the history of American musical life; and finally, to lay the groundwork for the argument that African Americans would uniquely and disproportionately benefit from music education. These ideas were clearly articulated in Rosamond's work, and the brothers often made similar arguments about race and national culture, applying them to whatever project they were working on at the moment in their respective fields of music and literature.

The Autobiography of an Ex-Colored Man was James's effort to make the argument through literature about recognizing certain forms of ragtime as art and their creators as representative of African Americans' talents. This novel was a materialization of his oft-stated belief that "the final measure of the greatness of all peoples is the amount and standard of the literature and art they have produced."[32] The Johnson brothers also understood their work as having a "direct bearing on the most vital of American problems."[33] If the argument of black inferiority could be dismantled, then the United States would be forced to reassess its view of African Americans. Beginning at least in 1898, James would constantly reiterate that no great people ever existed who did not have a coherent written history.[34] In countless essays, articles, and public speeches, he repeated the idea that recuperating a history was crucial to the advancement of the race, especially because African Americans had been denied a place in U.S. history because their labor and culture had been repeatedly appropriated to suit the needs and desires of whites. This had been noted, although obliquely, as part of his experience as a songwriter in Tin Pan Alley. "The status of the Negro in the United States," he argued, "is more a question of national mental attitude toward the race than of actual conditions."[35] Americans were already forgetting that ragtime originated with African Americans, and whites were rapidly appropriating jazz as well. For Johnson, one consequence of not knowing the racial history of syncopated music would be the erasure of African American genius. Europeans were identifying ragtime and jazz as "American music" without adding any racial signifiers, which seemed to offer third-party validation of the distinctiveness and aesthetic value of African American culture but also threatened to write that very culture out of U.S. history or to dismiss it as a mere imitation of white culture. To insist on the truth of the music's origins was, then, to seize upon a golden moment to frame a larger antiracist argument concerning Jim Crow segregation, racial violence, and the denial of African Americans' civil rights. To reframe U.S. racial history in this way was to control the discussion of race, national culture, and national progress.

For Bob Cole and Rosamond Johnson, the way to remind their public was to write the history of African Americans into their music, repeatedly using their compositions as knowledge-producing devices and as cultural histories. By insisting on the black origins of ragtime, African Americans could avoid becoming mired in the same debate about origins that surrounded the spirituals, for example, and the revisionist history that had begun as early as the 1890s with ragtime songs. Also at stake was the issue of financial remuneration for the work of African American artists, an issue that vexed the black composer Will Marion Cook until the end of his life. Black songwriters were regularly cheated out of the "products of their mind," as Cole described the theft of his compositions and sketches while performing with the famed Black Patti Troubadours.[36] In his 1908 essay, Rosamond noted, "In the days of slavery I would have known nothing of the science of music, and some man like [Stephen] Foster might have written down my expressions in music just as I have done for many white song writers of to-day, who were unable to write music for themselves."[37] This was true. Gussie Davis was said to have paid a white man to transcribe his songs for him because he could not read music, while other black songwriters never committed their songs to paper for fear that they would be stolen. Ragtime and jazz pianist Eubie Blake published two of his rags with Joseph Stern and Company without reading the fine print of the contract. "I signed a contract that left all the recording rights for the publishers. They used to do things like that to us—we didn't know any better." Blake added that some of the pieces African American musicians played for publishers would be written down by a hidden transcriber and stolen outright by the publisher.[38] Blake's memory of being deceived by white publishers left him so disgusted that he hardly ever performed the two pieces he published with Stern.

The Johnson brothers were aware of this from the moment they embarked on their careers as songwriters. Their first summer in New York, the Johnson brothers met the light opera composer Reginald De Koven and the librettist-lyricist Harry B. Smith while playing selections from their opera for Isidore Witmark, one of Tin Pan Alley's leading music publishers. The men had suggested the trio play something for them, adding kiddingly that they "might be able to steal something from it." Having been forewarned about the possibility of theft, the brothers made a quick exit. James Weldon Johnson dismissed the incident as an example of their naïveté in the early years and as something they joked about later with Smith and De Koven. But early in their collaboration, the trio was surprised at how little they netted from their royalties, despite the fact that the popular white comedic actress May Irwin was among the first to sing their songs. Despondent when they learned they had overdrawn their account with Joseph Stern and Company by $1500, Cole and Rosamond wondered aloud about what to do. As the story went, the more philosophical James questioned whether they had to do anything, insisting, "I think we've done very well. As far as I can see our publishers are the ones to worry."[39] Although the incident was presented as a lighthearted tale—a human interest story about familiar figures—for struggling songwriters, especially African Americans and those without musical training, theft was a real and pervasive problem that literally took money out of their pockets.

As part of their mission of depicting the interiority of African Americans, the trio emphasized songs that presented black music as a historical narrative, documenting ragtime as the creation of African Americans and presenting blacks as capable of originality rather than as imitators. Cole's and the Johnson brothers' argument complements those of James's protagonist in *The Autobiography of an Ex-Colored Man*, particularly in those moments when the Ex-Colored Man observes African American life as an insider. As Cole remarked, "Negro music is undergoing a constant change, still it retains some traits of every period, from 'savage' or 'jungle' music of Africa, to the music of the slave plantation, ragtime's first gasp of freedom from slavery, and the Negro's coming into his own as a ragtime composer."[40] Cole and Johnson drew attention to their piece "The Evolution of the Negro" in Marc Klaw and A. L. Erlanger's *Mr. Bluebeard*, which they described as a "regular jungle song with its boom-boom accompaniment like the pounding of log drums" and which traced African American history "up through all the stages of the Negro development as shown in his music." When a journalist asked if it would be psychological as well as musical, Cole agreed, "Yes, that's the idea. We will treat this theme in all the ways Negro music has been known—in the Jim Crow style, the Stephen Foster manner, the march song, and so on until it reaches the cakewalk period with all its exuberance. Beginning plaintively it will [grow] brighter and brighter until it becomes the joyous thing we have now."[41]

James Weldon Johnson used his novel to dramatize the broad contours of this debate. Ragtime's place in the cultural hierarchy, white appropriations of black cultural forms, and the question of whether a music that has both folk sources and commercial appeal could function as the true musical representation of "American" culture all served as thematic pivot points. While working as the personal musician to a wealthy white man, the Ex-Colored Man tellingly achieves clarity as to his own purpose and the racial and aesthetic importance of ragtime, taking on from abroad the debates that raged in the

United States. This is significant because central to Johnson's argument about ragtime's value was that Europeans championed the music as both "art" and "American." As the Ex-Colored Man notes, "Whatever is *popular* is spoken of as not worth the while." Nevertheless, "nothing great or enduring, especially in music, has ever sprung full-fledged and unprecedented from the brain of any master" (*The Autobiography*, 100). Through his protagonist, Johnson also remarks on the bans placed on ragtime by musicians and music teachers in the United States, official prohibitions whose failure was imminent, in his opinion, because of the "one strong element of greatness" that ragtime possessed: that it "appeals universally" (100).

Rosamond supplemented his brother's arguments in the field of music as he gained even greater fame in the music world after Cole's death in 1911. Following a stint in the military during World War I, he entered a new phase of his career in which he developed national and international influence as a pianist, singer, and music educator. From 1912 to 1914, he served as the musical director of London's Hammerstein Opera House with the specific mission of developing ragtime by using Western classical techniques and then served as the director of the Colored Music Settlement in New York City from 1914 to 1918. In the African American *New York Age*, Rosamond Johnson laid out his argument for a reevaluation of ragtime's value on paper, which was directed at the white music intelligentsia who believed that what had been put forth as "Negro music" in the United States had largely derived from European and European American music and that African American folk music was no more representative of the United States than other "American" folk musics, including Euro-American and Native American musical traditions.[42] At the core of Johnson's rebuttal was a threefold argument: *all* national musics had "lowly" origins among the peasants and the folk; the musical elements of ragtime were, like European folk idioms, characteristic enough to serve as a national folk music; and even if white composers were unwilling to do so, African Americans were at a stage in their historical evolution as a people to develop ragtime as a national classical music.

Comparing ragtime to the Spanish bolero, as already mentioned, Rosamond drew parallels between that European folk form and African American folk music, observing that both styles of music had originated among the peasant class and had been used to accompany "sensuous" forms of dance that aristocratic elements of each society considered repugnant. Despite this, the bolero had emerged as a defining musical idiom of Spain, and ragtime, he asserted, could do the same in the United States. Echoing his brother's argument, Rosamond noted, "Likewise, with American music, as it is known here and the world over, it is the direct expression of the American peasant, the Negro." And like James, Rosamond identified both the plaintive sounds of the spirituals and the syncopation of ragtime as "the only music that the musical centers of the world and the great musicians of the world recognize as American music."[43] In his call for American composers to draw on ragtime, Rosamond carefully accented his brother's ideas, especially the argument that African Americans should be recognized in their own country for the unique gifts they had given to the broader national culture; they had not simply absorbed the cultural, religious, and moral lessons of living in the United States but had made key contributions to the country's culture. He then compared these contributions to those of Native Americans, whom he dismissed as a "morbid" and unmusical race that had not produced anything on the level of the spirituals "Go Down Moses" and "Steal Away." "Had they been set to the broken rhythm of two beats in one measure, five in the next and so on, with the discordant harmonies known as Indian music, they would never have caught the ear of the American people. And if there is to be such a thing as American music it must be a music that the American people enjoy." Americans loved the song "Dixie," he noted, because it was a typical African American tune; ragtime, invested with authentic black folk music, in turn created an authentic American musical form.[44]

If James embodied his protagonist's literary aspirations, Rosamond as a composer, arranger, and educator was the Ex-Colored Man's musical counterpart, the "Negro composer" who often appeared in the brothers' musical plays who used his art to elevate black music to national prominence and respectability. Rosamond performed and arranged spirituals in recitals with the singer Taylor Gordon, and his Colored Music Settlement had as its mission the development of musical talent among black youth. By drawing a historical trajectory that emphasized the links between the folk work of slaves and the modern musical compositions of educated black musicians, Rosamond made two primary assertions: the roots of ragtime, even as a popular music, could be found in the folk culture of enslaved black people, and a conservatory education did not dilute African American composers nor make them second-rate derivatives of European musicians. Rather, they were uniquely capable of musically interpreting Americans to themselves. Had he been born in slavery, Rosamond Johnson observed, he would have been ignorant of the science of music, but as a former student of the New England Conservatory of Music, he had knowledge of music theory and the compositional techniques of European masters. Blacks no longer needed to look to whites to create a record of their historical musical progress. In a strategy of reversal, Rosamond also noted that as a representative of the modern, conservatory-educated "Negro composer," he now had the compositional technique and music theory not only to compose his own music but to perform that same service for uneducated white musicians. Rosamond obliquely addressed the issue of whites' appropriation of black music: the historical theft of black music by whites had led Americans to believe that black music was really white but, he artfully noted, much of his work as a music professional entailed transcribing music for white clients who did not have the education to do so themselves. In this configuration, European Americans, despite their association with a dominant European classical music culture, needed at times to rely on black musicians to record their musical ideas for posterity.

Despite the work of black songwriters like Cole and the Johnson brothers, history has largely written them out of Tin Pan Alley. As Johnson feared, U.S. national memory of early ragtime has failed to take into account the music produced by the various Cole-Johnson combinations and the invisible work that they and other African Americans performed for white productions as writers, editors, and arrangers of popular music in Tin Pan Alley and musical theater.[45] The brothers' later accomplishments in civil rights and in musical performance, education, and theater have eclipsed their Tin Pan Alley success in the memory of African Americans. Yet their writings on musical culture, with *The Autobiography of an Ex-Colored Man* at the center, provide an important corrective to the history of ragtime, one in which the composer—the music professional rather than the untutored "perfessor"—advances musical composition, musical professionalization, and the reassessment of black cultural contributions in writing and interpreting America.

NOTES

1. James Weldon Johnson, *The Autobiography of an Ex-Colored Man* (1912; rpt., New York: Hill and Wang, 1960), 98–99. Future references to this work are provided parenthetically in the text. I reference the anonymously published 1912 edition in order to emphasize Johnson's intentional creation of a protagonist who moves between black and white worlds and both culturally and physically between the United States and Europe. The Ex-Colored Man's initially ambiguous racial identity uniquely reinforces Johnson and his brother's argument that black people can easily move between European classical music and African American popular music and do so with just as much authenticity as white American composers. As well, the 1912 publication appeared at the moment of ragtime's demise and jazz's emergence as the culturally defining genre of black life in the United States. Ragtime's legacy and how the story of its origins was told was most crucial at this moment.

2. James Weldon Johnson, *Along This Way: The Autobiography of James Weldon Johnson* (1933; rpt. New York: Da Capo, 1991), 156.

3. *Los Angeles Herald*, February 26, 1905, 35.

4. "The Negro a Composer," *Cleveland Plain Dealer*, undated clipping, James Weldon Johnson and Grace Nail Johnson Papers, Beinecke Rare Book and Manuscript Library, Yale University, hereafter JWJ BRBL.

5. Johnson, *Along This Way*, 187–88.

6. Edward A. Berlin, for instance, argues against the idea of ragtime as a compilation of African American folk tunes, especially because most of the melodies strung together into a piano rag cannot be traced to specific folk songs. See Berlin, *Ragtime: A Musical and Cultural History* (Berkeley: University of California Press, 1980). Johnson's argument, however, is not that these melodies have recognizable roots in black folk tunes but that they convey a folk spirit, especially with their reliance on black syncopation.

7. J. Rosamond Johnson, "Why They Call American Music Ragtime," *New York Age*, December 24, 1908, 2.

8. Ibid.

9. W. E. B. Du Bois, *The Souls of Black Folk* (1903; New York: Dover, 1994), 155.

10. "Ragtime Older than Man," *New York Sun*, March 14, 1902, 8.

11. *American Musician* (July 1901), quoted in Karl Koenig, *Jazz in Print, 1859–1929* (Hillsdale, N.Y.: Pendragon, 2002), 63.

12. George Seltzer, *Music Matters: The Performer and the American Federation of Musicians* (Metuchen, N.J.: Scarecrow, 1989), 6.

13. "The Case of Ragtime," *New York Tribune*, July 15, 1917, 38; Moderwell, "Ragtime," *New Republic*, October 16, 1915, 284–86.

14. James Weldon Johnson, ed., *The Book of American Negro Poetry* (1922; rpt., New York: Harcourt, Brace, 1931), vii.

15. James Weldon Johnson, "Negro Poets and Poetry," address at Howard University, 1904, JWJ BRBL.

16. Johnson expressed these ideas in a speech, noting that white imitators of black culture go to extremes of hardness and drabness, incapable of capturing in their work the "sheer joy of living" found in black culture ("American Minorities—the Negro" (n.d.), JWJ BRBL). In other public addresses and writings, Johnson impressed on his audiences the assertion that "the Negro has long been a giver as well as a receiver, a creator as well as a creature," and a "vital force in the making of America" (Johnson, Address to Fisk University, Chicago, 1938, JWJ BRBL). See "Race Prejudice and the Negro Artist," in Johnson, *The Selected Writings of James Weldon Johnson*, ed. Sondra Kathryn Wilson (New York: Oxford University Press, 1995). Also see Johnson's differentiation between the aims of the dialect poet and the black folk artist in *Along This Way*, 158–61.

17. A handwritten manuscript by Johnson entitled "Down the Nile" (n.d.) suggests that the brothers had at one time considered bringing the theme of a "great" Negro composer to the musical stage. A mere sketch, the manuscript puts forth the idea of a black American composer "obsessed" with uncovering the African roots of rhythm and makes the argument that African Americans contributed to America a completely original musical style (JWJ BRBL). See also Johnson's prefaces to *The Book of American Negro Poetry* (New York: Harcourt, Brace, 1922) and *The Books of American Negro Spirituals: Two Volumes in One* (1925, 1926; rpt., Boston: Da Capo, 2002), 1–50.

18. James Weldon Johnson, speech delivered at the National Book Fair, 1936, JWJ BRBL.

19. Johnson, *Book of American Negro Poetry*, ix.

20. "James W. Johnson Replies to Criticisms of His Preface," *New York Tribune*, April 9, 1922, 49.

21. Henry Krehbiel, *Afro-American Folksongs: A Study in Racial and National Music* (New York: G. Schirmer), 1914.

22. John Rosamond Johnson, ed., *The Books of American Negro Spirituals: Two Volumes in One* (New York: Viking, 1940), 16.

23. Ibid., 30.

24. Quoted in *New York Sun*, n.d., clipping file, JWJ BRBL.

25. Undated newspaper clipping, JWJ MSS II, JWJ BRBL, quoted in Eugene Levy, *James Weldon Johnson: Black Leader, Black Voice* (Chicago: University of Chicago Press, 1973), 88.

26. Johnson, *Along This Way*.

27. "From Sunday School to Stage," *New York Sun*, n.d., JWJ BRBL.

28. See, for example, Johnson's discussion about creating universal appeal (and greater profitability) in the lyrics he penned for the trio's "The Maiden with the Dream Eyes," in *Along This Way*, 179–80.

29. On Dvořák's role in shaping American music culture, see John C. Tibbetts, *Dvořák in America, 1892–1895* (Portland, Ore.: Amadeus, 1993); Maurice Peress, *Dvořák to Duke Ellington: A Conductor Explores America's Music and Its African American Roots* (New York: Oxford University Press, 2004); Thomas L. Riis, "Dvořák and His Black Students," in *Rethinking Dvořák: Views from Five Countries*, ed. David R. Beveridge (Oxford: Clarendon, 1996), 265–73; and the insightful essays in Michael B. Beckerman, ed., *Dvořák and His World* (Princeton, N.J.: Princeton University Press, 1993).

30. Rosamond Johnson, "Why They Call American Music Ragtime," 2.

31. Ibid.

32. Johnson, *Book of American Negro Poetry*, 9.

33. Newspaper clipping, n.d., JWJ BRBL.

34. As early as his college years, Johnson wrote in an issue of the *Tuskegee Student* (1898) that blacks needed a history to be considered great. In his speeches as a consular official and as the executive secretary of the NAACP, he emphasized the same arguments. Newspaper clippings, n.d., JWJ BRBL.

35. Johnson, *Book of American Negro Poetry*, 9.

36. Quoted in James Weldon Johnson, *Black Manhattan* (New York: Atheneum, 1968), 101–2. See also Thomas L. Riis, "'Bob' Cole: His Life and His Legacy to Black Musical Theater, Black Perspective," *Music* 13 (Fall 1985): 135–50; and Riis, *Just before Jazz: Black Musical Theater in New York, 1890–1915* (Washington, D.C.: Smithsonian Institution Press, 1989).

37. Rosamond Johnson, "Why They Call American Music Ragtime," 2.

38. Quoted in Terry Waldo, *This Is Ragtime* (New York: Da Capo, 1991), 108.

39. Johnson, *Along This Way*, 150.

40. "Profits of Song-Writing," *Baltimore News*, n.d., JWJ BRBL.

41. *Cleveland Plain Dealer*, n.d., JWJ BRBL. Originally composed as an orchestral suite, *Mr. Bluebeard* was performed by a 150-voice chorus. Composing the piece for orchestra was clearly central to the trio's goal of communicating an epic classicism and a grand emotional racial statement in their composition, particularly since, as Cole noted, they *still* intended to publish "The Evolution of the Negro" as an orchestral work.

42. Rosamond Johnson, "Why They Call American Music Ragtime," 2.

43. Ibid.

44. Ibid.

45. Johnson noted in his autobiography that the Cole-Johnson Trio was often called on to fix ailing musicals and to provide arrangements of music for other productions. See Johnson, *Along This Way*, 191.

James Weldon Johnson's *The Autobiography of an Ex-Colored Man*, Archived and Live

NOELLE MORRISSETTE

On June 3, 1886, a young James Johnson received an award recognizing his "general proficiency, regular attendance and good conduct" in "Eighth Grade Jacksonville Graded School." Stanton School, Jacksonville, was the city's grade school for African Americans; Johnson's prize was *The Life and Times of Frederick Douglass*.[1] Later that year Johnson had the rare opportunity of hearing Douglass speak in Jacksonville, an event that resoundingly shaped his aspiration to create an archive adequate to the task of reflecting the speech, performance, and "elusive undertone" of African American culture.[2] "I wanted to hear him speak and catch his words," Johnson recalled. "As I watched and listened to him, agitator, editor, organizer, counselor, eloquent advocate, co-worker with the great abolitionists, friend and adviser of Lincoln, for a half century the unafraid champion of freedom and equality for his race, I was filled with a feeling of worshipful awe. Douglass spoke, and moved a large audience of white and colored people by his supreme eloquence."[3] Johnson carefully preserved this compelling memory and also Douglass's book with its inscription. It is now part of the James Weldon Johnson Memorial Collection housed at Yale University's Beinecke Rare Book and Manuscript Library.[4] The following year Johnson completed his studies at Stanton. There was no grade higher than eighth in the state of Florida for Johnson, or any other black student, to attend. After completing his preparatory studies at Atlanta University, Johnson entered its freshman class. Johnson would go on to "eulogize" Douglass while the older man was still living in a speech given while he completed his BA. As the president of the Phi Kappa Society and a recognized orator, Johnson delivered the Emancipation Day speech "A Tribute to Frederick Douglass."[5]

That Johnson received as his award Douglass's third autobiography—his *Narrative of the Life* (1845) and *My Bondage and My Freedom* (1855) preceded *The Life and Times* (1881)—underscored for the younger man the power of self-declaration by and through narrative. From this power of self-declaration achieved in narrative and through performance, Johnson recognized his challenge: to create an archive of sound in print in a more technologically and discursively complex time. He would first need to build the archive into which he would place prominent African American authors of the nineteenth century, such as Frederick Douglass, and eventually himself and his (as yet unwritten) works. Douglass, an orator who intervened in American letters, and Johnson, writing after him, narrated the self through writing *and* its emanations. That Douglass had written three narratives of his life helped Johnson see biography as an archive with many versions, many cultural locations.

Johnson created this more dynamic and inclusive archive while writing from the margins. He animated the exclusionary boundaries; he did not come at the archive through the lettered privilege of a Matthew Arnold, say, or a William Wordsworth.[6] Instead, by moving the margins, making them dynamic, Johnson demonstrated that this shared archive cannot be contained and that text is inadequate as its mode of representation.

Johnson's innovation of the archive for the twentieth century is reflected strongly in *The Autobiography of an Ex-Colored Man*, his prefaces to *The Book of American Negro Poetry* and *The Book of American Negro Spirituals*, and his history *Black Manhattan*. His endeavors to create, or enliven, an archive came at a time in which there was a rush to institutionalize American history and literature for university study—largely propelled by the explosion of anthologies edited and framed by literary notables, such as Harriet Monroe, William Stanley Braithwaite, and Louis Untermeyer. Johnson's anthology *The Book of American Negro Poetry* declared what he repeated throughout his writing, beginning with *The Autobiography of an Ex-Colored Man*: the archive cannot be contained, and its users and the sounds within are involved in a continuously evolving relation. As Brent Edwards has noted of Johnson's preface to this work and the shaping of the anthology overall, "the book splits its own binding"[7]: Johnson's preface is intentionally resistant to categorization, its very elusiveness pointing to Johnson's idea of a moving archive capable of reflecting black expressive culture beyond text.

Johnson, inspired by meeting Douglass through both his texts and his speech, used a people's poetry to create a more inclusive, dynamic, and even physically present archive composed of individuals, poets, and a political collective of bodies. He was equally influenced by Walt Whitman's *Leaves of Grass*, particularly the "body electric": the poet's acts of cataloging, encircling, and flowing through bodies while galvanizing an individual spirit to create a fully democratic, shared citizenship of men and women, black, white, and immigrant. The aspiring author Johnson was, by his own account, "engulfed and submerged" by Whitman's *Leaves* at the turn of the twentieth century.[8] As Johnson realized, "Song of Myself" is really a song of others—a song of relation to and alteration through others. Johnson, drawing on Whitman to advance a more inclusive archive and citizenry, established an idea that has since been built upon by African American authors as varied as Margaret Walker in "For My People," Ralph Ellison in *Invisible Man*, and June Jordan in *Passion*.[9] As the narrator of *Invisible Man* states at the conclusion of his text, "Who knows but that, on the lower frequencies, I speak for you?" Johnson engineered his literary presence through an archive that he composed of Douglass, Whitman, and the bodies and voices in between.

Johnson's Archive

Johnson's lifetime of achievements, predating and following his authoring of *The Autobiography of an Ex-Colored Man*, overwhelmingly outdo his narrator's artistic and heroic ambitions, even in that fictive character's most boastful moments. Johnson, a poet, educator, and statesman, also became a New Negro Renaissance literary luminary and a civil rights advocate. His "firsts" are also impressive, seeming almost too much for one man to have undertaken, let alone achieved: first black man to pass the Florida state bar; founder of the first black high school in the state of Florida; first black member of the NAACP's executive branch; and primary author of the first federal anti-lynching bill. Some of his compositions, the works for which he is best known—"Lift Every Voice and Sing" (lovingly called the "Negro National Anthem," coauthored with his brother, John Rosamond Johnson) and *God's Trombones*, his volume of poetic sermons—became very popular with white and black audiences, and they continue to live as beloved works, outsinging his narrator's undeveloped folk and musical arrangements in *The Autobiography of an Ex-Colored Man*.[10]

Much like the narrator of his *The Autobiography of an Ex-Colored Man*, Johnson carefully documented and archived himself in his lifetime, not just the accomplishments with which his contemporaries were familiar, but the dreams and ambitions that led to their completion or at least their persistent presence in manuscript form, the evidence of which can be found in his papers at the Beinecke Library.[11] This archive emphasizes origin, trajectory, and achievement, yes, but it also reveals Johnson's performativity in creating its documentation.[12] Unlike his narrator, Johnson's self-archiving was a public declaration of value as well as a personal act of self-authoring. He traced his letters—the tangible, written works—and also his endeavors as a writer, from his earliest notebooks to his final lecture notes for Columbia University's and New York University's teachers colleges. He documented not only texts but also the more ephemeral practices surrounding writing.

Johnson's process of archiving—mirroring his attitude toward biography as a continuously mutable, adaptive form—asserted moving, relational meanings and values, rather than static categories of knowledge. He documented both praise and base insult in the reactions to his works through correspondence and journalistic reviews.[13] Johnson also persistently courted responses to his published works from established poets, such as Louis Untermeyer and Gertrude Stein; from government officials local and federal, such as Fiorello La Guardia and Franklin Delano Roosevelt; and from well-known literary and cultural critics, such as Heywood Broun and Carl Van Doren. He solicited collaboration with composers, such as Leonard Constant Lambert, and translators, who carried his works abroad to Norway, Germany, and France, among other nations. Often Johnson initially wrote to these potential readers unintroduced, with only the enclosed volume and a brief note as explanation. His works thus became diplomatic overtures, the correspondence a documentation of his ambitions and relational strategies. In a telling example, Johnson sent his autobiography, *Along This Way*, to Roosevelt for inclusion in the presidential library, a forcefully symbolic act. In this instance, Johnson plotted—behind the scenes and confrontationally also—the continued integration of the presidential library, which until 1933 contained only Booker T. Washington's *Up from Slavery* (1900) as the representation of black authorship, culture, and experience.

These diplomatic acts began with Johnson's anonymous publication in 1912 of *The Autobiography of an Ex-Colored Man*. Through this work and other diverse examples of the author's writing it is possible to attend to Johnson's performativity—through his texts and as an author—as the means through which he established an archive, one that presents the practice of composition as *acts* of, rather than simply textual foundations of, African American cultural knowledge. Johnson placed the ambivalent and ambiguous nature of African American cultural sounds at the heart of *The Autobiography* to create this emphasis on acts of composition, using sound to draw attention to the mutual contingencies and the interdependence of American and African American cultures.[14] More than simply employing sound thematically in this work, Johnson defined his role as an interlocutor between black expressive culture and mainstream American culture and politics.

He made his book and his body commodities of exchange that, like the ambitious artists encountered in the novel by the narrator at the club, "would compel the public to recognize" him (*The Autobiography*, 64), even from—particularly from—his obscured role as anonymous. Writing therefore was a means of creating and authorizing a self through performance and in this way bridging text and vernacular culture. His self-commodification and the commodification of his writing were problematic acts, even perilous, as Johnson knew, and yet such acts were declarations of the inherent value of black expressive culture.[15] This peril of commodification is clearly articulated in the action of *The Autobiography of an Ex-Colored Man*, where America is known to the world through two divergent acts: the appropriative and "world-conquering" cultural form of ragtime (54) and the unspeakably destructive violence of lynching.

Johnson, even more than his narrator, saw the creative potential for a sound-based culture in which listening to America's noises—controlled and uncontrollable—might form better citizens and encourage broader participation in U.S. social, political, and artistic life across traditionally segregated and artificial divisions of culture, identity, and critical practice. His novel articulates this potential, which is also, as he writes of his beloved Harlem in *Black Manhattan*, "still in the process of making."[16]

Johnson's message acknowledges both the materiality of sound and its transcendent potential. His concept of sound was informed by Walt Whitman as much as by the popular musical compositions he wrote with Rosamond and Bob Cole. In his lecture notes for Fisk University, where, beginning in 1931, he held a named chair as a distinguished professor, Johnson wrote his recollection of a well-known line from the fourth section of Whitman's "A Song for Occupations" in *Leaves of Grass*: "all music is what awakes in you when you are reminded of the instruments," planning to impart this line and its ethos to his students of American literature.[17] Johnson's awareness of the potential for transcendence provided by and through the instruments—God's trombones, in the sermons he later wrote, or those who lift their voices, in his commemoration of the Emancipation Proclamation—therefore draws on a prior century's idealism as well as on the modern conditions shaping such instrumentation and its audibility.[18] Both Whitman and Johnson were aware of and concerned for the common men and women who labored to create the unique sound composition of America. Yet Johnson was not deceived by the false reasoning of chronology as a guaranteed, steady march toward progress. The continuous presence of black expressive culture's song, with or without its transcription, demanded the skill and facility of its listeners; it sat not unmoving but unceasing in movement, located not in a distant history but in the present.

Johnson, like Whitman before him and Ralph Ellison, Albert Murray, and the Reverend Joseph Lowery after him, believed in listening for "Jones."[19] Ellison recounted his friend Murray's observation: "Franklin D. Roosevelt Jones might sound like a clown to someone who looks at him from the outside ... but on the other hand ... he might just lie back in all that comic juxtaposition of names and manipulate you deaf, dumb, and blind—and you not even suspecting it, because you're so thrown out of stance by the name! There you are, so dazzled by the F.D.R. image—which you *know* you can't see—and so delighted by your superior position that you don't realize that it is *Jones* who must be confronted."[20] Listen for Jones, Murray says, for sound is the true bearer, the body the instrumentation of the song of America. Johnson's "unknown bards," his "trombones," and "every voice" noted this presence and imparted this lesson too—through the Mozart Jackson, Jasper Jones, and Singing Johnson of his written works—even as such sounds moved, altered, and eluded the ear.[21] *The Autobiography of an Ex-Colored Man* first articulated this ethos of listening.

The Autobiography of an Ex-Colored Man, the 1912 work that inaugurated James Weldon Johnson's literary career, continued to inform his life and writing in complex ways, indicating its—and Johnson's—adaptive, performative capability. This novel, which has so often been mistaken for the author's life because of its claim to be autobiography, was intertwined closely with Johnson's story, but not in the ways that readers often presume. The author's endeavors to advance this work in what might be called the dual archives of letters—one black, one white—comprising the nation created the autobiography of its title. Although he published it anonymously, Johnson worked industriously through correspondence, conversation, and anonymous reviews to bring his work to the attention of a wide and interracial readership.[22] His persistence kept the novel alive, and Johnson, who described it in 1912 as a "biography of the race," saw its continued and evolving relevance to America's rapidly changing culture.[23]

In Johnson's mind, the adaptive life of *The Autobiography of an Ex-Colored Man* easily continued through America's present and near future. He wrote the literary critic Heywood Broun as much in 1924, loaning him the sole remaining copy he possessed of *The Autobiography* and stating that, although the novel concludes in the first decade of the twentieth century, he had "often thought of bringing it down through the Great War."[24] It is Johnson and not Carl Van Vechten, the author of the introduction to the work in its 1927 reissue, who should be credited with seeing *The Autobiography of an Ex-Colored Man* through to republication at the height of the Harlem Renaissance, for Johnson shared the novel and his ideas for its extension and revision with anyone in the New York, Boston, and Chicago literary scenes who might pay attention, from about 1915 on.[25] In a curious way, Johnson's promotion of his literary career through *The Autobiography of an Ex-Colored Man* confirms his use of biography as a technique for the continuous reinvention of the work and himself, while his archiving of the novel through reviews, correspondence, and even the guise of its anonymity points to his will to create, declare, and propel—rather than simply conserve, as archives are often thought to do—the meaning of both the composition and its creator in the record.[26]

Johnson's will to archive his novel while authoring himself indicates his conception of the archive *as* biography, as a shifting frame of record propelled by lives, particularly through the sounds of modern America. His conception of an archive composed of lives and sound has significance for current critical conversations about the archive and the concerns of what has been termed the "ethnic archive," repositories whose issues are often distinct from the formulations of categorized knowledge offered by Michel Foucault and Jacques Derrida.[27] Johnson has often been figured as a censoring archon of African American culture who confirmed his elitism by selectively presenting its cultural origins outside a black vernacular tradition.[28] Such a characterization is a profound misreading of Johnson's practices and the legacy he created through the archive, however. Johnson presented and developed a theory of transcription of black vernacular culture, as Brent Edwards has shown, which declared its meaning and value while avoiding the risk that it become a static, isolated abstraction in modern America. I argue that Johnson's concept of the moving archive addresses the problem of black expressive culture's transcription by offering a strategy not of translation to text but of text to composition beyond the page—a process that suggests a different, more imperative reading of *The Autobiography of an Ex-Colored Man* and his authorship of this work.[29] Johnson knew that knowledge and value are derived from institutional power. He knew, too, that redefining this knowledge base was as important for the archive he wished to bring into existence as it was for his role as author. Johnson wrote for two archives, willing them into one; he understood "letters" not only as writing, but also as its emanations in prior and subsequent cultural forms. This is the nation of Uncle Tom and Wendell Phillips, *The Autobiography of an Ex-Colored Man* argues, as well as the nation of ragtime and Harry T. Burleigh and of all the elite and popular acts in between them.

Johnson was conscious of the playfulness and subterfuge accompanying the simultaneously improvisational and pointed act of declared authorial anonymity, particularly the potential of autobiography to conceal more than it reveals about a life.[30] The ambiguity and provocation of *The Autobiography of an Ex-Colored Man* prompted numerous inquiries into the fact and fiction of the work in relation to Johnson's life, both contemporary to its publication and in the decades of literary criticism since.[31] Joseph Skerrett and Valerie Smith, both of whom evocatively studied the relation of the narrative to Johnson's experiences and his developing ideas of culture and politics, point to the ironic distancing of the narrator's and Johnson's lives, which diverge as the antihero of the text advances the race leader Johnson.[32] More recently, Brent Edwards, Katherine Biers, and Mark Goble have explored the presence of translation and recording in Johnson's text, as they convey the relation of difference and black culture in the modern era of communication.[33] Both foundational and current criticism of Johnson's work suggests but has not fully explored the theoretical importance of biography and sound in Johnson's concept of the archive, which may also inform contemporary conversations about the archive, writing, and knowledge practices.

Johnson, the lyricist and unseen member of the Cole and Johnson Brothers Broadway trio, wrote of the immersive experience of American sounds in *The Autobiography of an Ex-Colored Man* while making the claim for black expressive culture's unique and elusive presence in the modern United States. Taken together, these sounds represent the audibility of an archive that speaks beyond the texts commonly understood to comprise such a collection. The author's anonymity in *The Autobiography* was therefore a more sweeping cultural gesture, inclusive of both the writer and the larger experience of African Americans. The archive was both a declaration of a framework for understanding—hearing, recognizing, interpreting—black culture in America and an acknowledgment of the ephemeral nature of this living, breathing presence in the nation.

Sound, at once material and ephemeral, provided Johnson with a way of thinking about black expressive culture beyond imposed limitations and distortions. Its emphasis in *The Autobiography of an Ex-Colored Man* enables sensitivity to the "fugitivity" of black expressive culture emerging from experiences that might otherwise seem mute. This 1912 work aptly articulates African American expressive culture's dilemma of transcription, which is one of audibility as well as record—the transcript itself. The contemporary poet and critic Nathaniel Mackey's evocative phrasing of the phenomenon of "fugitivity" in relation to black expressive culture—what he calls "telling inarticulacy"—underscores the complexity of these sounds.[34] There is the persistent characterization of African American culture's failure of expression—its silencing—and its potential to tell and to be heard. Johnson's novel represents these extremes of sonic experience, from cultural violence to creative force, to emphasize African American culture's distortions and silencing, on the one hand, and the ways in which those silences speak, on the other.

Added to the archival framework of his novel, which revealed through anonymity broader cultural dilemmas for African Americans, Johnson's endeavors as an author underscore the potential of the archive itself to enunciate its "telling inarticulacy." In *The Autobiography of an Ex-Colored Man*, African American expressive cultural transcription and interpretation is a problem that is expressed not only through the narrator, but through Johnson's audience's attunement to the sounds composing American culture. It is the obscured author who facilitates this attunement. The dual advancement of the anonymous writer and Johnson's biographical practice of self-archiving provide an interpretative framework for the novel while also developing an aesthetic that guided all of Johnson's subsequent works.

Through writings as varied as the poem "O Black and Unknown Bards" (1908), *The Autobiography of an Ex-Colored Man* (1912), essays for the *New York Age* (1914–23), and critical prefaces to *The Book of American Negro Poetry* (1922) and *The Book of American Negro Spirituals* (1925), Johnson emphasized that African American cultural practices are not bound to text or notation.[35] Instead, African American expressive culture often has evaded the matter of text while continuing to adapt and transpose matters such as the Bible contains through sound, which Johnson showed in his primary examples of spirituals, sermons, and ragtime. Johnson as author also enacted this process both in distributing his written work and in suggesting *The Autobiography of an Ex-Colored Man*'s potential transformation through time and different readers, its status as "alive" and breathing, its contingency in relation to its audibility. This archive moves, and this work's author is situated both in the text and between texts.

Archive, Expressive Culture, and Voice

Without acknowledgment of "telling inarticulacy," the archive, while purporting to reveal an objective or conclusive truth, has the potential to perpetuate silence; the repertoire of real-time and continuous acts of change may be rendered mute. An archive of African American culture has the potential to overshadow the relational complexities of time, space, and sound in the store of African American culture by emphasizing progress and accomplishment—ends and ascension. Gayatri Chakravorty Spivak's now-classic intervening essay, "Can the Subaltern Speak?," which interrogates critical practices and the exclusivity of the speaking subject, emphasizes the importance of noting absences—in the linguistic register and in categories of knowledge—that limit critical understanding of alterity.[36] In a development of this crucial interrogation, Diana Taylor has asked how one might reconsider the function of the archive through the "live"—performance culture inclusive of political, representational, and artistic acts—in order to examine what one thinks is known about an archival record.[37] While the terms "archive" and "live" may seem to articulate the familiar and oversimplified tensions in literary study between formalism and cultural history, or even between oral and literate cultures, Taylor instead considers the concepts of archive and live in relation, *not* in opposition, to one another, proposing ways of interpreting the archive to achieve breath, bodies, and voices not immediately apparent or audible. The live, she suggests, is not fully absent from the archive but rather has the potential to be sensed and acknowledged.

Johnson's archive employs the idea of multiplicity to form a possible theory of transcription of black expressive culture. The tension between the archive and the live, between conclusive and continually changing ways of knowing and remembering, is characterized in *The Autobiography of an Ex-Colored Man* by the "fast-yellowing manuscripts" of the narrator's endeavors, which are contrasted to the continuation and alteration of the song of black culture that Johnson composed in this and subsequent works to be taken up by his auditors. The body of the performer connects sound and its notation, presenting Johnson's work as a sonic encounter with the audibility and transcription of black expressive culture as it bears on modern black identity.[38] In *The Autobiography* and in Johnson's later works, such sounds are elusive, recordable only through their transmission by the voices of others. These sounds cannot be contained by the author, the narrator, or the page.[39] The performance of black culture undoes the original-copy binary as the means of understanding cultural practices and differences. As Weheliye points out, this binary has been used in critical practices to perpetuate notions of difference, on the one hand, and to render black cultural practices unreadable, on the other.[40] Moreover this expressive culture remains an undeveloped consideration in crucial matters of meaning and existence, particularly in speech and writing.[41]

Undoing the alterity, or color line, of the original-copy divide, Johnson used performance to capitalize on the prevalent idea of black culture as elusive, using the anonymous publication of *The Autobiography of an Ex-Colored Man* to enhance this notion of performativity.[42] But not only did its anonymity lend the work an air of believability. The fact that the author framed the novel in multiple ways—anonymously promoting the work to potential readers as urgent, authoring its preface (signed "THE PUBLISHERS"), and possibly even writing newspaper reviews of the work for syndication[43]—points to Johnson's exploitation of the very terms of black textual/authorial voice. As Johnson recalled more than twenty years after its initial publication, "I did get a certain pleasure out of anonymity, that no acknowledged book could have given me."[44] Although wishing the credit for himself, Johnson welcomed the ambiguity and confusion prompted by its anonymous publication as improvisational potential, exemplified by the young man who claimed falsely, in Johnson's company, to have written *The Autobiography of an Ex-Colored Man*.[45] Such an assertion confirms the narrator's complex motivations in collecting the songs of his "mother's people" for individual and shared gain: he positions himself as an outside collector *and* as an insider aware of the best-kept cultural secrets, a kind of "freemasonry," as the narrator—and the preface—term it.[46] The need to claim ownership of something as elusive as the sounds and biographies emanating from the pages of the unnamed author's work emphasizes black expressive culture's "fugitivity," its resistance to capture by the narrator and by his author, a fact that was understood and exploited by Johnson, even as others claimed the novel's authorship.

Contingency and Audibility: The Archive

The Autobiography of an Ex-Colored Man confronts the dilemma facing Johnson—of archiving sound while voicing its compositions, making them audible in an archive expansive and supple enough to acknowledge but not contain sound. Can an archive sing the voices, the aspirations of a people, as the narrator seems to believe, concomitant with his desire to be "a great man, a great colored man, to reflect credit on the race and gain fame for myself" (*The Autobiography*, 29)? For Johnson, this was a pressing question that needed to be answered carefully. His narrator attentively collects and documents black cultural practices, such as sermons and spirituals from southern camp meetings. The Ex-Colored Man clearly wishes to "catch the spirit of the Negro" and, in doing so, form an archive (102). Yet he also acknowledges its fleeting, ephemeral nature, "that elusive undertone, the note in music which is not heard with the ears" (107). As the archivist of this collection, he speaks of his material as "the Negro in his relatively primitive state" (102), also "gloat[ing]" over "the immense amount of material ... material which no one had yet touched" (85), acts that delineate the difference of the collector from his collection. He will declare its value to a different audience while possibly also appropriating the material for his individual use along the way. Johnson shows that the narrator believes it is his status as an archivist, not as a participant in the culture, that enables the collection's valuation; it is he who can adapt, or transpose, its compositions for appreciation of its difference and his difference.

The narrator's act of adaptation for broad appreciation may sound like Johnson the interlocutor, but there is a vital difference between the two. The author of *The Autobiography* dramatizes composition and writing as simultaneously obscured and revealed—revealed only through a living, mutually altering practice. The narrator's endeavors to collect are a responsibility that makes him accountable to the lives of those whose cultural practices he observes, yet he proves himself unprepared for the task. The Ex-Colored Man's archive is not one of possibilities; indeed, at the close of the text his box of manuscripts is a secret he keeps. Unable to assume an active, public curatorial role—to "command" in the Derridean sense of the archive—the narrator finds by the close of the novel that the lives of those he has observed have been stifled, even laid to rest in his archive. The author, this work shows, must do more than "catch" or "mine" the cultural composition of African America.

Johnson, in contrast, wishes to create a dynamic archive, one that takes up a framework introduced in W. E. B. Du Bois's *The Souls of Black Folk* (1903), in which an unidentified bar of notated music was placed by a widely recognized verse by a British or American poet.[47] Johnson broadens the musical framework in his novel to create a soundscape of the American environment. Providing a soundscape that includes popular, classical, and ragtime forms as well as oratory, opera, camp songs, and spirituals, Johnson draws attention to two distinct issues: a new musical culture inclusive of commodity and the modern experience of the world through sound broadly construed.[48] The control of aural experience has taken different forms in the modern era, from copyright protections for authors to sound ordinances distinguishing noise from music. Such efforts to control sound in the modern era are attempts to understand and impose value on certain kinds of sound through shared sensibilities created by the experience of sound itself.

Johnson uses sensibility and sentiment to chart the biography of the narrator who in effect uses the "ear" to privilege meaning, as demonstrated by his emotive musical improvisations.[49] This is one aspect of sound in the novel. Yet noise and silence account for much of the work's exploration of sound and experience, emphasizing the significance of biography as an incomplete and elusive musical composition. Johnson uses sound—music and linguistic practices, silence and noise—and the conflicts between its central and marginal uses as the basis of the modern experience and its archive. The author's innovative incorporation of spirituals and hymns, classical and romantic scores for piano, opera, abolitionist oratory, Broadway songs from New York's Tenderloin, and especially ragtime shows their imperative and continuous alteration through both performance and the novel itself. The biography of this American soundscape underscores the play between the works themselves and reaches beyond them to articulate a varied, continual composition of modernity through sound, interpolation, and songs that the narrator is only beginning to hear—a process of attunement that experientially places him in an immersive setting alongside his reader.

In a process similar to how Johnson, Rosamond, and Bob Cole composed many of their hit songs using the tunes of the spirituals, the model of the Ex-Colored Man involves more reciprocity than critics have attributed to it, and his actions cannot be so readily condemned as the ironic opposite of best-foot-forward racial heroics (*The Autobiography*, 55). Johnson's use of a ragged Mendelssohn's "Wedding March" in *The Autobiography of an Ex-Colored Man* is a means of indicating American sounds' simultaneous variations, rather than delineating distinctions between original and copy.[50] This ragged piece is the narrator's signature. While it hardly seems original—North references the easy parody of "semiclassical chestnuts" like it—this may actually be the point.[51] Biers points out, "To those in the know, the narrator's transcription of the 'Wedding March' would have provided a stark contrast [to the pieces played by the black ragtime musician who composes all his works 'by ear']. It was in fact a real tune published by the leading white popularizer of ragtime, Axel Christensen."[52] Yet, as North points out, claims to originality within the logic of the work are easily and conspicuously undercut by the inconsistencies facilitated by ragtime.[53] There is little certainty that Axel Christensen was the originator of the ragged "Wedding March": the pattern the narrator describes, of taking set classical pieces and ragging them, does not point to the extreme polarities of black and white compositions and the misguided, inadvisable act of the narrator in working from the classical rather than the racial (of the spirituals) in creating his ragtime. In Johnson's *The Autobiography of an Ex-*

Colored Man, the "Wedding March" was not simply the original musical work but a creation of Bert Williams and Will Marion Cook for their 1906 show *Abyssinia*; their composition "The Tale of the Monkey Maid" appropriated Felix Mendelssohn's "Wedding March" from the incidental music for Shakespeare's play *A Midsummer Night's Dream* and perhaps from the ragtime composition of Christensen.[54] Johnson, with Cole and Rosamond, carried the biography of this composition through its multiple enactments of difference, wherein origins were not so much invented as obscured by quoting, interpolation, and just plain theft—of what could not be owned or controlled but that nonetheless had "real social and political consequences."[55]

In this use of Mendelssohn and many others in Johnson's soundtrack, the emphasis of musical composition is placed on its enactments and performances, whereby difference is emphasized but in such multifarious variety as to destabilize the idea of a singular original. For example, the character Shiny becomes the interlocutor of Wendell Phillips's "rhetorical ... even ... bombastic" abolitionist speech, and in its performance he forces a physical response from his listeners, who "actually rose to him" in an "electric" response; and while Shiny is "a natural orator," it is more the juxtaposition of voices, performances, and realities that, when recognized, "loosed the pent-up feelings of his listeners" (*The Autobiography*, 28). More pointedly, Shiny's name alludes to a popular song of the Tenderloin period in black musical production: "That's Why They Call Me Shine" (1907), which references the New York City riot of 1900.[56] Johnson had been present in New York when the riot occurred, as he later described in his autobiography, *Along This Way*. This song, with words by Cecil Mack (R. C. McPherson) and music by Ford Dabney, is about a man nicknamed Shine who was with George Walker when they were badly beaten during the riot, according to the blues composer Perry Bradford. Shiny of *The Autobiography of an Ex-Colored Man* is the valedictorian of a school that permits the attendance of black students; he is an exemplary leader, an electric speaker, an unlikely but brave opponent, "waging with puny, black arms so unequal a battle" against his white audience's predisposition toward black speaking subjects, "Anglo-Saxon love of fair play" notwithstanding (29). Johnson repeats and elaborates on the context of the riot and "That's Why They Call Me Shine" in his 1930 work, *Black Manhattan*: "The cry went out to get Williams and Walker."[57]

The idea of sound and its performance, where one voice is superimposed on another in an effort to control the sonic environment or to force recognition of its multiplicity, is also found in Johnson's referencing of Charles Gounod's wildly popular *Faust*. There is a good possibility that Johnson saw a performance of Gounod's opera when the Cole and Johnson Brothers trio traveled to France in 1905, since Johnson's referencing of it invokes not only Gounod's version but Theodore Drury's production in the Lexington Opera

House and the Metropolitan Opera House, where Johnson attended the entire 1902–3 season.[58] Johnson mentions the baritone Drury's "enterprise which annually, for four or five years, gave Negro New York a one-night season of grand opera ... in the Lexington Opera House for Drury's productions of Verdi, Wagner, Gounod, and Bizet," starting a few years after the turn of the twentieth century.[59] (A decade after the publication of *The Autobiography of an Ex-Colored Man*, Black Swan Records, for which Johnson's father-in-law, John B. Nail, was a board member, would record many of these arias, including those by Gounod.)

Since Mendelssohn was Bert Williams and George Walker's and Gounod was Theodore Drury's, Frédéric Chopin, also wildly popular and frequently played in American parlors, registered something more in Johnson's work than a simple marking of the classical as European and of the popular as classical. One would do well to remember the observation made by Ralph Ellison that Duke Ellington's "Black and Tan Fantasy" has "mocking interpolations from Chopin's B-flat minor piano concerto, to which ... it was once popular to sing the gallows-humored words 'Where shall we all / be / a hundred years / from now?'"[60] Johnson's use of Chopin's thirteenth nocturne (op. 48, no. 1, in C minor) as the courtship song of the narrator and his amour (*The Autobiography*, 123–24) marks the long history of this tradition of interpolation, with the narrator's alteration of the nocturne's concluding chord from a minor to a "major triad" (124) tracing one of Rosamond's distinct compositional practices of altering phrases from minor to major and ending lines on a triad—here combined into a single action in Johnson's work. The song in a minor key, which seems to represent the narrator's sonic experience in the novel—both his fondness for "the black keys" (6) and the predominating key of C minor in the pieces he performs or hears: Beethoven's "Pathétique" piano sonata, Gounod's aria "Avant de quitter ces lieux," and Chopin's nocturne—is altered as he composes a new resolution in a major key.

In these complex, layered borrowings of music described in the novel, Johnson references the specialized lexicon of the composer, who must know the significance of any musical sequence in order to successfully alter it.[61] Indeed, this is the function of the interlocutor. Johnson extends this function by referencing popular culture's interpolations of these texts, as in the case of Chopin. Composing thus becomes a collective, mutual act of borrowing shaped by all who care to listen. Johnson showcases his brother's signature musical voice, effectively producing a biography of the composer by interpolating Rosamond's voice into the text. And indeed, it will be Rosamond who performs the spirituals at Carnegie Hall, the concert to which the narrator of Johnson's novel is merely a spectator (*The Autobiography*, 125). In this way, the novel begins to sing in the voice of someone else, carrying Johnson's interpolation—also singing in the voice of someone else—beyond the pages of the work.

Johnson's creation of an archive in and between his writing and his life is not a store of disembodied voices, nor is it the immobile, distant archive of a historical or originary past. Rather, Johnson's archive, replete with interpolations, borrowings, and explicit references to silences and theft, is a mutually altering composition. His archive implicates the listener in the sounds of America and its great potential—a futurity that is, like its past, contingent on African Americans and African American culture in motion.[62] The writer and his writing are sounded through human instruments; the "biography of the race" that Johnson's draft of the publisher's preface claimed the work to be is a biography of the nation, sounded through human instruments.

Coda

Read from the perspective of twenty-first-century issues and attitudes toward information, people, and power, Johnson's *The Autobiography of an Ex-Colored Man* questions contemporary assumptions about the accessibility, function, and transference of knowledge.[63] The work acknowledges text- and sound-based archives of knowledge and exploits the swing between them. Well before postcolonialism gave credence to the idea of heterogeneity, of in-betweenness, Johnson's text capitalized on travels between high and low, black and white, public and private, South and North, America and Europe, collective and individual knowledge, fact and fiction, and sound and text.[64] Johnson, an astute listener to the sounds of modern American culture, narrates the story of his age's changing relationship to discourses, technologies, and peoples, particularly African-descended cultures. He makes the case not only for African Americans' humanity—made evident by the constantly changing composition of U.S. civilization through their significant contributions—but also for their crucial role in America's future.[65]

Johnson makes this case by demanding acknowledgment of a larger and more inclusive archive: he figures African American culture at the center of America's transformation to greatness through its civilization—its arts. At the turn of the twentieth century, this civilization was a moving archive, working against its opposite: the destructive, savage force of lynching, an anticultural violence. Johnson shows the multivalent potential of music to shape public opinion—the attitudes of the educated, the uneducated, and the miseducated—through its combination with both printed material and black vernacular culture. The effect is the creation of a shared knowledge and a collective conscience. Such knowledge could redirect the "electric current" propelling a man to his fate as he is lynched to the more constructive and revolutionary concept of shared frameworks of knowledge—popular and elite, black and white, sound and text—composing the American nation.

Widely recognized as a founder of the African American literary canon, Johnson has been described also as an elitist archon of black culture. This perception is, to a large extent, derived from the memorial archive established at Yale by Johnson's friend Carl Van Vechten after Johnson's death. Johnson as archon reflects the status of this archive as elite, exclusive, and unmoving, tied to Yale's past associations with slavery, eugenics, and other racially oppressive legacies. Yet Johnson, were he to learn of the location of his archive, might find satisfaction in his works' integration of a static archive of white letters, as well as in the digitally accessible form of his papers. But such symbolism is never enough, as the historian David Levering Lewis has pointed out and as Johnson himself knew.[66] Johnson understood that the acts surrounding composition could revise the very concept and motion of knowledge, indeed of raced peoples, in a world of nations. As Williams and López observe, "Archival findings are ... as capable of establishing genealogies as they are of destabilizing the ethnic histories and selves we thought we already knew."[67] Johnson and his archive, both familiar to many, now offer, through new archival study, a voice of resistance rather than regulation, of creation rather than control. Johnson's archive at the Beinecke Rare Books and Manuscript Library breathes and can sing.

In Johnson's biographical practice, the writer-composer is constituted through and between his works and through the works of other composers in the shared culture of African Americans in America. These are the "instruments" of Whitman's music—instruments of a nation whose futurity can only be realized through them, making imperative the alteration of all by their incorporation.

Responses to Johnson's death and subsequent remembering through the establishment of an archive and many performances of his works reveal contentiousness over the ownership of his life and his creative legacy, which resound in more contemporary debates over the meaning of an African American archive.[68] Divergent ideas of Johnson's value, initiated by different publics—popular and academic among them—suggest the fruitful tension of an archive that encompasses competing ideas of African American cultural practices—practices that speak and yet elude fixity. The archive as a moving practice of cultural biography helps one understand how value and meaning are formed from literature and interpretative practices. Historical sequencing reveals little about individual literary works, much as the mere sequence of a life reveals little about its subject. The representational acts of the reading public carry *The Autobiography of an Ex-Colored Man* and Johnson beyond themselves, to the living, breathing, continuously altered compositions that not only are read, but heard. Attending to Johnson and the archive, we may move away from the commitment to singular, divided literary and cultural traditions and toward the idea of truth's multiplicity, evasions, and incompletions—and further toward the creative and continuous processes of making meaning. In this 1912 work's prescient version of futurity, the far-reaching techniques of modern black composers draw together a spontaneous people's culture of America, which has been collectively propelled forward by greater technological innovations, facilitating exposure through sound.

As one looks forward to a world of information that seems radically altered by technological innovation, one might consider readings of *The Autobiography of an Ex-Colored Man* paired with the practices of gathering and interpreting knowledge so as to make the archives speak with the diverse voices of a common humanity. This archive and America's future are not raceless, nor are they postracial. Our endeavors, like Johnson's, might embrace Douglass's and Whitman's works through and beyond the text to advance the futurity of African America, laying claim to democratic impulses that might not yet exist, but take refuge in a recognized, shared, fugitive spirit of democracy.[69]

NOTES

1. Frederick Douglass, *The Life and Times of Frederick Douglass: Written by Himself* (Hartford, Conn.: Park, 1881). Johnson's edition is preserved in the Beinecke Rare Book and Manuscript Library, Yale University (hereafter BRBL), JWJ Zan D747 881 Lb. It is not known who inscribed the copy of Douglass's autobiography to Johnson.

2. Johnson, *The Autobiography of an Ex-Colored Man*, ed. Noelle Morrissette (New York: Fine Creative Media, 2007), 107. Future references to this work are given parenthetically in the text.

3. Johnson, *Along This Way: The Autobiography of James Weldon Johnson* (New York: Viking, 1933), 61.

4. See also Johnson, *Along This Way*, 60–71, 280.

5. Johnson, "A Tribute to Frederick Douglass," in *The Selected Writings of James Weldon Johnson*, ed. Sondra Kathryn Wilson (New York: Oxford University Press, 1995), 2:427–30.

6. Lawrence Oliver's evocative essay in this collection on Brander Matthews's influence on Johnson's work provides a crucial example of how Johnson used mainstream literary forms and expectations to make the margins move.

7. Brent Edwards, *The Practice of Diaspora: Literature, Translation, and the Rise of Black Internationalism* (Cambridge, Mass.: Harvard University Press, 2003), 50.

8. Johnson, *Along This Way*, 158.

9. Walker, "For My People" (1937), in her *This Is My Century: New and Selected Poems* (Athens: University of Georgia Press, 1989); Ellison, *Invisible Man* (1952; rpt., New York: Vintage, 1995); Jordan, *Passion: New Poems, 1977–1980* (Boston: Beacon, 1980), esp. the preface, "For the Sake of a People's Poetry: Walt Whitman and the Rest of Us," ix–xxvi.

10. Johnson, with John Rosamond Johnson, "Lift Every Voice and Sing" (1901), in Johnson, *God's Trombones* (New York: Viking, 1927). Johnson writes cryptically in his autobiography, *Along This Way*, that the publishers of "Lift Every Voice" "consider it a valuable piece of property," but it is "commonly found" in copies "in the backs of hymnals and songbooks," which he believes "is the method by which it gets its widest circulation" (155).

11. The formation of the James Weldon Johnson Memorial Collection at Yale University is a coda to this essay's consideration of the archive. I tell the story of its founding in the afterword to Noelle Morrissette, *James Weldon Johnson's Modern Soundscapes* (Iowa City: University of Iowa Press, 2013), 185–206.

12. See Michael Nowlin's essay in this collection for an alternative discussion of Johnson's productivity as an author and his use of the archive.

13. See Lori Brooks's discussion of Henry Krehbiel in her essay in this volume.

14. See Morrissette, *Modern Soundscapes*, particularly the introduction, where I discuss Johnson's use of sound.

15. See Jeff Karem's discussion of Johnson's intentional construction of evaluative measures of black culture in his essay in this collection.

16. Johnson, *Black Manhattan* (New York: Knopf, 1930), 281.

17. Fisk University lecture notes, contemporary American literature, lecture 2, JWJ MSS 220, BRBL.

18. Contemplating "the instruments," I am immediately brought to Augusta Savage's 1938 sculpture for the 1939 New York World's Fair in homage to Johnson's "Lift Every Voice and Sing"—the choral members standing in line, ascending in height to create a harp, heads uplifted in song. The sculptor lovingly carried forth Johnson's vision and her own in this piece, which became familiarly known as *The Harp*, despite the artist's and Grace Nail Johnson's dislike of this name. See Augusta Savage to Grace Nail Johnson, March 21, 1939, JWJ MSS 49, box 35, folder 201, BRBL.

19. Lowery's inaugural benediction for President Barack Obama demonstrates this intent listening: "God of our weary years, God of our silent tears, Thou who has brought us thus far along the way," Lowery began, not just quoting but animating Johnson's lyrics to "Lift Every Voice and Sing." He concluded: "Lord, in the memory of all the saints who from their labors rest, and in the joy of a new beginning, we ask you to help us work for that day when black will not be asked to get back, when brown can stick around—(laughter)—when yellow will be mellow—(laughter)—and when the red man can get ahead, man (laughter)—and when white will embrace what's right." "Rev. Lowery Inauguration Benediction: Transcript," *Washington Post*, January 20, 2009, http://voices.washingtonpost.com/inauguration-watch/2009/01/transcript_of_rev_lowerys_inau.html/

20. Ralph Ellison, "Hidden Name and Complex Fate," in *The Collected Essays of Ralph Ellison*, ed. John Callahan (New York: Random House, 1995), 194.

21. See Morrissette, *Modern Soundscapes*, 28–32.

22. Johnson wrote to his brother, Rosamond; his wife, Grace Nail Johnson; his brother-in-law, John E. Nail; his literary mentor, William Stanley Braithwaite; and his Atlanta University classmate George Towns to "keep the secret," because if the author's identity were known, the book would "fall flat." Johnson also pressed the book upon

a U.S. naval captain, representing the narrative as real and claiming not to know the author. Miles Jackson, ed., "Letters to a Friend: Correspondence from James Weldon Johnson to George A. Towns," *Phylon* 29, no. 2 (1968): 182–98. See also Lawrence Oliver's discussion of Brander Matthews's influential relationship with Johnson in this collection.

23. Johnson calls the work a "biography of the race" in his proposed preface to the work, sent to the publishers, Sherman, French and Company, on February 7, 1912 (box 18, ser. 1, JWJ Correspondence, BRBL). See Diana Paulin's and Bruce Barnhart's essays in this volume for a discussion of futurity in *The Autobiography of an Ex-Colored Man*.

24. Johnson to Broun, May 2, 1924, box 4, folder 62, ser. 1, JWJ Correspondence, BRBL.

25. In addition to corresponding with Broun, who was unresponsive to the author's proposition, Johnson saw to it that *The Autobiography of an Ex-Colored Man* was reissued in serialized format in the *Chicago Defender* in 1919.

26. The term "conserve" is derived from Jacques Derrida's discussion of the archive in *Archive Fever: A Freudian Impression*, trans. Eric D. Prenowitz (Chicago: University of Chicago Press, 1995).

27. Foucault, *The Archaeology of Knowledge*, trans. A. M. Sheridan Smith (1969; rpt., New York: Routledge, 2002); Derrida, *Of Grammatology*, trans. Gayatri Chakravorty Spivak (1976; rpt., Baltimore, Md.: Johns Hopkins University Press, 2016); and Derrida, *Archive Fever*.

28. Amiri Baraka, "The Revolutionary Tradition in Afro-American Literature" (1979), in *The LeRoi Jones/Amiri Baraka Reader*, ed. William J. Harris (New York: Thunder's Mouth, 1991), 311–22.

29. Dana A. Williams and Marissa K. López, "More than a Fever: Toward a Theory of the Ethnic Archive," *PMLA* 127, no. 2 (2012): 357–59. About the ethnic archive, the authors observe, "Because knowledge is perpetually translated, interpreted, and then mediated through power relations, archival methodologies must be organic; they must evolve along with their objects of inquiry" (358).

30. The proposition of Paul de Man's "Autobiography as De-Facement" in his *The Rhetoric of Romanticism* (New York: Columbia University Press, 1984)—that the story an autobiographer tells conceals more than it reveals—is productive when one begins to consider what one thinks is known about James Weldon Johnson.

31. Reviews contemporary to the work's publication responded to its provocation—initiated through the question of racial authenticity—coming down on the side of truth or fiction as a result of what its readers considered possible or typical for a "Negro author." One reviewer found that the narrative was prone to "embellishment," as was "the African" (Springfield *Union*, June 15, 1912). Others responded to what they perceived as the internal "color peril" of the nation, which was more threatening than the "yellow" peril: "The color peril is right at our doors. It comes from the South, not the Far East. It is not yellow, but black" (Philadelphia *Telegraph*, August 21, 1912). The narrative was further seen to describe "the dangers of race amalgamation," as one reviewer put it (New Orleans *Picayune*, July 21, 1912).

32. Joseph T. Skerrett Jr., "Irony and Symbolic Action in James Weldon Johnson's *The Autobiography of an Ex-Coloured Man*," in *Critical Essays on James Weldon Johnson*, ed. Kenneth M. Price and Lawrence J. Oliver (New York: G. K. Hall, 1997); Valerie Smith,

"Privilege and Evasion in James Weldon Johnson's *The Autobiography of an Ex-Colored Man*," in Price and Oliver, *Critical Essays*.

33. Brent Edwards, *The Practice of Diaspora: Literature, Translation, and the Rise of Black Internationalism* (Cambridge, Mass.: Harvard University Press, 2003); Katherine Biers, "Syncope Fever: James Weldon Johnson and the Black Phonographic Voice," *Representations* 96 (Fall 2006): 99–125; Mark Goble, *Beautiful Circuits: Modernism and the Mediated Life* (New York: Columbia University Press, 2010).

34. Mackey, *Discrepant Engagement: Dissonance, Cross-Culturality, and Experimental Writing* (New York: Cambridge University Press, 1993), 268–69. As Biers has observed, "Historically, forces of political and social modernization ... have constructed the spectacle of black linguistic and gestural excesses and emphasized the materiality of the black body in order to deny their own entanglements with writing and voice" ("Syncope Fever," 100).

35. Ben Glaser's essay in this collection deepens this consideration of poetics through Johnson's satiric poem "Saint Peter Relates an Incident" (1930).

36. Spivak, "Can the Subaltern Speak?" in *Can the Subaltern Speak? Reflections on the History of an Idea*, ed. Rosalind Morris (New York: Columbia University Press, 2010).

37. Taylor, *The Archive and the Repertoire* (Durham, N.C.: Duke University Press, 2003).

38. See Ben Glaser's discussion in his essay in this collection of Johnson's mediation of anger and irony through metrical and rhythmic experimentation. This experimentation with phonographic voice is arguably a defining feature of Johnson's poetics.

39. See Morrissette, *Modern Soundscapes*, 31.

40. Alexander Weheliye, *Phonographies: Grooves in Sonic Afro-Modernity* (Durham, N.C.: Duke University Press, 2005), esp. 30–36; see also Fred Moten, *In the Break: The Aesthetics of the Black Radical Tradition* (Minneapolis: University of Minnesota Press, 2003), 74–84, 183–86.

41. For example, as Moten has shown, Derrida's formulations of the feeling and improvisation of language, of writing and speech, reproduce a "color-line. How does it feel to be a problem of feeling?" (*In the Break*, 77). By interrogating this binary, one begins to perceive a powerful African American archive that is not exclusively nor primarily text-based. As Weheliye's and Moten's critiques of deconstruction show, its critical practices diminish black expressive culture, which is both present and absent in the formulations of its practitioners. Weheliye observes that Derrida's early foundational concept of writing—that it "must be repeatable—iterable—in the absolute absence of the addressee or of the empirically determinable set of addressees" and that "writing needs to be discernible beyond the immediate context of its re/production"—"plac[es] a significant barrier between signifier and signified" because in this formulation speech is unmediated and always present, "acting as [a] humble servant of interiority and meaning." Weheliye instead offers "not repetition with a difference so much as the repetition *of* difference, wherein the original/copy distinction vanishes and only the singular and *sui generis* becomings of the source remain in the clearing. This repetition of difference does not ask how 'the copy' departs from 'the source' but assumes that difference will, indeed, be different in each of its incarnations" (*Phonographies*, 32). From such an alternative formulation, sounds, whether recorded as

"graph" or not, become more audible, independent, and equal; variation does not move from source to copy but exists in multiple, simultaneous forms.

42. See Michael Nowlin's and Jeff Karem's essays in this volume for a more thorough treatment of anonymity and authorship in *The Autobiography of an Ex-Colored Man*.

43. For example, Johnson encouraged members of the U.S. Navy whom he encountered during his diplomatic posting to Nicaragua to read the book without revealing that he was the author. His writing of the preface was only established in 1990. See James Weldon Johnson, *The Autobiography of an Ex-Colored Man*, ed. William L. Andrews (1912; rpt., New York: Viking, 1990). Further, Johnson avidly collected reviews of this work contemporary to its 1912 publication, and much later engaged Richetta Randolph, then his secretary at the NAACP, to arrange the reviews in a scrapbook. Some of them echo the syntax and voice of Johnson's writing, particularly the preface: "The book gives a new and striking portrayal of the race drama, and explains why the prejudice against the negro is forcing those [of] fair skin into the ranks of whites, where intermarriage takes place with the blood taint all unguessed" (*Times Union*, Albany, N.Y., September 23, 1912). While this similarity may be the effect of the review's presentation of the text—maybe even an effort to let the text speak—I find it far more likely that Johnson himself authored one or more reviews for syndication, in effect extending the framing work he had already done in writing the preface. Perhaps the best evidence of Johnson's authoring is the review that echoes the part of Johnson's letter to his publisher proposing the preface that was not used: "If true autobiography, this man's story is stranger than fiction" (*Western Christian Advocate*, December 18, 1912). Johnson's unused portion of the preface claimed, "This story is stranger than fiction—or, romance." Johnson to Sherman, French and Company, February 7, 1912, box 18, ser. 1, JWJ Correspondence, BRBL.

44. Johnson, *Along This Way*, 238.

45. Ibid., 238–39.

46. See Jeff Karem's essay in this collection for a fuller discussion of secrets, promises, and authenticity.

47. W. E. B. Du Bois, *The Souls of Black Folk*, ed. Farah Jasmine Griffin (1903; rpt., New York: Fine Creative Media, 2003).

48. David Suisman makes this distinction in *Selling Sounds: The Commercial Revolution in American Music* (Cambridge, Mass.: Harvard University Press, 2009), 9.

49. A version of this argument appears in Morrissette, *Modern Soundscapes*, 53–54.

50. I make this argument in Morrissette, *Modern Soundscapes*, 57–60.

51. Michael North, *Camera Works: Photography and the Twentieth-Century Word* (New York: Oxford University Press, 2005), 179.

52. Biers, "Syncope Fever," 123n62.

53. North, *Camera Works*, 179–80.

54. Thomas Riis, *Just before Jazz: Black Musical Theater in New York, 1890–1915* (Washington, D.C.: Smithsonian Institution Press, 1989), 64.

55. Suisman, *Selling Sounds*, 13; Morrissette, *Modern Soundscapes*, 57.

56. Tim Brooks dates this song to 1907 in *Lost Sounds: Blacks and the Birth of the Recording Industry, 1890–1919* (Urbana: University of Illinois Press, 2004), 397.

57. Johnson, *Black Manhattan*, 127.

58. Johnson, *Along This Way*, 174, 192.

59. Ibid., 174.

60. Ellison, "Homage to Duke Ellington on His Birthday," in *Living with Music: The Jazz Essays of Ralph Ellison*, ed. Robert G. O'Meally (New York: Random House, 2001), 79.

61. See Lori Brooks's essay in this collection on the associations of the composer and the "perfessor."

62. Diana Paulin's essay in this volume discusses Johnson's concept of futurity with that of his contemporary Pauline Hopkins.

63. Robert Stepto's essay in this volume emphasizes the relation to the archive itself of the "schoolhouse blues" of a racial education on African American subjects and subject matter.

64. Daphne Lamothe's essay in this volume aptly extends these travels and the exploration of a racial cosmopolitanism to the contemporary novelist Teju Cole's peripatetic *Open City* (2012).

65. Bruce Barnhart's essay in this volume discusses the relationships among race, subjectivity, and temporality in *The Autobiography*.

66. David Levering Lewis, *When Harlem Was in Vogue* (1979; rpt., New York: Penguin, 1997), 147–48. Lewis assesses the impulses of Johnson and other New Negroes to claim a symbolic and yet contradictory progress as "the genuine convictions of upper middle class status" (148).

67. Williams and López, "More than a Fever," 358.

68. See "Remembering James Weldon Johnson," in Morrissette, *Modern Soundscapes*.

69. At this essay's writing, the violent events of racial profiling and police brutality in Ferguson, Missouri; Staten Island, New York; and other locations throughout the nation weigh heavily on many Americans' minds. The last words of New Yorker Eric Garner—"I can't breathe"—as he was struggling in a chokehold before dying in police custody have become a desperate and outraged slogan for the dispossessed.

PART FOUR

Legacies

In the following essay, Robert Stepto returns to his pathbreaking monograph of African American narrative traditions, *From behind the Veil* (1979), which firmly established the major tropes of racial literacy, ascent and immersion, and authorial control in works by eighteenth- and nineteenth-century African American authors. That was "the call." His chapter "Lost in a Quest: James Weldon Johnson's *The Autobiography of an Ex-Coloured Man*" occupies a special place in that work, initiating the second half of his study. It commences "the response" to this series of racial rhetorics, or tropes, in the writing of racial forebears. The authors James Weldon Johnson, Richard Wright, and Ralph Ellison, Stepto argues, revoice and intentionally alter these tropes, creating new narrative forms in the process of responding to prior texts. Stepto demonstrates an interwoven and at times secretive narrative conversation that has taken place within African American literature as it has unfolded over time between two significant periods in African American experience and authorship.

The essay included in this collection was originally delivered as part of the 2009 W. E. B. Du Bois Lecture Series at Harvard University. Stepto discusses several scenes of racial education, both fictional and autobiographical, from major works by twentieth-century African American authors: Johnson's *The Autobiography of an Ex-Colored Man*, Du Bois's *The Souls of Black Folk*, Zora Neale Hurston's *Their Eyes Were Watching God*, and Barack Obama's *Dreams from My Father*. The "search for race" involves the recognition and navigation of racial tropes by subjects who find themselves made into objects at the center of the racial lesson. Tracing the writers' authority dramatized in these works—not only through the racialization depicted but also through the differentiation created by the authors, who are distinct from their subjects—Stepto shows the navigation of the autobiographical form as a means of possibility for Johnson, Du Bois, Hurston, and Obama. Placed in a broader discursive context of American autobiography, Stepto shows, these works more effectively convey "identities assumed and identities imposed" and register the giving and receiving of "gifts"—the interracial sharing of this understanding of ourselves.

In his preface to the second edition of *From behind the Veil* (1991), Stepto wrote, "*Veil* studies how freedom occasions literacy and how, even more impressively, literacy initiates freedom. In the process the point is made that reading and writing are empowering activities for African Americans (among others), that they have always been so, and that our writers have always written about such activities—fantasized about them, even. Obviously this is a productive line of inquiry for me personally.... But there must be a public benefit as well: the public needs to be reminded (far more than I do) that an African American written culture exists and endures" (x–xi). Setting out to write his lectures in 2008–9, Stepto knew that "there was a project to pursue that involved being attentive to how we read African American literature at the present moment, knowing, and actually being stunned by the fact, that an African American writer is our president."[1] Johnson's *The Autobiography of an Ex-Colored Man*, Stepto shows, occupies an important position in this consideration of African American narrative's interventions in American autobiography—indeed, its interventions in the biography of America. —NM

NOTES

1. Robert Stepto, *A Home Elsewhere: Reading African American Classics in the Age of Obama* (Cambridge, Mass.: Harvard University Press, 2010), 3.

W. E. B. Du Bois, Barack Obama, and the Search for Race
School House Blues

ROBERT B. STEPTO

> Everybody remembers the first time they were *taught* that part of the human race was Other. That's a trauma. It's as though I told you that your left hand is not part of your body.
>
> —Toni Morrison

The schoolhouse episode is a staple event in African American narratives no doubt because it is remembered or imagined as a formative first scene of racial self-awareness. It is not a moment when race is adopted—that may come later; it is instead a moment when race is imposed. The episode may involve a graduation exercise, with all the attendant questions regarding what, exactly, is commencing. Though set in a hotel ballroom, the battle royal in the first chapter of Ralph Ellison's *Invisible Man* is one such monumental episode. More likely, though, the episode is an earlier moment, perhaps the first day of school, in which the narrative's protagonist is "schooled" in being colored, sometimes made aware for the first time that he or she is colored. Obama's *Dreams from My Father* offers a schoolhouse episode that is singular in its complexity, partly because it is a series of evolving scenes and because the events are complicated by the presence of family members—Obama's white Kansan grandfather and black Kenyan father in particular—who hover and haunt and literally enter the schoolhouse during Obama's first weeks in an American classroom. (He had been in school in Indonesia before.) These features of the episode, which takes up most of the narrative's chapter 3, render Obama's version of the schoolhouse story virtually unique. Even so, his story is of a piece with the stories that have come before: these are stories about the onslaught of insult and difference, about young people first becoming aware of how unaware they are of themselves in the world.

Before discussing the schoolhouse episode in *Dreams from My Father*, I would like to review certain features of the episodes famously offered by

W. E. B. Du Bois, James Weldon Johnson, and Zora Neale Hurston. Each of these episodes occurs in the opening pages of a canonical African American text; each has features that direct us to assessing particular attributes of Obama's chapter. Let me begin with the visiting-card affair right at the beginning of Du Bois's *The Souls of Black Folk* (1903). Given the fact that Du Bois was writing during terrible times for the American Negro, a period historian Rayford Logan called "the nadir" of African American history,[1] it is striking that he begins *Souls* with an incident of insult, not atrocity, set among the green hills of New England's Berkshires, not the red clay of the South's Cotton Belt.

In his opening sentences, Du Bois presents a "wee wooden schoolhouse" and describes himself as "a little thing," clearly suggesting the young, naïve innocence of the self and circumstance to be sullied. What happened that fateful day, "when the shadow swept across me," was at first just an occasion of childish frivolity: "something put it into the boys' and girls' heads to buy gorgeous visiting-cards—ten cents a package—and exchange."[2] "The exchange was merry," Du Bois recalls, "till one girl, a tall newcomer, refused my card,—refused it preremptorily, with a glance" (*Souls*, 38).

There is something to observe in almost every word offered in this passage of remembrance. The "shadow" that sweeps across Du Bois prefigures his famous trope of the Veil, which is variously that which shuts him (and others) out of "their world," that which he himself can put in place in seeking a self-protective isolation, and that which he will triumphantly live above, in time. But first, it is a shadow, rendering him a shadow. One notes that the visiting-cards are "gorgeous" and that they were, for a boy whose only meager funds came from the occasional odd job, costly: "ten cents a package."

Anger is expressed in that detail: even as an adult, Du Bois is still seething about actually having paid good money for what happened to him. The girl is not named, perhaps because Du Bois wishes to expose the behavior of a whole class of people, not that of one individual alone. She is described as a "tall newcomer." It has been appropriately suggested that in this remark Du Bois is retaliating by "othering" the girl as one of the new immigrant girls.[3] "Tall" is an interesting detail as well, since we know that Du Bois was short. What rage (and contempt) is thus expressed in characterizing the girl as "new" and "tall," the point being that it is rage of this order that must be controlled and channeled into the special energy and dedication that brings the sunny days with "bluest" skies when "the strife [is] . . . fiercely sunny" (*Souls*, 38).

"Refused" is twice written, lingered over, and then modified by "preremptorily," the very sort of two-dollar word Du Bois spelled correctly "when I could beat my mates at examination-time." The card is refused "with a glance," and that is a key to the scene. What happened to Du Bois that day was that he was initiated into double-consciousness, which is precisely the "peculiar sensation" of "looking at one's self through the eyes of others." And so Du Bois directs us to the tall girl's eyes and instructs us in the pain that even a glance can inflict. Even a merry moment in a New England schoolhouse can be what Saidiya Hartman has termed a "scene of subjection."

Du Bois revels in beating his fellow students in examinations and in footraces, adding that beating "their stringy heads" was pretty good, too. Yet he calls them his mates, which suggests that an allegiance exists along with his animosity. This expresses a twoness that is mirrored in how Du Bois situates himself with other black youth, or more precisely, other black boys. He refers to "us" and includes himself among the "sons of night," but he is the one who knows the light of the "bluest" days. He is determined not to be of that black number whose "youth shrunk into tasteless sycophancy, or into silent hatred of the pale world ... or wasted itself in a bitter cry" (*Souls*, 38). Life above the Veil is, in short, life above a lot of people of many circumstances, which suggests that seeking the true self-consciousness that lies beyond, or above, double-consciousness can be a self-isolating activity, or is necessarily self-isolating. Du Bois does indeed appear to be alone in his schoolhouse episode. There are no adults, not even a teacher; no students have names or otherwise materialize as individuals except the tall newcomer girl. Other black boys are cited in the episode's paragraph but not explicitly as fellow students, and no one black boy emerges as a friend or a relative with a name, or as a knowing compatriot who shares the strife. In short, Du Bois's "we" contains a lot of "me"; filling "we" with "me" is something that began that day in the "wee schoolhouse."

James Weldon Johnson's young colored male in *The Autobiography of an Ex-Colored Man* (1912) also attends public school in a New England schoolhouse. In this instance, the hero-narrator lives and attends school in Connecticut, not Massachusetts, which puts him and his mother close enough to New York so that, on at least one occasion, his father can visit them while on business in New York. Connecticut is at once the convenient yet distant site where this white gentleman can situate his colored family and the site of opportunity for his colored son who would have next-to-no opportunity in the South. The Yankee schoolhouse, which we and the Ex-Colored Man enter in the second half of chapter 1, complete with all the town's children—black, white, brown—attending school and learning together, exemplifies the opportunities available in the North and unheard of in the South. And so, Johnson's novel begins there, as if to suggest that nothing important did happen, or could happen, before our hero's mother relented and enrolled him at the schoolhouse.

Adults matter in Johnson's schoolhouse episode: the Ex-Colored Man is assigned to "a teacher who knew me," and we learn this detail: "my mother made her dresses." This hints at a social hierarchy that we are to take into account and strongly suggests that the teacher knows our racially ambiguous-looking protagonist is colored and has a colored mother. The most interesting detail about the teacher is this: "She was one of the ladies who used to pat me on the head and kiss me."[4] We tend to think of the Ex-Colored Man's amours with white women commencing with the young ladies with whom he later plays duets, just as we assume that whatever Du Bois was up to with white women began with fräuleins in Berlin, not tall newcomers to the Berkshires. But something warm and ardent is present in the way the Ex-Colored Man attaches to his teacher. If nothing more, school is going to be manageable because she is the other mother who has patted him and kissed him. This must be seen in order to comprehend the magnitude of our hero's sense of betrayal when his teacher very publicly "outs" him as a colored child. She, not his real mother, is the mother who does that.

Which brings us to his mother. She is a transplanted southerner who has delayed enrolling her son in the public school apparently to put off the day of his inevitable schoolhouse lesson in race. While the effort to protect her son is understandable, the result is that she has raised what we might term a racial misfit. This is suggested when he rattles on about calling the really smart black boy in his class "Shiny," adding idiotically, "to that name he answered good-naturedly during the balance of his public school days" (*The Autobiography*, 9), and it is confirmed when it turns out that he is one of the boys who walks behind the colored children on their way home from school chanting, "Nigger, nigger, never die, / Black face and shiny eye" (10). On one occasion, a colored boy turns and hurls his slate, which gashes a white boy, and runs, as do the other colored youths. The Ex-Colored Man then relates, "we ran after them pelting them with stones" (10). This is, of course, a very revealing "we."

When our hero arrives home that day and tells his mother what occurred, her behavior is as extraordinary as his has been. Furious with her son, she lights into him, saying, "Don't you ever use that word [nigger] again ... and don't you ever bother the colored children at school. You ought to be ashamed of yourself" (*The Autobiography*, 10). Left out of all this, most obviously, is the point that he is colored, too, and so is she. One senses that this is but the most recent moment when the mother could have "schooled" her son about his racial identity but has refused to do so. What she doesn't realize is that in avoiding the subject she creates a space in which other ideas and behaviors may take hold.

It is a wonder that it is not until the end of his second term of school that the Ex-Colored Man learns of his race. For whatever reason, the school principal arrives at his classroom and asks "all the white scholars to stand for a moment." This is what happens next: "I [the Ex-Colored Man] rose with the others. The teacher looked at me and, calling my name, said: 'You sit down for the present, and rise with the others.' I did not quite understand her, and questioned: 'Ma'am?' She repeated, with a softer tone in her voice: 'You sit down now, and rise with the others." I sat down dazed. I saw and heard nothing. When the others were asked to rise, I did not know it. When school was dismissed, I went out in a kind of stupor" (*The Autobiography*, 11).

One thing that conveys this young boy's confusion is the ambiguity of who the "others" are in this scene. He rose with "the others," but then is told (twice) to sit down and rise with "the others." And once "the others" sat down, "the others" rose? Not surprisingly, the boy ends up not standing with either group of others. He is initiated into that particular status as well. His teacher turns out to be the mother who schools him on race, and she is in this scene both instructive and maternal. She is honest, but she speaks softly, and if she seems slightly evasive in her language it is because she cannot help attempting to protect this boy at the same time that she is exposing him, in several senses of the term.

In Du Bois's schoolhouse episode, we have no idea how the others reacted to young Du Bois being rebuffed by the tall newcomer girl. We do not know if they were aware of the incident, or if aware of it, whether they even deemed it racial. In Johnson's novel, the remainder of the episode is carefully designed to display a gamut of reactions to the young Ex-Colored Man's outing. We are told right off that a few of the white boys jeered: "Oh, you're a nigger too" (*The Autobiography*, 11). We don't learn how the white girls reacted, but some of the black children were heard saying, "We knew he was colored" (11). The "We" in that utterance is as conspicuous as "nigger" is in the dialogue attributed to the white boys. The smart black boy whom our young hero unforgivably has called Shiny shows that he is already some kind of moral force when he tells the black children, "Come along, don't tease him" (11). "Red Head," a big slow-witted white boy who is the one other child in this episode with a name (and note that it is also, arguably, a racially descriptive name), walks our young boy home, and additionally expresses his compassion by carrying his friend's books and promising a present the next day. So there are good guys, two of them, one black, one white, one smart, one slow, and so forth. "Twoness" in this episode is not strictly the "two souls" or "two warring ideals in one dark body" (*Souls*, 38) that is Du Bois's subject; it is in this instance less spiritual.

As we will also see in Obama's schoolhouse episode, returning home after "that day" at school can be part of the story. Our young boy arrives home and, finding his mother busy with a customer, rushes to his room and to the looking-glass on his wall. Clearly, this is this episode's enactment of "looking at one's self through the eyes of others." Soon, he will also scrutinize his mother's visage in a way he has never done before. What is extraordinary about this moment is that he stands before the mirror searching for race and discovers instead his own beauty. One finds in the literature occasional passages in which a colored man's good looks are almost erotically described; think of Douglass's account of Madison Washington's "heroic" appearance in "The Heroic Slave" or of how Ellison's Invisible Man introduces us to Tod Clifton. But there is nothing, certainly not before 1912, when Johnson's novel appeared, quite like the Ex-Colored Man's gaze upon himself. Here is the passage:

> I had often heard people say to my mother: "What a pretty boy you have!" I was accustomed to hear remarks about my beauty; but now, for the first time, I became conscious of it and recognized it. I noticed the ivory whiteness of my skin, the beauty of my mouth, the size and liquid darkness of my eyes, and how the long, black lashes that fringed and shaded them produced an effect that was strangely fascinating even to me. I noticed the softness and glossiness of my dark hair that fell in waves over my temples, making my forehead appear whiter than it really was. How long I stood there gazing at my image I do not know. (*The Autobiography*, 11–12)

What we may see here is a child's genuine confusion: he has been informed at school, by his teacher no less, that he is colored, and out on the street he's been called a nigger, but he looks in the mirror and what he's been called is not what he sees. But to push the matter further: what he sees is beauty, white beauty; that is what he recognizes for the first time and what he is "conscious" of. What he sees is not just a white boy but a pretty white boy. No one detail confirms this; they all do. It may be anxiety that is taking over, it may be anger; either way, he's driven to build his case. In psychoanalytic terms, what he seeks is "relief from otherwise unbearable constellations of identification and wishing."[5]

The events of the day have given our young fellow the vocabulary with which to ask his mother some burning questions: "Tell me mother, am I a nigger?" And after she fumbles with that he asks, "Well, mother, am I white? Are you white?" (*The Autobiography*, 12). These are, of course, questions and issues she has been carefully avoiding, especially in conversations with her son. Thrown off balance, the mother stumbles into another morass: the subject of who our young boy's father is. What she most revealingly manages to say to her son about his father is "the best blood of the South is in you" (12). This declaration may convey the mother's admiration for her child's father, but it also suggests that her thoughts on this difficult subject are bundled up inside timeworn clichés. That is how she manages; that is why the conversation she promises to have with her son "some day" is likely to be unhelpful, if it occurs at all.

All of the protagonists in the schoolhouse episodes under discussion appear in circumstances of remove from one or both parents. Du Bois lived with his mother as a young boy, his father having left them when Du Bois was two, but, as we have seen, there is no parental voice or presence in what he chooses to remember and to present of the visiting-card incident at school. Johnson's young Ex-Colored Man lives with his mother and, one could say, has another mother in his teacher at school. Learning more about race from his "white mother" than from his colored mother proves to be a feature of his dilemma. His father is present as an absence, as a subject to be broached in the future—not now, never now. In Obama's narrative, young Barack has returned to Hawaii—to America—from Indonesia to live with his grandparents while he matriculates at Punahou Academy. His mother remains in Indonesia; his father, who left the family when Barack was an infant, is far away in his native Kenya. As we will see, Obama's schoolhouse episode turns on the reentry into young Barack's life of both his mother and his father.

In *Their Eyes Were Watching God* (1937), Zora Neale Hurston's Janie Crawford begins the story of her life with this information:

> Ah ain't never seen mah papa. And Ah didn't know 'im if Ah did. Mah mama neither. She was gone from round dere long before Ah wuz big enough tuh know. Mah grandma raised me. Mah grandma and de white folks she worked wid. She had a house out in de back-yard and dat's where Ah wuz born.[6]

Right off we learn that Janie is virtually an orphan, that she speaks a thick folk speech, and that she and her grandmother reside within a particular proximity to the white people in their lives. As we have seen, the presence or absence of names is important in these narratives. Janie's grandma is nanny to the white Washburn children and is called "Nanny"; she has no other name. Janie also calls her grandma "Nanny," which is presented as evidence that Janie "was wid dem white chillen so much till Ah didn't know Ah wuzn't white till Ah was round six years old" (8).

We have good reason to anticipate that what happened to Janie when she was six was that she entered school and, perhaps on the first day, got a race lesson. But this episode unfolds a bit differently, partly because the setting is the South, not Du Bois's and Johnson's New England, and Janie is destined for a segregated all-black school, not an integrated one. In this instance, discovering one's race is a preparation for school; other lessons await at the schoolhouse.

In Johnson's novel, the young protagonist peers at himself in the mirror; in Hurston's tale, young Janie looks for herself—futilely at first—in a photograph taken of her and the Washburn children, white children who are about to go off to their own segregated school. Janie relates: "So when we looked at de picture and everybody got pointed out there wasn't nobody left except a real dark little girl with long hair standing by Eleanor. Dat's where Ah wuz s'posed to be, but Ah couldn't recognize dat dark chile as me. So Ah ast, 'where is me? Ah don't see me'" (*Their Eyes*, 9). Janie sees a "dark little girl" standing next to a white girl with a proper name and knows, just knows, she isn't "dat dark chile," the lapse into dialect in itself conveying the status she assigns to what she sees and can't "recognize."

Miss Nellie, a white Washburn woman who is a widow and a mother, points to the "dark one" in the picture and says to Janie, using her nickname as a term of endearment, "Dat's you, Alphabet, don't you know yo' ownself?" Janie's response is, "Aw, aw! I'm colored!" (*Their Eyes*, 9). This prompts much hard laughter, from everybody. Miss Nellie is not unlike the teacher in the young Ex-Colored Man's episode: she is the white mother who fills in, somewhat, for the colored mother who is variously missing from the action.

The curious nickname with which she addresses Janie is explained by Janie as follows: "Dey all useter call me Alphabet 'cause so many people had done named me different names" (*Their Eyes*, 9). What's disturbing here is not just that the colored girl has a comic name in contrast to Eleanor, the white girl standing next to her, but that the nickname results from people habitually calling her anything they want to call her. Hurston is as interested as all our authors are in presenting these everyday moments for what they are: scenes of subjection.

Janie's tormentors at school are led by "uh knotty head gal name Mayrella." One of their sports is to taunt Janie about being illegitimate; they especially like the part in the gossip about how her father was hunted down by Mr. Washburn and the sheriff and the hound dogs "for whut he done tuh mah mama" (*Their Eyes*, 9). Of this, Janie pointedly observes that the children always remembered "de bloodhound part" but not her father's name. While we wonder about all the reasons why Mr. Washburn might be so exercised about catching the man who impregnated Janie's mother, who is, in a sense, a colored member of the family, this is not necessarily a racial incident: bastards and their parents have been berated for time out of mind in every society. What is racial, intraracial, is the grief Janie receives about her dress and her looks. Janie knows she is colored; what awaits her at the schoolhouse is the accusation from black children that she isn't colored enough.

We are told that Mayrella "useter git mad every time she look at me" (*Their Eyes*, 9). What she sees is Janie's long hair, which has already been remarked upon several times in the novel's early pages. Mayrella is especially frenzied by the bows that adorn Janie's hair, and by the clothes Janie wears that, even as hand-me-downs from the white children, are better than what the black children are wearing. Egged on by Mayrella, the children pick at Janie, push her away from "de ring plays," and tell her "not to be takin' on" over her looks. Janie is colored, she is Nanny's granddaughter, but she is dressed for school and otherwise fussed over by the white Washburn women: this is her twoness, this is what is exposed and problematized in the school setting. Janie does not act privileged (as far as we know), but the spectacle and threat of privilege prompts the black children to taunt and ostracize her because she lives "in the white folks' back-yard" (9). This last thing is the matter Nanny acts upon. Janie tells us: "Nanny didn't love tuh see me wid mah head hung down, so she figgered it would be mo' better fuh me if we had uh house. So she got the land and everything and then Mis' Washburn helped out a whole heap wid things" (10). And this is how Nanny acquires the gatepost at which she later spies a teenage Janie kissing Johnny Taylor.

Janie's schoolhouse episode ends with Nanny finding a house for them, perhaps even buying a house for them. One imagines that this no more satisfied the black schoolchildren and their parents than it did the mostly male African American critics (I'm thinking mainly of Sterling Brown, Alain Locke, and Richard Wright) of the late 1930s who criticized Hurston for not presenting the "real problems" before the Negro in the South.[7] Nanny's acquisition of a house, with help from Miss Washburn, likely does nothing to allay the novel's black community's suspicions of Janie's sense of privilege, based in white support. And that may be Hurston's point: black women successfully seeking rooms of their own, in America, achieve something and nothing. Janie may well recall what the black folks said about her Nanny's house when she returns from "the muck" and hears the folks sniping about her having a house all her own in Eatonville. What she is recalling is part and parcel of what her formative schoolhouse episode first instructed.

In *Dreams from My Father*, ten-year-old Barack Obama's flight to Hawaii to begin classes at Punahou Academy may be characterized as a young boy's return to America for race lessons. Whereas the features of the episode border on the unique—Hawaii is not part of the mainland, Punahou is a prestigious private school, Obama lives with his white grandparents, he is African American because his father is really African—the episode as a whole is something of a twice-told tale, an age-old rite of passage.

Preceding the events at school is the remarkable moment of Obama's arrival at the airport in Honolulu and his recollection of how he was overwhelmed by a sense of transition and of twoness, and how he acted out that twoness, while searching the crowds for his grandparents. He tells us that he was carrying an Indonesian mask and that he suddenly put it on, took in its "nutty, cinnamon smell," and felt himself "drifting back across oceans and over the clouds, into the violet horizon, back to the place where I had been."[8] But then his name is called, and he drops the mask to his side and sees his grandparents. Yet there is more: Obama, "without thinking," returns the mask to his face and performs a little dance for his grandparents, who are amused. This goes on until a Customs official taps him on the shoulder and asks if he is an American. With that, the mask is again lowered.

What a piece of business this is: at the very least, we see a biracial child greeting and attempting to please his white elders, using the props at hand, which include the faces of his identity. The masking and unmasking stops with the question about official citizenship; the Customs officer wants to see a passport. But it seems as if he is also policing the racial order: put that mask away, he seems to be saying. This is America!

Obama's first day of school begins with Gramps (the grandfather) proudly escorting him to the well-appointed campus, arriving early in fact, full of excitement. While it is suggested that Gramps is busy fantasizing about what it would have been like if he had attended a fancy school, he is also, by plan or nature, on a mission: to clarify who his colored grandson is and how he's the boy's grandfather and part of the picture. This is not a schoolhouse episode in which the subject of race is avoided or whispered about. Obama's grandfather walks right up to the teacher and introduces himself. By the time he is done, he has told the teacher, Miss Hefty (the only teacher in this discussion to have a name), that Obama's mother is his daughter and that his father is Kenyan and living in Kenya, and much more. Miss Hefty cannot begin the school day until Gramps has completed his introduction.

Unintentionally, Gramps creates one confusion: he calls Barack "Barry" and introduces Barack to a Chinese boy named Frederick as "Barry." One assumes that Barack is "Barry" to everyone he's met that morning until Miss Hefty calls the roll and the mostly white school children hear a strange name: "Barack Hussein Obama." Immediately, "titters break across the room" (*Dreams*, 59). Miss Hefty hears the titters and attempts to address the situation by asking Barack if he prefers "Barry," while declaring at the same time, "Barack is such a beautiful name." Once again, the names deployed in a schoolhouse episode are telling us much about identities assumed and identities imposed. Barack is Barack, but he is also, especially while a schoolboy, Barry; even his Kenyan father, who is also named Barack, calls him Barry. This is a lot for a ten-year-old to process and to put in place.

Miss Hefty reminds us of the teacher in the Ex-Colored Man's episode: she is kind, she has personal reasons for feeling attached to her colored pupil (Miss Hefty has lived in Kenya), and she doesn't seem to be aware of the pain she is causing when she "outs" Barack. What the Ex-Colored Man calls his teacher's "swordthrust" comes in Obama's first-day episode when Miss Hefty asks Barack, "Do you know what tribe your father is from?" (*Dreams*, 60). He is speechless. Being asked, in effect, to other yourself in front of strangers who have already laughed at your name is unbearable. When he finally answers, he says, "Luo." Miss Hefty's question does not create respect for Barack, the new boy; to the contrary, "a sandy-haired boy . . . repeated the word [Luo] in a loud hoot, like the sound of a monkey" (60), and pandemonium breaks out in the classroom. Apparently, even at a young age, these children know intuitively that racism's project is to primitivize the other (*Hating*, xvii); in this scene, monkey sounds do that work.

The sandy-haired boy, like Du Bois's tall newcomer, gets no other name. It is not so much that he doesn't "deserve" a name in the narrative but that he is a specter in a memory that is painful to assemble. He is not the only such figure Barack encounters in the "daze" of the rest of the school day. There is the "red-headed girl" who wanted to touch his hair and "seemed hurt" when he refused. And there is the "ruddy-faced boy" who asked if Barack's father ate people. Once again, names are not offered because this is not, in truth, individualized, idiosyncratic behavior. These children represent a shared mindset, an ignorance that is at best a part of their innocence.

The first day of school begins with the grandfather and ends with him as well. As he merrily prepares dinner, he asks, "So how was it? Isn't it terrific that Miss Hefty used to live in Kenya? Makes the first day a little easier, I'll bet" (*Dreams*, 60). Well, actually, it did not make the first day easier. But she had good intentions; Gramps has good intentions. Good intentions abound. But good intentions did not prevent the day of school Barack just endured. Little wonder, then, that in a sentence starkly centered on the page, in a paragraph unto itself, Obama next writes, "I went into my room and closed the door" (60).

The schoolmate who does have a name is Coretta. She is "plump and dark" and the one other black child in Obama's class. Before his arrival, she has been the only black student in their grade. Just as we cannot help being alert to the fact that she is named, we cannot help but wonder at the name bestowed on her. If, indeed, Obama changed the names of most of the persons in his narrative (*Dreams*, xvii), what alchemy, what civil-rights-laden, historical gesture, led him to name this particular black girl "Coretta"? Young Barack and Coretta avoid each other but watch each other, as if to gain lessons on how to deal with their classroom situation without doing something as obvious and "tribal" as openly conversing and being friends. But there comes a day, a "hot, cloudless day," when Barack and Coretta spontaneously begin to play with each other, and fall to the ground, "breathless." When Barack looks up, he discovers to his horror that he and Coretta are surrounded by white classmates screaming, "Coretta has a boyfriend!" (61).

Perhaps especially for preadolescents, any innocent episode with unwanted sexual implications is devastating. But this moment is exceedingly unbearable for young Barack because the equation includes race as well as sex. Barack is down on the ground not just with any girl but with the black girl, and the taunts from the white children carry the suggestion that he and the black girl are out on the playground doing what black people do, when given the chance. No wonder, then, that Barack screams back that he is *not* Coretta's boyfriend, and gives her a shove, to boot.

Among the key features of this schoolhouse scene is the fact that Obama's memory recalls that Coretta chased him; it was not the other way around.

This suggests Obama's conviction, as an adult, that this episode, or one similar to it, was bound to happen—bound to catch up with him. It is also notable that the taunting white children are on high, pointing down at Barack and Coretta, assuming, as it were, a hierarchical position at the same time that they are "faceless." Earlier in *Dreams*, the offending children have sandy hair or red hair or a ruddy face; these children on the playground are faceless and even more specter-like. Most extraordinary in the scene is Obama's acute awareness of how in pushing Coretta away and yelling "leave me alone!" he was also letting her down. This is, in his words, his "betrayal" of Coretta. Just as Du Bois will never forget the glance of the tall newcomer girl, Obama will forever recall the look on Coretta's face after he pushed her. He tells us that the look brimmed with "disappointment" and "accusation" (*Dreams*, 61). And he admits that "somehow I'd been tested and found wanting" (61). But there are lessons in failures: the episode with Coretta schools Obama to seek the "true self-consciousness" (Du Bois's term) that hopefully disappoints no one, including one's self.

A telegram arrives, and suddenly Barack and his grandparents are nervously aware that Barack's father is coming from Kenya to see him and is staying through the Christmas holidays. Barack's mother is soon arriving in Hawaii as well, two weeks before his father, but the consternation is not about her, it is about Barack Senior. The thought of him is what creates a "moment the air was sucked out of the room" (*Dreams*, 62) and what later prompts Gramps to say, "Should be one hell of a Christmas" (63).

During the weeks Barack and his mother have together before Barack Senior arrives, she "stuffs" Barack with information about Kenya and its history. One might think that a bit of schooling on Kenya would abate the confusion enveloping both Barack and his mother, but it doesn't work. He writes, "But nothing my mother told me could relieve my doubts, and I retained little of the information she offered" (*Dreams*, 64). Part of the problem is that young Barack wants stories, myths even, and images, not facts. His own attempts to find or create those stories are unsuccessful and rather self-incriminating. But Obama nonetheless carries on with this aspect of the story so that we might see how a boy attempts to contend not so much with the familiar matter of his father's absence but with the new dilemma of his pending return.

School is the venue for one key scene of story creation. Another child might have dealt with the confusion of having a mysterious parent arriving from another part of the world by being secretive about the whole matter. Not so our young Barack. He's voluble on the subject; he's got stories, including the inevitable tale some anxious black children tell about how, back in the motherland, "my father was a prince" (*Dreams*, 63). The boys at his lunch table get interested, and that's an added bonus: Barack is negotiating his status at the schoolhouse as well as his personal befuddlement. One of the boys has a question: "I mean, will you go back and be a prince?" Barack replies, "Well ... if I want to, I could. It's sort of complicated, see, 'cause the tribe is full of warriors" (63). It sure is complicated, and not just because of the warriors! It's complicated because Barack is attempting to make whole cloth out of remnants, "the scraps of information I'd picked up from my mother" (63). He is trying to find the useable story, the story that meets needs and that can be altered "on a whim" or ignored "when convenient" (63). He seeks the story he can depend on because he already knows it is too risky to depend on his father.

Barack Senior arrives, and Barack is let out of school early that day by Miss Hefty, who wishes him good luck. This occasions the second long walk home from school in the chapter, the first having been the trudge home after the humiliations of the first day of school. Obama describes the walk home in these terms: "I left the school building feeling like a condemned man. My legs were heavy, and with each approaching step toward my grandparents' apartment, the thump in my chest grew louder. When I entered the elevator, I stood without pressing the button" (*Dreams*, 64). In this instance, what makes the walk home excruciating is not something that happened at school but what awaits him at home, his father, the stranger.

When Barack's grandmother opens the door and says, "Come on, Bar ... come meet your father" (*Dreams*, 65), we realize that he may well be *meeting* his father. What is there for him to remember of the man? Perhaps to amend the grandmother's use of the word "meet," Barack Senior stresses that "it is a good thing to see you after so long" (65), and he addresses his son as "Barry." Calling him "Barry" is an act of affection meant to put young Barack at ease; it is also a familial gesture, a way of saying I, too, am of the family that calls you Barry. But when Barack Senior calls Barack "Barry," he is also calling attention to the fact that Barack is his American son, his son from his (first?) marriage to an American woman. When Barack's father calls him "Barry" there is another lesson in twoness in that.

School is a subject or an issue throughout the family's strange month together. Barack Senior immediately asks young Barack about school in their first conversation, letting him know that he's already heard about how well Barack is doing in his studies. This at first seems to be idle, conventional talk, but he is actually pursuing an important concern: he is initiating friendship with his son while proclaiming him an Obama. At one point, he says, "Have I told you that your brothers and sisters have also excelled in their schooling? It's in the blood, I think" (*Dreams*, 65). Of course, this is a way of underscoring for his son an important thing he wants him to know about himself: that he was a good student and is a studious man. There is risk in this: every adult in that small living room knows that he left his family rather than pass up graduate school at Harvard. But in the beginning of the month together, on the first day in fact, everyone is on good behavior.

Weeks into the visit, however, resentments burn, and tempers begin to flare. The eruption Obama reports occurs one evening just before the Christmas recess at school. Barack turns on the television to watch *How the Grinch Stole Christmas*, and his father summarily orders him to turn it off and go to his room and study, so the adults can talk. Toot (the grandmother) suggests that Barack watch the show in the bedroom; his father says no. Barack's mother tries to explain that it's almost Christmas and that the cartoon is a Christmas favorite and that Barry's been looking forward to it all week. His father says, "Anna, this is nonsense. If the boy has done his work for tomorrow, he can begin on the next day's assignments. Or the assignments he will have when he returns from the holidays" (*Dreams*, 68). And he has more words for his son: "I tell you, Barry, you do not work as hard as you should. Go now, before I get angry at you" (68). With that, all hell breaks loose; everybody's yelling and furious. The scene turns from *How the Grinch Stole Christmas* to How the Father Stole Christmas. While the ensuing argument was inevitable, and could have been about almost anything, it is revealing that Barack Senior makes it an argument about school. This is another matter from which Barack retreats to his room.

The next day, his mother has some news for him: "By the way, I forgot to tell you that Miss Hefty has invited your father to come to school on Thursday. She wants him to speak to the class" (*Dreams*, 69). His response is: "I couldn't imagine worse news. I spent that night and all of the next day trying to suppress thoughts of the inevitable: the faces of my classmates when they heard about mud huts, all my lies exposed, the painful jokes afterward" (69). Clearly, with the mention of the classmates' faces, we have in Obama's reaction another phrasing of double-consciousness, of "looking at one's self through the eyes of others" (*Souls*, 38). This is a feature of our other narratives; consider Du Bois remembering the glance of the newcomer girl or Hurston's Janie unhinged by the looks from Mayrella. What may be singular about Obama's circumstance is that the faces of his classmates include Coretta's face; what will be her look this time? What also may be unique is that Barack's anxieties about how the children will look at him are totally bound up with how they will see his father. What will they see?

What they see is a highly educated man from Kenya who has been introducing his country, and himself, to myriad audiences for a good long while. Barack Senior is especially deft at speaking to an American audience: Africa is in his narrative, but so is America. And so, while there are wild animals and tribal customs in what he describes, there is also a surprisingly familiar story of a country's struggle for freedom from British colonial rule. This is what Obama remembers of that part of the speech: "And he told us of Kenya's struggle to be free, how the British wanted to stay and unjustly rule the people, just as they had in America; how many had been enslaved only because of the color of their skin, just as they had in America; but that Kenyans, like all of us in the room, longed to be free and develop themselves through hard work and sacrifice" (*Dreams*, 70).

Barack's father's speech at the school is a lesson in inclusiveness, in what is shared. *Dreams from My Father* offers the rare schoolhouse episode in which the parent actually comes to the school, and everyone, including the child who dreaded the parent's appearance, is the better for it. The schoolhouse scenes in *Dreams* begin with Gramps coming to school and end with Barack Senior coming to school; this is typical of the kind of symmetry Obama often constructs in telling his stories. Symmetry is additionally offered when classmates who appeared in the early scenes reappear right after his father's address. For example, the ruddy-faced boy who on the first school day asked if Barack's father eats people comes up to Barack to say, "Your dad is pretty cool" (*Dreams*, 70). In a more complicated way, Coretta is part of the moment as well. As before, she does not speak; she says nothing to Barack or to his father. Off to the side, she watches his father say goodbye to some of the children. Since she and Barack are the only colored children in the class, this means, of course, that she is watching Barack's father say goodbye to white children. What is she looking for? What does she see? Obama tells us that "her face showed only a simple satisfaction" (70). What does that mean?

Barack Senior's arrival and departure are marked with gifts to his son. The evening of his arrival, he gives Barack three wooden figurines: "a lion, an elephant, and an ebony man in tribal dress beating a drum" (D*reams*, 66). Barack doesn't know what to say, perhaps because gifts from his father are so rare, or perhaps because these figurines represent the very sort of images of Africa that prompt children like his classmates to giggle and crack jokes. His mother urges him to say thank you; Barack mutters his thanks. The figurines are described as being "lifeless in his hands" (66). The question is thus raised as to whether the figurines, and the father who bestowed them, will, in some measure, come back to life for Barack. Will they and the father become something more than curios from a dark place far away?

Barack Senior comes to life, at least for a golden moment, when he gives his departing gifts to his son. The gifts are records, 45s, which he gives to Barack, saying, "Barry! Look here—I forgot that I brought these for you. The sounds of your continent" (*Dreams*, 71). The records bring the continent alive as the figurines never could because the music begins and Barack's father begins to dance. Though still hobbled from his automobile accident, the man knows his steps and can move. And then he does a wonderful thing: he invites Barack to join him in the dance. His very words are "Come, Barry, ... you will learn from the master" (71). As they dance, Barack watches his father tingle with life and pleasure, his eyes closed, his whole self transported. But suddenly he opens one eye and peeks at his son and grins a silly grin; he's keeping track of his boy; he's schooling him in something indescribable. Obama remembers it this way: "I took my first tentative steps with my eyes closed, down, up, my arms swinging, the voices lifting.... And I hear him still.... I follow my father into the sound" (71).

Barack's grandfather was right in his prediction: especially with Barack Senior around, it was going to be one hell of a Christmas. Barack Senior came to town, came to school, in fact. In the photos Obama has of that visit (the only photos he has of himself with his father), he and his father stand before the Christmas tree, his father sporting the tie he has just received as a gift from Barack. Barack is next to his father, holding an orange basketball, his father's gift to him. These are the "official" Christmas gifts, the ones recorded in photographs, the ones with no strings attached. But other gifts, wanted and unwanted, were no doubt exchanged—the figurines and records, yes, but others, too: some tangible, some ephemeral, some known to be gifts only with the passage of time. We learn from the giving and receiving of gifts, and this can be a part of our schooling, as we know from reading the schoolhouse episodes in African American narratives. Obama learned much during his first months of American schooling, thanks in part to the gifts and dreams from his father.

NOTES

This chapter is reproduced from *A Home Elsewhere: Reading African American Classics in the Age of Obama* by Robert B. Stepto (Cambridge, Mass.: Harvard University Press), Copyright © 2010 by the President and Fellows of Harvard College. The epigraph to this chapter is from Bonnie Angelo, "The Pain of Being Black: An Interview with Toni Morrison" (1989), in *Conversations with Toni Morrison*, ed. Danielle Guthrie-Taylor (Jackson: University Press of Mississippi, 1994), 258, emphasis added.

1. Rayford W. Logan, *The Negro in American Life and Thought: The Nadir, 1877–1901* (New York: Dial, 1954).

2. W. E. B. Du Bois, *The Souls of Black Folk*, ed. David W. Blight and Robert Gooding-Williams (1903; rpt., Boston: Bedford, 1997), 38. Future references to this edition are cited parenthetically in the text.

3. See, for example, Shamoon Zamir, *Dark Voices: W. E. B. Du Bois and American Thought, 1888–1903* (Chicago: University of Chicago Press, 1995), 138.

4. James Weldon Johnson, *The Autobiography of an Ex-Colored Man* (1912; rpt., New York: Penguin, 1990), 6. Future references to this edition are given parenthetically in the text.

5. Donald Moss, "Introduction: On Hating in the First Personal Plural: Thinking Psychoanalytically about Racism, Homophobia, and Misogyny," in *Hating in the First Person Plural: Psychoanalytic Essays on Racism, Homophobia, Misogyny, and Terror*, ed. Moss (New York: Other Press, 2003), xxxiii. Future references are given parenthetically in the text.

6. Zora Neale Hurston, *Their Eyes Were Watching God* (1937; rpt., New York: Harper Perennial, 1990), 8. Future references to this edition are given parenthetically in the text.

7. See Mary Helen Washington's summary of the critical response to Hurston from Brown, Locke, and Wright in her foreword (*Their Eyes*, vii–viii).

8. Barack Obama, *Dreams from My Father: A Story of Race and Inheritance* (New York: Three Rivers, 1995), 54. All future references are given parenthetically in the text.

AFTERWORD

The Ex-Colored Man for a New Century

NOELLE MORRISSETTE AND AMRITJIT SINGH

James Weldon Johnson, who thought of *The Autobiography of an Ex-Colored Man* as a living, moving work—a "biography of the race"—no doubt would have had much to add to his novel as he viewed more than a century of African American experiences following its publication. The novel has proven prescient in the way it anticipated the ongoing story of African American life. This story, still unfolding in the twenty-first century, is central to everything the United States as a nation stands for. As Ralph Ellison reminds readers in his essay "Twentieth-Century Fiction and the Black Mask of Humanity," it is important that "we view the whole of American life as a drama acted upon the body of a Negro giant, who, lying trussed up like Gulliver, forms the stage and scene upon which and within which the action unfolds."[1] In reading *The Autobiography* today, one cannot possibly ignore Ellison's notion of the centrality of race to every aspect of American life. While *The Autobiography* explores binaries of social class as well as the creative tensions between ragtime and European classical music, it also narrates the practices and categories shaping literary study: nationally bounded formations of canon and tradition, transnational crossings and affiliations, and the place of literature and literary study in the world.

In his autobiography, *Along This Way*, Johnson refers to "collateral knowledge" as a driving concept that links cultural and historical contexts and literary texts. Johnson's "West Indian cobbler," who served as his teacher for a brief time when he was away from Atlanta University, possessed, in Johnson's estimation, "a considerable store of collateral knowledge" that "stir[red] my curiosity and interest in what I studied."[2] "This collateral information not only made it [Johnson's study] interesting, but gave it sense and connected it up with life" (*Along This Way*, 93). Johnson's orientation to his studies and to the world was critically altered by his time spent with this man, whose name is now forgotten and who "disappeared" within the year (99). "The only other teacher who made a subject as interesting to me as did this little cobbler was

Brander Matthews at Columbia. I wonder just what it was that kept him down on a cobbler's bench?" Johnson asks rhetorically (93).

Like his many successors in nonviolent resistance to oppression—Martin Luther King Jr., Mahatma Gandhi, and Nelson Mandela, among them—Johnson trained as a lawyer and expansively directed this expertise to the larger endeavor of human understanding. Through writing, scholarship, and activism Johnson devoted his life to providing an understanding of race and expounding on the meaning and promise of America. In almost all areas of his layered career, he strove to confront the Janus-faced United States on the issue of freedom and slavery. In the process, he troubled the mythic claims of liberty associated with "America," bidding the ancestral bards of African American experiences to speak and be heard. Through these endeavors, he insisted on addressing the past and present of racial oppression and on changing public policy not only through law but also through sociocultural outlook. Reaching for that future—as yet ungraspable—in which African American culture and citizenship can be fully realized, Johnson directed the nation's focus to its history of slavery and racial oppression in order to imagine and realize a better future for all. He devoted his life to this future.

Such a future nation would be composed of world citizens, "cosmopolites." While the concept of cosmopolitanism has not been fulfilled in its quest for universal understanding and human mutuality and has been associated with imperialism, nationalism, and parochialism, it persists as a useable, if shifting, measure of academic and real-world relations.[3] Johnson's distinct use of the term in his writings referenced not its widely held negative association with the contradictory claims of world citizenship and world imperialism, but its usefulness as a concept of intercultural understanding and tolerance.[4] This collaborative framework operated for Johnson through the productive tension between the nation and national belonging, to which he remained committed, and transnational cultural identifications created by the conditions of modernity. African Americans of necessity possess this greater awareness. The Black Atlantic, framing modern life for African peoples through the transatlantic slave trade, was immediately and forcibly recognizable to its descendants as part of their "collateral knowledge." As Paul Gilroy points out, this diasporic condition created a "countercultural" modernity in which thinkers like W. E. B. Du Bois and Johnson could productively challenge the politically oppressive framework of the nation, even while remaining committed to it.[5] The violent modernity that made the Black Atlantic became, in the writings of Johnson, an innovative concept that enabled transnational movement and the affiliation of raced and colonized peoples beyond limiting, nationally bounded discourses of identity and homeland. In this search for greater freedom and its attendant justice, other peoples might join African Americans and share a heightened sense of affiliation and identification.

The Autobiography stands in solidarity with a few works of African American fiction from the first half of the twentieth century—such as Nella Larsen's *Quicksand* (1928) and *Passing* (1929), Jessie Fauset's *Comedy: American Style* (1933) and *Plum Bun* (1929), George S. Schuyler's *Black No More* (1931), and Chester Himes's *The Third Generation* (1954)—that have brought a sharp perspective on the social disease of colorism that emanates from facing the daily "burden of the dwarfing, warping, distorting influence which operates upon each and every colored man in the United States."[6] At the same time, the National Association for the Advancement of Colored People's nomenclature of "colored people" instead of "Negroes" signaled an early recognition of inclusiveness that began to embrace all those who are dispossessed and marginalized. As texts such as Du Bois's *Dark Princess* (1928) and *The World and Africa* (1947), Richard Wright's *Black Power* (1954) and *The Color Curtain* (1956), Ian Haney López's *White by Law* (1996), and Matthew Frye Jacobson's *Whiteness of a Different Color* (1998) demonstrate, "race" in theory and praxis is both capacious and contextual, going well beyond the black-white binary in the United States.

Not simply the cosmopolitanism of individuals, but also the nature of our lives indicates our global interconnectedness.[7] As U.S. Supreme Court justices debate the place of other nations' laws in America's consideration of fairness and legitimacy, their very conversations make apparent the nation's best and worst dispositions in the search for social justice. On the one hand, U.S. courts claim the nation's uniqueness, which may be used to justify the evasion of obligations to international contexts and other peoples. On the other, court debates have demonstrated at least partial recognition of the shared human condition of injustice and made the case for interdependence.[8] Global interconnectedness makes obvious our obligation to each other, while also revealing the inequities of new systems of slavery, capitalism, and power.

Cosmopolitanism's early twentieth-century moment of globalization and imperialist crisis resounds in this twenty-first-century moment. The nativist and xenophobic turn in the 2015–16 presidential debates has turned on its head the powerful antinativist timbre of W. E. B. Du Bois's "Of Our Spiritual Strivings" (1903) and Randolph Bourne's "Trans-National America" (1916). The loud anti-immigrant sentiments of 2016 appear to echo Theodore Roosevelt's claim in 1904 that "we cannot have too much immigration of the right kind, and we should have none at all of the wrong kind. The need is to devise some system by which undesirable immigrants shall be kept out entirely, while desirable immigrants are properly distributed throughout the country."[9] Discussion of U.S. citizenship simultaneously entails, however, acknowledgment of U.S. imperialism, as Johnson knew. Both his editorial "Why Latin America Dislikes the United States" (1913) and his "Style of Business Correspondence" (1909), submitted in triplicate to the State Department at the start of his diplomatic posting to Nicaragua, demonstrate Johnson's awareness of these interdependent concerns.[10] Contemporary debates on immigration, combined with continuing concerns about the citizenship rights of African Americans within the republic, demonstrate a nativist, exclusionary privilege of white citizenship and its racial order that has both national and global implications. There is a reluctance to confront white supremacy at home or to acknowledge the economic exploitation of other, often nonwhite nations that undergirds globalization and neoliberal capitalism.[11]

As a diplomat and public intellectual, Johnson was involved with several of the events that founded this order in the twentieth century: the Platt Amendment permitting U.S. intervention in Cuba and establishing the U.S. naval base at Guantanamo Bay (1901, approved 1903); Roosevelt's corollary to the Monroe Doctrine (1904), as well as the Venezuelan crisis (1902–3) that prompted it; and the postcrisis situation into which Johnson was introduced as a U.S. diplomat to that nation (1906–9). In hindsight it is obvious that the Monroe Doctrine protected U.S. imperialist interests in the hemisphere, particularly but not limited to Latin America. Roosevelt's corollary took the protectionist doctrine a step further, using it to justify U.S. intervention in and annexation of those nations. The Platt Amendment, which removed the U.S. occupation of Cuba, also ensured a continued American presence through the naval base there and by justifying U.S. intervention when needed to defend Cuban "sovereignty." American interventions have often been couched in terms of business and financial obligations, as was the case in Haiti (U.S. occupation of that nation stretched from 1914 to 1934).

Johnson would have recognized in this twenty-first-century discourse of immigration and citizenship rights the perpetual "us" versus "them," which is defined not simply by war but by the American imperialist agenda imposed on French- and Spanish-speaking as well as African-descended peoples of the hemispheres of America.[12] No doubt he also would have recognized in the twentieth-century segregationist practices imposed on U.S. citizens of Mexican descent their similarity to African American oppression. Today's waves of Mexican American migration and Mexican immigration not only help to sharpen recall of Native American genocide, but also illuminate African American experiences of displacement and second-class citizenship, which has included systemic practices that define contingent labor forces and even contingent citizenship.[13]

The landscapes of memory, spectral and symbolic in Johnson's 1912 novel, continue to mark national attitudes toward the past and present in the United States, which is decisively defined by slavery and continued forms of oppression. Discursively engaged with the myth and reality of America and with the brutal logic of terror enacted on raced subjects, be they Haitian, Mexican, Native American, or African American, Johnson would have recognized the documented examples of twenty-first-century police brutality and terror from Ohio, South Carolina, New York, and Texas. The high stakes that have been placed on romanticizing the past of slavery have enabled the imposition of continued acts of terror on slavery's survivors. The slaying of nine African American churchgoers in Charleston, South Carolina, in 2015 was both an act of white supremacy and an attempt to control the history of slavery.[14] To discuss the promise of the United States, Johnson argued, it is also necessary to address its betrayals of that promise to the peoples within its gates—peoples whose lives provide evidence of the nation's shameful, oppressive practices. Only through such acknowledgment can the nation reach its ideal, better future—altered by the recognition and inclusion of all of its peoples.[15] There are similar notes in the fictional writings of Johnson's contemporaries, such as Abraham Cahan, Mary Antin, and Anzia Yezierska.[16]

Literature, in order to succeed, must bear a relation to the real world, even if that bond is forged through a relation that does not yet exist. Literary study is a necessary act that affirms this human connection. Johnson recognized the importance of university study, especially the disciplines of history, literature, drama, art, and education. He was acutely aware of his role as an African American educator, humanist, and cosmopolite at Columbia's and New York University's teachers colleges. The very scene of those classrooms could cultivate the moral imagination of individuals in conversation with each other. As one assesses the meaning and value of education in the digital age, one ought to recall Johnson's description of his 1912 narrative as a "human document": a complex work contemplating human thoughts, actions, and works of art. To place the Ex-Colored Man in the twenty-first-century classroom is to recognize the urgency of freeing knowledge from a perceived uniformity and facticity through human contact and a commitment to multiple "discrepant engagements"—to "collateral knowledge" and to the "family bookshelf" of African American literature.[17] Studying Johnson's *The Autobiography of an Ex-Colored Man* today affirms the crucial nature of such readings. Personal and ancestral literary readings open consciousness and enable shared intellectual, cultural, and racial expansion.

The archive, Johnson knew, has a life of its own: its liveliness points toward this collection of essays more than a hundred years after *The Autobiography of an Ex-Colored Man*'s initial publication. The essays offered here bring together a wide range of perspectives on *The Autobiography* and its creator. They are reevaluations of Johnson's work, and they acknowledge the power of *The Autobiography* and its literary interpretations in the twenty-first century. The record of black cultural expression has expanded in the hundred years since its publication, but the promise of a more attentive and attuned nation has yet to be fulfilled. *The Autobiography of an Ex-Colored Man*'s retrospective framework of seeming regret ("I cannot suppress the thought that... I have sold my birthright for a mess of pottage"; the shadowy recollections of his origins in slavery and Reconstruction) leaves Johnson's readers poised on the edge of a new, modern reality. Johnson's tale was not a historical retelling, nor was it exclusively engaged with the representational strategies of the culture of uplift. Rather, its "forward glance" anticipated the intellectual work of Afrofuturism—a historical and cultural foundation of black popular culture extended into the future through technology and knowledge formation.[18]

Reading *The Autobiography of an Ex-Colored Man* now, one might consider how crucial are current endeavors to interpret issues of human existence in the digital age: what is available, and how, and what it means about "us." The new critical tools—whether the recognition of an "ethnic archive," the interrogation of the "literary classic," or a more expansive theorization of knowledge practices—do not replace the older concepts of knowledge, but instead make them relevant and more widely acknowledged. Interpreters must integrate their encounters with other individuals, ideas, and cultures; absorb, copy, and make intimate the random knowledges offered by the archive. To be transformed is also to transform our understanding of humanity, to be explained as well as to interpret ourselves to each other. These interpretative and biographical processes help reveal the ways in which literature and literary study shape our experiences and articulate our transformations in the modern world. As the inheritors of Johnson's beautiful work, let us imagine and produce the still-unwritten chapters of this ongoing narrative.

NOTES

1. Ralph Ellison, "Twentieth-Century Fiction and the Black Mask of Humanity," in *The Collected Essays of Ralph Ellison*, ed. John Callahan (New York: Random House, 1995), 85.

2. James Weldon Johnson, *Along This Way: The Autobiography of James Weldon Johnson* (New York: Viking, 1933), 93, 100. Future references are given parenthetically in the text.

3. Janet Lyon, "Review of Rebecca L. Walkowitz, *Cosmopolitan Style: Modernism beyond the Nation*," *Politics and Culture* (October 2, 2009): n.p.

4. Stephen Toulmin, *Cosmopolis: The Hidden Agenda of Modernity* (Chicago: University of Chicago Press, 1990).

5. Gilroy, *The Black Atlantic: Modernity and Double Consciousness* (Cambridge, Mass.: Harvard University Press, 1993).

6. Johnson, *The Autobiography of an Ex-Colored Man*, 13.

7. Daphne Lamothe's essay in this collection poignantly demonstrates this point.

8. Stephen Breyer documents this debate among the justices in *The Court and the World: American Law and the New Global Realities* (New York: Knopf, 2015).

9. Jacob Riis, *Theodore Roosevelt, the Citizen* (1904; rpt., e-book, Bartleby.com, 2000), 46. See also Kitty Calavita, *U.S. Immigration Law and the Control of Labor, 1820–1924* (London: Academic, 1984).

10. Johnson, "Why Latin America Dislikes the United States," in *The Selected Writings of James Weldon Johnson*, ed. Sondra Kathryn Wilson (New York: Oxford University Press, 1995), 2:195–97; Johnson, "Style of Business Correspondence," Diplomatic Records, Nicaragua, register 84, vol. 308, National Archives II, College Park, Md. See my discussion of this report in Morrissette, *Modern Soundscapes*, 75–76.

11. In line with the twisted ironies that often mark U.S. history, the U.S. Congress offered an apology in 2012 for the 1882 Chinese Exclusion Act and its sundry progeny, which kept Chinese and other Asian immigrants out of the United States between 1882 and 1965, when President Lyndon Johnson signed into law the Immigration and Nationality Act.

12. See John Cullen Gruesser, *The Empire Abroad and the Empire at Home: African American Literature and the Era of Overseas Expansion* (Athens: University of Georgia Press, 2012), esp. chap. 4, "Annexation in the Pacific and Asian Conspiracy in Central America in James Weldon Johnson's Unproduced Operettas."

13. Mexicans living in the current southwestern region of the United States were colonized by America as the result of the Mexican-American War (1846–48). The United States has used soldiers of Mexican descent in every conflict since World War II, while still denying them citizenship. The Bracero Program of 1942–64 brought Mexican workers to labor in America, while President Dwight D. Eisenhower's Operation Wetback (1954) deported them. The internment of U.S. citizens of Japanese descent during World War II provides another example of contingent citizenship.

14. A dispute had unfolded in Charleston in 2014, when, after rancorous debate, Denmark Vesey had received a statue acknowledging his place in the city's history. Vesey had organized a widespread rebellion against slavery in 1822, but the plot was exposed just days before the insurrection was to take place. He and five other men were publicly hanged as a consequence.

15. Several contemporary works demand this acknowledgment, including Randall Robinson, *The Debt: What America Owes to Blacks* (New York: Plume, 2001); and Ta-Nehisi Coates, "The Case for Reparations," *Atlantic Monthly*, June 2014, http://www.theatlantic.com/magazine/archive/2014/06/the-case-for-reparations/361631/. See also Coates's *Between the World and Me* (New York: Spiegel and Grau, 2015).

16. For example, the protagonist in Yezierska's "America and I" (1923) is disillusioned as she searches for her "big idea" of America: "I felt that the America that I sought was nothing but a shadow—an echo—a chimera of lunatics and crazy immigrants." In *Heath Anthology of American Literature*, vol. D: *Modern Period, 1910–1945*, 7th ed., ed. Paul Lauter et al. (Boston: Wadsworth, Cengage, 2014), 2323.

17. Nathaniel Mackey, *Discrepant Engagement: Dissonance, Cross-Culturality, and Experimental Writing* (New York: Cambridge University Press, 1993). As Robert Stepto recalls, he was "initially a 'family bookshelf' Afro-Americanist," and writing *From behind the Veil* was "a revisitation of family bookshelves and a brave effort to render the academic world more familiar—if not exactly familial—by writing myself into the intellectual impulses and traditions which were responsible for there being in the first

place any *family* books to shelve" (*From behind the Veil: A Study of Afro-American Narrative*, 2nd ed. [Urbana: University of Illinois Press, 1991], x).

18. The phrase "forward glance," taken from the conclusion of *Along This Way*, demonstrates Johnson's future-oriented narrative framing of black cultural politics in the United States. Afrofuturism, a multivalent term for countless genres, styles, and authors from the 1970s on, conveys the presence and importance of race in technology and the future. See Alondra Nelson, ed., *Afrofuturism: A Special Issue of Social Text* 71 (June 3, 2002). Johnson anticipated this concept in his interest in the "scientific basis" of ragtime and its performativity in technology and future modalities of time, space, and reproduction.

SUGGESTED FURTHER READING

Andrews, William. Introduction to *The Autobiography of an Ex-Colored Man* by James Weldon Johnson. New York: Penguin, 1990.

Badaracco, Claire Hoertz. "*The Autobiography of an Ex-Coloured Man* by James Weldon Johnson: The 1927 Knopf Edition." *Papers of the Bibliographical Society of America* 96 (2002): 279–87.

Baker, Houston A., Jr. "A Forgotten Prototype: *The Autobiography of an Ex-Colored Man* and *Invisible Man*." In *Critical Essays on James Weldon Johnson*, edited by Kenneth M. Price and Lawrence J. Oliver, 31–42. New York: G. K. Hall, 1997.

Biers, Katherine. "Syncope Fever: James Weldon Johnson and the Black Phonographic Voice." *Representations* 96 (Fall 2006): 99–125.

Brooks, Daphne. *Bodies in Dissent: Spectacular Performances of Race and Freedom, 1850–1910*. Durham, N.C.: Duke University Press, 2006.

Bruce, Dickson D., Jr. *Black American Writing from the Nadir: The Evolution of a Literary Tradition, 1877–1915*. Baton Rouge: Louisiana State University Press, 1989.

Clements, Amy Root. *The Art of Prestige: The Formative Years at Knopf, 1915–1929*. Amherst: University of Massachusetts Press, 2014.

Collier, Eugenia. "The Endless Journey of an Ex-Colored Man." *Phylon* 3 (Winter 1971): 372–432.

Cooper, Patricia A. *Once a Cigar Maker: Men, Women, and Work Culture in American Cigar Factories, 1900–1919*. Urbana: University of Illinois Press, 1987.

Doyle, Laura. *Freedom's Empire: Race and the Rise of the Novel in Atlantic Modernity, 1640–1940*. Durham, N.C.: Duke University Press, 2008.

Edwards, Brent Hayes. *The Practice of Diaspora: Literature, Translation, and the Rise of Black Internationalism*. Cambridge, Mass.: Harvard University Press, 2003.

———. "The Seemingly Eclipsed Window of Form: James Weldon Johnson's Prefaces." In *Jazz Cadences of American Culture*, edited by R. G. O'Meally, 580–601. New York: Columbia University Press, 1998.

Fabi, M. Giulia. *Passing and the Rise of the African American Novel*. Urbana: University of Illinois Press, 2001.

Fleming, Robert. "Irony as a Key to Johnson's *The Autobiography of an Ex-Colored Man*." *American Literature* 43, no. 1 (March 1971): 83–96.

Gates, Henry Louis, Jr. "Introduction to the Vintage Edition." *The Autobiography of an Ex-Coloured Man* by James Weldon Johnson. New York: Vintage, 1989.

Goble, Mark. *Beautiful Circuits: Modernism and the Mediated Life*. New York: Columbia University Press, 2010.

Goldsby, Jacqueline. Introduction to *The Autobiography of an Ex-Colored Man* by James Weldon Johnson. New York: Norton, 2015.

———. "Keeping the 'Secret of Authorship': A Critical Look at the 1912 Publication of James Weldon Johnson's *Autobiography of an Ex-Colored Man*." In *Print Culture in a Diverse America*, edited by James P. Danky and Wayne A. Wiegand, 244–71. Urbana: University of Illinois Press, 1998.

———. *A Spectacular Secret: Lynching in American Life and Literature*. Chicago: University of Chicago Press, 2006.

Gruesser, John Cullen. *The Empire Abroad and the Empire at Home: African American Literature and the Era of Overseas Expansion*. Athens: University of Georgia Press, 2012.

Hutchinson, George. *The Harlem Renaissance in Black and White*. Cambridge, Mass.: Belknap, 1997.

Jackson, Miles M., ed. "Letters to a Friend: Correspondence from James Weldon Johnson to George A. Towns." *Phylon* 29 (1968): 182–98.

Jaji, Tsitsi. "Art Song Poetics: Performing Samuel Coleridge-Taylor's Setting of Paul L. Dunbar's 'A Corn Song.'" *J19: The Journal of Nineteenth-Century Americanists* 1, no. 1 (2013): 201–6.

Jarrett, Gene. *Deans and Truants: Race and Realism in African American Literature*. Philadelphia: University of Pennsylvania Press, 2006.

Johnson, James Weldon. *The Selected Writings of James Weldon Johnson*. 2 vols. Edited by Sondra Kathryn Wilson. New York: Oxford University Press, 1995.

———. *Writings*. Edited by William L. Andrews. New York: Library of America, 2004.

Kawash, Samira. "*The Autobiography of an Ex-Colored Man*: (Passing for) Black Passing for White." In *Passing and the Fictions of Identity*, edited by Elaine K. Ginsberg, 59–74. Durham, N.C.: Duke University Press, 1996.

Levy, Eugene. *James Weldon Johnson: Black Leader, Black Voice*. Chicago: University of Chicago Press, 1973.

Lewis, David Levering. *When Harlem Was in Vogue*. 1979. Rpt., New York: Penguin, 1997.

Logan, Rayford W. *The Negro in American Life and Thought: The Nadir, 1877–1901*. New York: Dial, 1954.

Marks, Edward. *They All Sang: From Tony Pastor to Rudy Vallee*. New York: Viking, 1934.

Mirabal, Nancy Raquel. "The Afro-Cuban Community in Ybor City and Tampa, 1886–1910." *OAH Magazine of History* 7, no. 4 (Summer 1993): 19–22. http://www.jstor.org/stable/25162907.

Morrissette, Noelle. Introduction to *The Autobiography of an Ex-Colored Man* by James Weldon Johnson. New York: Fine Creative Media, 2007.

Oliver, Lawrence J. *Brander Matthews, Theodore Roosevelt, and the Politics of American Literature, 1880–1920*. Knoxville: University of Tennessee Press, 1992.

———, ed. *The Letters of Theodore Roosevelt and Brander Matthews*. Knoxville: University of Tennessee Press, 1995.

Page, Amanda. "The Ever-Expanding South: James Weldon Johnson and the Rhetoric of the Global Color Line." *Southern Quarterly: A Journal of the Arts in the South* 46, no. 3 (Spring 2009): 26–46.

Pascoe, Peggy. *What Comes Naturally: Miscegenation Law and the Making of Race in America*. New York: Oxford University Press, 2008.

Price, Kenneth M., and Lawrence J. Oliver, eds. *Critical Essays on James Weldon Johnson*. New York: G. K. Hall, 1997.

Radano, Ronald. "Hot Fantasies: American Modernism and the Idea of Black Rhythm." In *Music and the Racial Imagination*, edited by Radano and Philip Bohlman, 459–80. Chicago: University of Chicago Press, 2000.

Riis, Thomas. *Just before Jazz: Black Musical Theater in New York, 1890–1915*. Washington, D.C.: Smithsonian Institution Press, 1989.

Roberts, Brian Russell. "Passing into Diplomacy: U.S. Consul James Weldon Johnson and *The Autobiography of an Ex-Colored Man*." *Modern Fiction Studies* 56 (Summer 2010): 290–316.

Russell, Heather. *Legba's Crossing: Narratology in the African Atlantic*. Athens: University of Georgia Press, 2009.

Scruggs, Charles. *The Sage in Harlem: H. L. Mencken and the Black Writers of the 1920s*. Baltimore, Md.: Johns Hopkins University Press, 1984.

Seltzer, George. *Music Matters: The Performer and the American Federation of Musicians*. Metuchen, N.J.: Scarecrow, 1989.

Seniors, Paula. *Beyond "Lift Every Voice and Sing": The Culture of Uplift, Identity, and Politics in Black Musical Theater*. Columbus: Ohio State University Press, 2009.

Skerrett, Joseph T., Jr. "Irony and Symbolic Action in James Weldon Johnson's *The Autobiography of an Ex-Coloured Man*." In *Critical Essays on James Weldon Johnson*, edited by Kenneth M. Price and Lawrence J. Oliver, 70–87. New York: G. K. Hall, 1997.

Smith, Valerie. "Privilege and Evasion in James Weldon Johnson's *The Autobiography of an Ex-Colored Man*." In *Critical Essays on James Weldon Johnson*, edited by Kenneth M. Price and Lawrence J. Oliver, 88–101. New York: G. K. Hall, 1997.

Somerville, Siobhan. *Queering the Color Line: Race and the Invention of Homosexuality in American Culture*. Durham, N.C.: Duke University Press, 2000.

Stecopoulos, Harilaos. *Reconstructing the World: Southern Fictions and U.S. Imperialisms, 1898–1976*. Ithaca, N.Y.: Cornell University Press, 2008.

———. "Up from Empire: James Weldon Johnson, Latin America, and the Jim Crow South." In *Our Americas: Political and Cultural Imaginings of the Americas*, edited by Sandhya Shukla and Heidi Tinsman, 34–62. Durham, N.C.: Duke University Press, 2007.

Stepto, Robert. "Distrust of the Reader in Afro-American Literature." In *Literary Criticism and Theory: The Greeks to the Present*, edited by Robert Con Davis and Laurie Fink, 828–42. New York: Longman, 1989.

———. *From behind the Veil: A Study of Afro-American Narrative*. 2nd ed. Urbana: University of Illinois Press, 1991.

———. "Literacy and Hibernation: Ralph Ellison's *Invisible Man*." In his *From behind the Veil: A Study of Afro-American Narrative*, 2nd ed., 163–94. Urbana: University of Illinois Press, 1991.

———. "Lost in a Quest: James Weldon Johnson's *The Autobiography of an Ex-Coloured Man*." In *Critical Essays on James Weldon Johnson*, edited by Kenneth M. Price and Lawrence J. Oliver, 43–69. New York: G. K. Hall, 1997.

Stokes, Claudia. *Writers in Retrospect: The Rise of American Literary History, 1875–1910*. Chapel Hill: University of North Carolina Press, 2006.

Sugimori, Masami. "Narrative Order, Racial Hierarchy, and 'White' Discourse in James Weldon Johnson's *The Autobiography of an Ex-Colored Man* and *Along This Way*." *MELUS* 36, no. 3 (Fall 2011): 37–60.

Suisman, David. *Selling Sounds: The Commercial Revolution in American Music*. Cambridge, Mass.: Harvard University Press, 2009.

Warren, Kenneth W. *So Black and Blue: Ralph Ellison and the Occasion of Criticism*. Chicago: University of Chicago Press, 2003.

———. *What Was African American Literature?* Cambridge, Mass.: Harvard University Press, 2011.

CONTRIBUTORS

BRUCE BARNHART is an associate professor of American literature and culture at the University of Oslo. He is the author of *Jazz in the Time of the Novel: The Temporal Politics of American Race* and *Culture Trading on Racial Futures*.

LORI BROOKS is a visiting assistant professor of history and American studies at Fordham University. She is the author of *Ragtime Cosmopolitanism: African American Men on the Popular Stage before the Harlem Renaissance* and is currently writing a history of African American comediennes.

BEN GLASER is an assistant professor of English at Yale University. His publications include the book *Modernism's Metronome* and essays in *PMLA*, *ELH*, and *Victorian Poetry*.

JEFF KAREM is a professor of English at Cleveland State University. He is the author of *The Romance of Authenticity: The Cultural Politics of Regional and Ethnic Literatures* and *The Purloined Islands: Caribbean-U.S. Crosscurrents in Literature and Culture, 1880–1959*.

DAPHNE LAMOTHE is an associate professor of Africana studies at Smith College. She is the author of *Inventing the New Negro: Narrative, Culture, and Ethnography* and essays on vernacular culture, cultural memory, and the making of modern black identities. She is working on a book about black subjects in urban spaces.

NOELLE MORRISSETTE is an associate professor and the Class of 1952 Distinguished Scholar of English at the University of North Carolina at Greensboro. She has published a monograph on Johnson and sonic experiences of African American culture, *James Weldon Johnson's Modern Soundscapes* and edited a Barnes and Noble Classics edition of Johnson's *The Autobiography of an Ex-Colored Man*.

MICHAEL NOWLIN is a professor of English at the University of Victoria. He is the author of *F. Scott Fitzgerald's Racial Angles and the Business of Literary Greatness* and the editor of Broadview editions of Fitzgerald's *The Great Gatsby* and Edith Wharton's *The Age of Innocence*. He is currently finishing a book tentatively titled "Literary Ambition and the African American Novel from Chesnutt to Ellison."

LAWRENCE J. OLIVER is a professor of English at Texas A&M University, where he teaches classes in African American and American ethnic literatures. His publications include *Critical Essays on James Weldon Johnson* (coedited with Kenneth M. Price) and several articles on the writings of W. E. B. Du Bois.

DIANA PAULIN is an associate professor of English and American studies at Trinity College. Her book *Imperfect Unions: Staging Miscegenation in U.S. Drama and Fiction* was the 2013 winner of the American Society for Theatre Research's Errol Hill Award for Outstanding Scholarship in African American Theatre Studies. Her current book project focuses on race and autism.

AMRITJIT SINGH is the Langston Hughes Professor of English at Ohio University and has held visiting positions at NYU, Wesleyan University, College of the Holy Cross, and the University of California at Berkeley. Books he has edited, coedited, or authored include *The Novels of the Harlem Renaissance*; *Memory and Cultural Politics*; *Postcolonial Theory and the United States*; *Collected Writings of Wallace Thurman*; *Interviews with Edward Said*; and *Revisiting India's Partition: New Essays on Memory, Culture, and Politics*. He received the MELUS Lifetime Achievement Award in 2007 and the SALA Distinguished Achievement Award in Scholarship in 2014.

ROBERT B. STEPTO is a professor of African American studies, American studies, and English at Yale University. His publications include *From behind the Veil: A Study of Afro-American Narrative*, *Blue as the Lake: A Personal Geography*, and *A Home Elsewhere: Reading African American Classics in the Age of Obama*.

INDEX

affiliation, 118, 125
Aframerican, 34
African American studies, 10, 52, 55
Alfred A. Knopf (publishing house). *See* Knopf, Alfred A.
Along This Way (J. W. Johnson), 1, 2, 23, 54, 192, 201, 230
American Federation of Musicians, 173–74, 186n12
Andrews, William, 18n26, 40n42, 64, 83n23
Anglo Saxon, 25, 30, 31, 34, 201
antihero, 48, 64, 67, 195
anti-immigrant, 232
anti-lynching, 2, 16n3, 31, 54, 191; Dyer Anti-Lynching Bill, 2, 16n3, 160
anti-miscegenation. *See* miscegenation
Antin, Mary, 6, 17n18, 234
antiracism, 172, 181
antislavery, 110
archive: African American, 14, 189–91, 196; knowledge and, 12, 194–95, 197–99, 203–5, 234–35
ars poetica, 148, 150, 154
Aubrey (character in Hopkins's *Of One Blood*), 91–92, 103, 104
authenticity, 14, 64–65, 71–72, 89, 176–78, 184
autobiography: as literary category, 6–7, 27–29, 64–67, 95–96, 189–90, 194–95; pseudo-autobiography, 55. *See also Along This Way*

Black Atlantic, 123, 231, 235n5; transatlantic, 156, 231
Black Manhattan (J. W. Johnson), 1, 2, 190, 193, 201
black studies, 10, 52, 55
Blake, Eubie, 181
Blue Jade Series (Knopf), 9, 49, 51
Book of American Negro Poetry (J. W. Johnson, ed.), 49, 52, 141–42n2, 149, 156, 175–77
Book of American Negro Spirituals (J. W. Johnson, ed.), 36, 83n23, 156, 177, 190, 196–97

Braithwaite, William Stanley, 35, 47, 190, 206n22
Broun, Heywood, 8, 192, 194, 207n24
Brown, John (character in Johnson's *The Autobiography of an Ex-Colored Man*), 139, 149–50, 151, 153–54, 157, 164
Brown, Sterling, 52, 61n53, 147, 153, 159, 221
Brown v. Board of Education, 51
Burleigh, Harry T., 179, 195

Chesnutt, Charles W., 43, 50, 57n6, 58n8, 64
Christensen, Axel, 200
Cole, Bob, 23, 44, 170, 181, 193, 200
Cole, Teju, 14, 112, 113–16, 120, 126
Cole and Johnson Brothers, 14, 201
Cole-Johnson Trio, 170–72, 185
Colored Music Settlement, 183–84
commodification, 9–10, 192, 199
consulate, 2, 8, 44–45, 99, 100
Cook, Will Marion, 179, 181, 201
cosmopolitanism, 9, 25, 30–37, 44, 115, 231–32
Crawford, Janie (character in Hurston's *Their Eyes Were Watching God*), 219–21, 226
Cullen, Countee, 147–48, 160, 161
Customs, as immigration or border-policing department, 221–22

Dianthe (character in Hopkins's *Of One Blood*), 90–92, 103–5
diaspora, 9, 87–93, 102, 104–5, 112–14, 231; postdiasporic, 164
digital age, 204, 234–35
diplomacy, 26, 32–34, 44, 66, 191–92, 233
double-consciousness, 26, 74, 134, 149–50, 214–15, 226
Douglass, Frederick, 64, 129, 154, 189–91, 205, 217
Dreams from My Father (Obama), 212, 213–14, 217, 219, 221–28
Drury, Theodore, 201–2

245

Dubey, Madhu, 121, 127n15
Du Bois, W. E. B., 218, 231; *The Souls of Black Folk*, 5–7, 26–27, 50–51, 74, 199, 214–15. *See also* double-consciousness
Dunbar, Paul Laurence, 45, 49, 55, 149–50, 178
Dvořák, Antonín, 179, 187n29
Dyer Anti-Lynching Bill, 2, 16n3, 160

economy: class and, 25, 79, 81, 136–37, 143n12; equality and, 51, 118, 129–32; globalization and, 114, 233
Ellison, Ralph, 5–6, 41–43, 56–57n4, 202, 213, 230
énonciation, 134
Euro-American, 80, 183–84
European American, 176, 183

Fauset, Jessie, 48, 58n23, 232
"Fifty Years" (J. W. Johnson), 42, 45, 47
Fifty Years and Other Poems (J. W. Johnson), 25, 37n2, 37n4, 47
Franklin, John Hope, 9, 52
freemasonry, 6, 67–69, 74–75, 81, 151, 198
fugitivity, 196, 198
futurity, 4–5, 88, 128–29, 131, 141, 203–5

globalization, 2, 14, 87–88, 104–5, 113–14, 232–33
God's Trombones (J. W. Johnson), 49, 150, 154–58, 176, 193–94, 206n10
Goldsby, Jacqueline, 46, 50, 53–55, 56n5, 65–66
Gounod, Charles, 201–2

Harlem Renaissance, 8, 42, 48–51, 114–15, 175, 194. *See also* New Negro Renaissance/Era
Hartman, Saidiya, 142n10, 215
Hefty, Miss (character in Obama's *Dreams from My Father*), 222–23, 225, 226
Hopkins, Gerard Manly, 153, 158–59, 160
Hopkins, Pauline Elizabeth, 14, 87–93, 105–7
Hurston, Zora Neale, 11, 42, 214, 219, 220–21, 226; *Their Eyes Were Watching God*, 56, 212, 219–21
hybridity: literary, 7, 67, 157; nationalism and, 32; racial, 89, 99, 102, 113, 115

immigration, 32, 99, 124, 232–33
internationalism, 9, 120

interracialism: culture and, 8, 119, 149, 212; literature and, 53, 90, 194; taboo of, 6, 79, 87, 91–93, 96, 100–102
intertextuality, 90, 112–13, 126n5
intraracialism, 10, 11, 220

Japanese American, 117, 120, 236n13
jazz, 139, 180, 181, 185n1
Jim Crow, 2, 5–6, 12–13, 42–43, 51–53, 181–82
Johnson, Charles S., 9, 18n26, 48
Johnson, Grace Nail (wife), 45, 57nn15–16, 206n18
Johnson, John Rosamond (brother), 44, 46, 170–72, 177–84, 200–202
Johnson, Singing (character in Johnson's *The Autobiography of an Ex-Colored Man*), 139, 150, 157, 194
Jones, Jasper (character in J. W. Johnson's manuscripts), 157, 167n35, 193
Julius (character in Cole's *Open City*), 114–26

Kasson, Byron (character in Van Vechten's *Nigger Heaven*), 50
Knopf, Alfred A. (publishing house), 9, 42, 49, 51, 115
Knopf, Blanche 50, 54–55, 62n72
Krehbiel, Henry, 177

labor, 6, 9, 173–74, 180, 233, 236n13
Larsen, Nella, 54, 57n6, 232
legibility, 68–72, 80–81, 94–95, 113, 121
"Lift Every Voice and Sing" (J. W. and J. R. Johnson), 3, 165, 191, 206n10, 206n18
literary destitution, 24, 43, 48–49, 52, 55, 56–57n4
Locke, Alain, 13, 48, 51, 115, 147, 221
Lowery, Joseph E., 3–4, 193, 206n19

Mackey, Nathaniel 196
Margetson, George Reginald, 147, 165–66n4
Matthews, Brander, 8–13, 23–40, 43–45, 47, 68, 231
Mayrella (character in Hurston's *Their Eyes Were Watching God*), 220, 226
McKay, Claude, 54, 155, 161
migration, 113–14, 116, 117, 123, 173, 233. *See also* immigration
miscegenation, 51, 87–89, 104–6; in Hopkins's *Of One Blood*, 90–92; in Johnson's *The*

Autobiography of an Ex-Colored Man, 93–103
modernism, 29, 31, 33, 53–54, 62n68, 112–13, 158
modern novel, 33, 53, 61
Morrissette, Noelle, 38n29, 82n26, 109n23, 166n15, 209n49
Murray, Albert, 193

Nadège (character in Cole's *Open City*), 116, 121, 124–25
nationalism, 14, 24, 30–32, 36–37, 101, 113, 231; culture and, 175–77, 179–81, 184
National League of Musicians, 174
National Urban League, 9
Negro Gold Star mothers, 148, 163, 165
Nelson, John Herbert, 60n53
New Negro, 3, 8, 12, 115, 210n66
New Negro (anthology), 50, 115
New Negro Renaissance/Era, 112, 114, 148, 172, 175, 191. *See also* Harlem Renaissance
New World, 1, 3, 5, 9
Nigger Heaven (Van Vechten), 50–51
North, the, 79, 98, 112–14, 203, 215

Obama, Barack, 3–4, 9, 14, 206n19; *Dreams from My Father*, 212, 213–14, 217, 219, 221–28
old-fashioned ideas, 54, 123
Old World, 33
Oliver, Lawrence, 13, 15, 62n66, 68, 82n2, 84n32, 205n6

pan-Africanism, 92, 100, 108n5
performance: African American literature as, 4, 14, 149, 165, 189; archive as, 191–92, 198; Ex-Colored Man as, 12, 98; of miscegenation, 88–89; of race, 94–99, 102–3, 137–39, 143–44n24, 198; of ragtime, 173–74
Phillips, Wendell, 152, 195, 201; "Toussaint L'Ouverture," 152
Plessy v. Ferguson, 43, 69, 113
poetics, 14, 25, 49, 148, 150, 158, 162, 165, 165–66n4, 208n35, 208n38
popular culture, 26–27, 170, 173, 176–77, 202; music and, 7, 14, 33, 172, 175, 184–85, 201–2
post-blackness, 112, 113, 126n1
postdiaspora, 164
postmodernism, 112, 113, 115, 121–22

postracialism, 9, 126n1, 205
poststructuralism, 12
precarity, 131
Progressive Era, 25, 26, 30, 87
Progressivism, 24, 26, 31, 32, 112, 125
pseudo-documentary, 55
Pudd'nhead Wilson (Twain), 28
Punahou Academy, 219, 221

ragtime: as American music, 7, 77, 169, 178, 180, 184; debates, 173–75, 177; hybridity and, 7, 230; interpolation in, 200–201; performance and, 136, 138–39; syncopation, 155, 171, 179; technique and, 33, 169–70, 176, 183
Randolph, Richetta, 16n3, 209n43
Reuel (character in Hopkins's *Of One Blood*), 91–92, 97, 101, 103, 104, 105
rhythm: poetics and, 148–62; subjectivity and, 129–30, 139–40; syncopation and, 171–72, 178
Richards, I. A., 158, 159

Saidu Caspar Mohammed (character in Cole's *Of One Blood*), 124
"Saint Peter Relates an Incident" (J. W. Johnson), 148–49, 156, 160–65, 166n7, 208n35
Saint Peter Relates an Incident (J. W. Johnson), 148
Saito, Professor (character in Cole's *Of One Blood*), 117–18, 121
secret of authorship, 6, 69–70, 79–81, 102, 199
Sherman, French and Company, 42, 46, 58n20, 59n27, 65, 209n43
Shiny (character in Johnson's *The Autobiography of an Ex-Colored Man*), 149, 150, 151–55, 157, 201, 216–17
Singing Johnson (character in Johnson's *The Autobiography of an Ex-Colored Man*), 139, 150, 157, 194
Skerrett, Joseph T., 11, 18n19, 63n73, 195, 207–8n32
Smith, Harry B., 181–82
Smith, Valerie, 9, 72, 94, 110n27, 195
Souls of Black Folk, The (Du Bois), 5–7, 26–27, 50–51, 74, 199, 214–15
sound: African American expressive practices and, 12, 178, 197; archive of, 190, 194–95, 197–200, 203; J. W. Johnson's aesthetic and, 14, 148, 156–57, 192–93, 196, 200;

sound (*continued*)
  recording and, 172, 199; soundscape, 17, 148; soundtrack, 201
South, the: blood and, 73, 218; as colonial enterprise, 9; Ex-Colored Man in, 78, 80, 103, 156, 215
Spencer, Anne, 55, 62n71
Spillers, Hortense, 109n16, 131–35, 136–39
spirituals, 36, 83n23, 156, 172, 177–79, 183–84, 200
Stepto, Robert, 10–11, 29, 68–69, 94, 110n27, 211–12
subjectivity, 89, 97, 129–33, 136–38, 141, 142n9
Sugimori, Masami, 67, 83n19

temporality, 129, 143n11, 210n65
Their Eyes Were Watching God (Hurston), 56, 212, 219–21
Toomer, Jean, 52, 57n6
"Toussaint L'Ouverture" (Phillips speech), 152
Towns, George A., 44–47, 52, 57n11, 59n29, 206–7n22
transatlantic, 156, 231; Black Atlantic, 123, 231, 235n5

transculturalism, 103, 156
translation, 1, 6, 12, 48, 99, 108n5, 153–54, 157, 192, 195
transnationalism, 14, 87–89, 91–93, 99, 103, 112–14, 230–31
Twain, Mark, 28

United States: black culture in, 3, 49, 76–77, 176–77; citizenship, 6, 25, 232; culture, 30, 106, 177; future of, 5, 173; imperialism, 105, 233; occupation of Haiti, 1, 93, 233; racial violence in, 68, 78–79, 81, 99, 104, 181; transnational movement and, 112, 115, 128, 132

Van Doren, Carl, 58–59n23, 192
Van Vechten, Carl, 8, 15, 36, 50–52, 55, 192; *Nigger Heaven*, 50–51

Wetmore, Judson Douglas, 1, 45, 55, 58n13
Williams (Bert) and Walker (George), 201–2

Yezierska, Anzia, 234

www.ingramcontent.com/pod-product-compliance
Lightning Source LLC
Chambersburg PA
CBHW011749220426
43669CB00022B/2958